Making Medicine a Business

Pierre-Yves Donzé

Making Medicine a Business

X-ray Technology, Global Competition, and the Transformation of the Japanese Medical System, 1895–1945

Pierre-Yves Donzé
Osaka University
Toyonaka, Osaka, Japan

ISBN 978-981-10-8158-3   ISBN 978-981-10-8159-0   (eBook)
https://doi.org/10.1007/978-981-10-8159-0

Library of Congress Control Number: 2018934672

Cover design: Fatima Jamadar

Printed on acid-free paper

This Palgrave Macmillan imprint is published by the registered company Springer Nature Singapore Pte Ltd. part of Springer Nature
The registered company address is: 152 Beach Road, #21-01/04 Gateway East, Singapore 189721, Singapore

ALSO BY PIERRE-YVES DONZÉ

A BUSINESS HISTORY OF THE SWATCH GROUP: The Rebirth of
Swiss Watchmaking and the Globalization of the Luxury Industry
FROM FAMILY BUSINESS TO GLOBAL BRAND: Longines
GLOBAL LUXURY: Organizational change and emerging markets
since the 1970s (*edited with Rika Fujioka*)
HISTORY OF THE SWISS WATCH INDUSTRY FROM JACQUES
DAVID TO NICOLAS HAYEK
INDUSTRIAL DEVELOPMENT, TECHNOLOGY TRANSFER,
AND GLOBAL COMPETITION: The Japanese watch industry
from 1850 to the present day
INDUSTRIES AND GLOBAL COMPETITION: A History of
Business Beyond Borders (*edited with Bram Bouwens and Takafumi
Kurosawa*)
ORGANIZING GLOBAL TECHNOLOGY FLOWS: Institutions,
Actors, and Processes (*edited with Shigehiro Nishimura*)

Preface and Acknowledgements

This book is the result of some twenty years studying the business and economic history of hospitals and healthcare systems. When I was a student in history in the mid-nineties in Switzerland, my first interest was the social history of medicine. Having read Michel Foucault, I wanted to carry out my own research on an institution of "social disciplinarization." I chose my hometown hospital, whose roots go back to the mid-eighteenth century, and started reading the minutes of the board. It was a big surprise, however, to see that the administrators of the hospital hardly discussed issues related to medicine and patients. Their major concern was money. The research gap was wide, with literature on the social history of medicine offering a discourse on society but usually without any discussion of economic background. I thus decided to shift my focus from social history to economic history and analyzed the management of the hospital. I pursued my research from this perspective through a Ph.D. thesis on the relations between technological change, hospital management, and health policy in the Swiss canton of Vaud. Later on, this research background gave me the opportunity to apply a similar approach to the case of Japan and examine the transformation of medicine into a business in a different environment.

My research in Japan was funded for five years by two organizations to which I would like to express my deepest gratitude. The Hakubi Project of Kyoto University (2012–2015) was undoubtedly the best experience a young scholar could have. It offered freedom, financial support, and ambition and enabled me to develop an international career. I also benefited from a grant from the Japanese Society for the Promotion of Science (Grant-in-Aid for Scientific Research C 25380424) between 2013 and 2017. Some parts of this book have been presented as research papers at various conferences of business history and history of medicine (Columbus, Frankfort, Lausanne, Leeds, Miami, Sapporo, Tokyo, Uppsala, and Yokohama). I thank all the participants at these sessions and workshops for their fruitful comments and discussion. Some parts of the first chapter are from an article that originally appeared in the journal *Business History Review* ("Siemens and the business of medicine in Japan, 1900–1945", vol. 87, no. 2, 2013, pp. 203–228) in 2013. Last but not least, I am grateful to Takafumi Kurosawa, who read and commented on previous versions of some parts of the manuscript.

Toyonaka, Osaka, Japan   Pierre-Yves Donzé
July 2017

CONTENTS

LIST OF FIGURES

LIST OF TABLES

CHAPTER 1

Introduction

Today, healthcare is a major sector of activity throughout the world. In 2015, health expenditures amounted to 16.9% of the GDP in the United States, 11.2% in Japan, and between 8 and 12% in Western Europe.[1] Moreover, considering the aging populations in Western and East Asian countries and growing income levels in emerging countries, many consider the healthcare industry to have immense potential for growth. According to the consulting firm Deloitte, global healthcare expenditures should rise to 8.7 billion USD in 2020, relative to just 2.6 billion in 1995 and 7.1 billion in 2015.[2] Health, one could easily argue, is one of the largest industries of the early twenty-first century.

Another characteristic of the healthcare industry is the rapid growth that it experienced during the twentieth century. While the databases of the Organization for Economic Cooperation and Development (OECD) and World Health Organization (WHO) do not include the years prior to the 1960s, making it nearly impossible to construct a global overview of this development, works by several economists and economic historians in the United States and Europe provide some evidence at the national level. Examining the United States, Melissa Thomasson estimated healthcare expenditures at about 2% of the total GDP in 1900 and 3–4% during the 1950s.[3] As for France, Sandrine Michel and Delphine Vallade put the expenditures at about 1% of the GDP in 1900 and around 3% in 1950.[4]

The causes of this continuous growth—especially since the 1960s—have caught the attention of numerous health economists, who have built models to highlight the impact of several factors. The literature discusses three main causes. The first set of factors comprises increasing life expectancy levels and aging populations. As more people get older, the demand for healthcare increases.[5] Most scholars generally share a consensus on this basic relationship. The second factor, technological change, prompts much more discussion.[6] Some economists have argued that certain innovations can also decrease costs, provided that the technologies improve the quality of patient life and thereby reduce the consumption of healthcare.[7] Gelijns and Rosenberg emphasized that the nature of the impact on costs depends on the type of innovation (new infrastructure vs. cost-saving technology).[8] In cases where there is a positive influence on rising costs, the level of national income is related to the speed of the adoption of new technology. Technological change is, in this case, an investment that requires sufficient capital.[9] Finally, the third factor centers on healthcare market organization and funding. Getzen argued, for example, that the main reason behind cost growth in the United States from 1960 to 1980 was "the system we have constructed."[10] "Physician-induced demand," or the use of diagnostic devices and other health services by doctors, usually grows when the number and density of practitioners increase.[11] Webster, a sociologist, maintained that "in market-based systems [...] new technologies have been much more quickly taken up in part because professional care is fee-based and specialist, and where patients are 'clients' with private health insurance, a physician competes with others in part through what state-of-the-art medicine they have to offer."[12] There are, however, some contradictions between studies emphasizing doctors' roles as patient agents (adapting health-service consumption to patients' needs and financial means, for instance) and physicians' self-interests.[13] Finally, for some authors like Michael Porter, healthcare systems based on the principle of a competitive market economy are the most effective organizations for providing good treatments at affordable prices.[14]

Consequently, health economists have emphasized that aging populations, new technology, and market organization all have an important impact in driving healthcare expenditures up. However, they have not focused on a more fundamental problem: why, when, and how medicine and healthcare transformed into a business. Until the late nineteenth century, medicine was essentially a charitable activity; the healthcare market was very limited, restricted to a social niche, while the overwhelming majority of the population used self-medication. Thus, the objective of this book is to understand the process of medicine's transformation into a business. In particular, it discusses the roles that technology and market structure played in the development. As the metamorphosis of the medical sphere since the nineteenth century has attracted the interest of numerous historians, the book builds on the broad base of literature discussing the history of medicine.

Until the 1990s, research on medical history was essentially dominated by medical doctors who wanted to study the past of their discipline. They followed a positivist and deterministic approach, focusing on the advances of medical science and the roles of "great men." George Rosen, himself a medical doctor, was one of the first to argue (in 1941) that medicine was a social science and, consequently, that examinations of its history needed to adhere to a social-science perspective.[15] It was several decades later when scholars finally took to observing the social history of medicine, with the influence of Michel Foucault and the "Ecole des Annales" driving the new approach.[16] While the history of medicine developed in an innovative and multidisciplinary field, the business and economic dimensions remain largely underdeveloped. For example, the main handbooks on the history of medicine published after 2000 have tackled a wide variety of themes—but not business.[17] Still, some works have focused on specific aspects of the history of medicine and contributed to a better understanding of how healthcare has transformed into a growing industry. The studies generally fall into five categories.

First, there are works on the business and economic history of hospitals. As hospitals established themselves as bastions of contemporary healthcare systems, many scholars have analyzed their historical development, mostly from the perspectives of social and cultural history. The economic dimension has pulled the discourse in two main directions. On the one hand, some research has focused on the issue of hospital funding, especially in the United Kingdom and United States[18] and recently in France.[19] Scholars have discussed the impact of declining philanthropy on finances, the increases in support from the state and health insurance providers, and the opening of hospitals to wealthy patients. On the other hand, some works have focused more on the issue of the organization and the management of hospitals.[20] The influence of Alfred Chandler is clearly evident in these works—and sometimes, the authors make explicit reference to Chandlerian concepts. The most important work in this category is undoubtedly the seminal book on the hospitals of Philadelphia and New York by Joel Howell, who showed how diagnostic equipment and laboratories changed the very nature of hospitals and supported their mutation toward bureaucratic organizations whose management draws primarily on scientific data and statistics.[21] Most of these hospital-centric works do not attempt to connect financial and technological issues. Historians focusing on hospital funding do not discuss the influence of new technology on hospital budgets, first of all, while their colleagues analyzing the impact of technology on hospital organization ignore the financial dimension of technology.

Second, some scholars have studied the organization and regulation of healthcare systems at the national, regional, or local level. Following a macroeconomic perspective, their analyses focus on the intervention of various actors (philanthropists, local and central governments, church, labor unions, and insurance providers, etc.) and the general dynamics of hospital development in specific spaces.[22] The works treat hospital development in its broad context, including demographic, social, and political dimensions. However, these works tend to be descriptive and avoid tackling major issues pertaining to healthcare business, such as the regulation of the market itself or the impact of new medical technology.

Works in the third category address the professionalization of medical doctors and the emergence of medical specialization. Researchers generally see specialization as a mere and direct consequence of the advances in medical science, which led doctors to focus on specific domains of medicine—as it had become impossible to master all aspects of healthcare, doctors naturally chose more exclusive fields.[23] As Rosemary Stevens asserted in a study on the British case, however, specialization may have been "an inevitable and desirable accompaniment of scientific advance"—but it occurred in a particular, formative context (given the growth of private specialized hospitals, development of health insurance providers, and birth of new medical associations, among other factors).[24] In a major comparative work on specialization in Germany, France, the United Kingdom, and the United States, George Weisz stressed the role of academic and professional associations of doctors, which adopted different types of certification for specialists.[25] He showed that specialization was not a natural result of the evolution of medicine but rather an outcome of social situations that changed between countries. However, these types of authors have usually underestimated the impact of a growing competitiveness on the medical market in the emergence of specializations as a building block for a niche market.[26] In his landmark study on medicine in the United States, Paul Starr adeptly demonstrated that medicine had become a real business in the early twentieth century; that development led doctors to concentrate in urban areas, which offered more professional opportunities.[27] In a case study on Philadelphia during the first half of the twentieth century, James A. Schafer traced a similar process. He argued that the organization of the medical market (free competition) significantly influenced the concentration of doctors in urban areas and their specialization.[28] This category also includes the innovative perspective of Takahiro Ueyama, who showed that, in the early twentieth century, some British doctors looking to establish careers as electrotherapists relied on alliances with industrialists, who wielded a mastery of the new technology.[29] The alliance between industry and doctors was a major step in the transformation of medicine into a business, as this book will demonstrate.

Fourth, there are works on the social history of medical technology. This is a wide field, one bearing a strong social-science influence, especially via the STS approach (Science and Technology Studies).[30] Numerous monographs on the social history of medical technologies, particularly on X-ray equipment and surgery, have shown that the diffusion and development of new technology was not a "natural" phenomenon resulting from the progress of science; rather, the outcomes were products of social forces. Social networks are frequent to explain how medical technology evolved, diffused in society, and made its way into use by doctors and patients.[31] For example, Stuart Blume's excellent book on medical imagery demonstrates that the process of specialization among medical professions strengthened the relations between science and medicine through the public's expanding demand for "scientific medicine" and insurance providers' demands for precise diagnostics.[32] John V. Pickstone eventually proposed a new analytical framework—Science, Technology, and Medicine (the STM approach)—to place the medical discipline within a larger socio-technological system and emphasize that medicine's evolution depends on the change of this larger environment, not just the "progress of science."[33] However, the most important shortcoming of this approach is that it fails to consider market mechanisms and the economic dimension in general terms. In a 1999 review article, Jennifer Stanton already professed her hopes "to see more about debates over the economic costs of medical technologies."[34] Now, nearly two decades since Stanton made that appeal, scholars still have yet to integrate economy and technology in a systemic explanation of medicine's evolution. As this book will demonstrate, however, technology played a major role in the evolution of medicine as a business.

Finally, the fifth approach includes research on the history of pharmaceutical companies. Since the 1990s, several works have analyzed the development of these firms through a classic approach to business history, focusing on innovation and organization—the internal factors of a firm's growth.[35] While some of the works of this type are excellent studies, few engage much in discussing the emergence and development of healthcare systems. Issues related to the regulation of drug demand (state intervention, insurances, and networks of drugstores, for instance) and other healthcare organizations like hospitals and private doctors are only minor themes in these works.

This short literature review shows that a broad range of articles and books have tackled the issues surrounding hospital funding, medical technology, and professionalization. However, none of them offers a comprehensive analysis of the transformation of medicine into a business since the end of the nineteenth century, a process that remains rather unclear. This book thus aims to investigate and discuss how medicine transformed into a growing business and what roles technology played in this process, adopting a systemic approach that integrates a broad range of actors (doctors, hospitals, state, insurances, private companies, and patients).

Figure 1 represents the healthcare market, indicating the positions of various actors who influence the overall organization. The market centers on care: The population demands care, which hospitals and doctors provide. The organization of the market results from the actions of various bodies and consequently differs between countries. There are five major groups of actors.

First, there is the state, which has both a direct and an indirect influence on the organization of the healthcare market through the adoption of laws and rules. Legal regulations can directly affect the market itself; legislation can shape hospital policy (by controlling the number and size of establishments), the existence of public health insurance providers, and controls on prices and fees, for example. Moreover, the state can regulate also other groups of actors through laws, directives, and norms governing the organization of the medical profession (certification for specializations, etc.), private insurance business, and drug-related research and development.

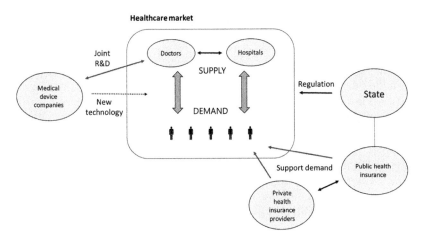

Fig. 1 Organization of the healthcare market (*Source* Created by the author)

Next are private health insurance providers, which include both non-profit organizations, such as providers belonging to trade unions, as well as companies. These entities negotiate agreements on fees and prices with other actors, particularly doctors and hospitals, and sometimes with pharmaceutical companies. They thus help organize the healthcare market by stabilizing prices and giving more people access to this market—and that boosts demand and market growth.

Doctors and hospitals, meanwhile, not only supply the care in the market but also engage in market organization, notably through associations that self-regulate fees. In the case of doctors, medical associations impact the organization of medical specialities and affect competitiveness through the control of access to the medical profession. Doctors also cooperate with medical device companies to codevelop new technology. The relation between doctors and hospitals is another important issue, with the former needing ways to access the new technical equipment—installed at hospitals—and offer the corresponding services to their patients.

The providers of new technology, namely medical device companies, also have a major impact on the healthcare market. Unlike other groups of actors, however, they do not exercise a regulating influence on the market; rather, they cultivate the market via launches of new products. The rate of technological diffusion and the scope of technological adoption are closely linked to market organization (free competition vs. state control) and structure (number and density of hospitals and clinics). Moreover, since the late nineteenth century, certain types of new medical technology like X-ray machines have had global reach but required adaptation to local conditions. From this perspective, cooperating with local doctors enables medical device companies to provide technology that fits well with specific markets.

Finally, patients are a major group of actors because they represent demand. When people get sick, they consult with doctors or visit hospitals—and thereby "consume" healthcare. Consumption is precisely the issue, as it transforms medicine from the non-commodity stratum that it occupied until the end of the nineteenth century to the business that it represents today. Increases in income, urbanization, and new medical technology have been important drivers of healthcare consumption since 1900. However, the growing costs of medical technology make it necessary to support the demand base through a system of health insurance—a structure that gives the healthcare market enough customers and thereby facilitates sustainability.

This book argues that a proper understanding of the historical conditions shaping the construction of the contemporary healthcare market requires a multifocal analysis that integrates the workings of these various actors. For its case study, it focuses on the development and diffusion of radiology and X-ray equipment in Japan leading up to World War II (WWII). I chose this specific technology because it was the first truly global medical technology and also because it had a decisive impact on the mutation of medicine throughout the world.[36] Japan is, in my view, undoubtedly the most suitable example for discussing the transformation of medicine into a business during the first part of the twentieth century. In most Western countries, including the United States, the tradition of Christian philanthropy and the early intervention of the state in social and health affairs led to the formation of healthcare markets based on the coexistence of numerous nonprofit organizations, state interventionism, and market principles. In prewar Japan, though, healthcare was basically an industry that operated on the principles of free competition (minimal state interventionism and profit-oriented medicine). The book thus offers a compelling case to probe the influence of new technology on the process by which medicine became a business, stressing the actions of X-ray equipment manufacturers and doctors, emphasizing the reactions of hospitals, and discussing the late intervention of the state to ensure the sustainable growth of the system.

The history of medicine in Japan is still a traditional academic field that tends to focus primarily on the activities of "great doctors," meaning that published works contribute relatively little to the understanding of the transformation of healthcare into a business and the roles that technology filled in the process.[37] Beyond the descriptive and determinist approach that characterized the field of history of medicine in Japan, one can find a few studies that shed light on the social, political, and economic dimensions of the development of medicine and healthcare. In particular, the moments of deep mutation in the healthcare system— the adoption of German medicine during the last third of the nineteenth century,[38] for example, or institutional changes during WWII and the postwar US occupation[39]—have attracted the attention of scholars in the social sciences. Moreover, some Western scholars have applied general issues in the social history of medicine to Japanese cases.[40] However, these works only rarely consider the economic dimension of this change. For example, Hoi-Eun Kim admirably demonstrated the differentiation in how Japanese doctors pursued medical training in Germany during the Meiji period: Recipients of state scholarships went to the University of Berlin, the formation center for the Japanese elite at the time, while young Japanese who studied abroad at their own expense chose Munich to undergo practical training in surgery or internal medicine.[41] However, Kim did not link the latter choice with the particular nature of the Japanese medical market, which would have explained the need for private doctors to strengthen their position in a highly competitive environment through practical training in Germany.[42] Therefore, these works on the social history of medicine lack the type of insight that would help answer the research question central to this book.

Among the rare authors who analyzed the economics of healthcare in Japan from a historical viewpoint, Takeshi Kawakami and Shuhei Ikai stand out. Kawakami, a medical doctor and a historian with a generally Marxist stance, published numerous books on the Japanese healthcare system during the 1960s and 1970s. He argued that the system experienced a profound metamorphosis during the second part of the nineteenth century with the co-emergence of Western and capitalist medicine. The lack of a Christian and philanthropist tradition in Japan resulted in the development of modern medicine with roots in free-market mechanisms. Capitalist medicine relied on two major elements: the freedom of commerce for medical doctors and the commodification of healthcare.[43] Ikai published a book in 2010 on the evolution of the Japanese hospital system during the twentieth century. According to Ikai, the high concentration of small and private hospitals in urban areas resulted from a competitive environment in which doctors accessed medical infrastructure in founding their own hospital.[44] These two works form an essential context for this book and figure prominently in the following chapters. However, the literature by Kawakami and Ikai does not discuss the issue of technological change or the impact of medical technology such as X-rays. As for the academic literature on the history of medical technology in Japan, the discourse includes the recent contributions of Miyoko Tsukisawa, who analyzed the adoption of Western techniques by Japanese doctors during the nineteenth century,[45] and research by foreign scholars, which I noted above. However, the economic approach is absent from these works.

This book, over five chapters, builds on this base of literature and adopts a multifocal perspective on both the construction and evolution of the healthcare market in Japan during the first part of the twentieth century and technology's function in the overall process. The first chapter starts by analyzing the suppliers of new technology, namely the producers of X-ray equipment. Although this technology was controlled by a handful of multinational enterprises (essentially General Electric and Siemens), the companies had to adapt their devices to various national markets. In Japan, the issue was to market cheaper equipment that could be sold to local hospitals, which were smaller than Western hospitals. The specificity of the Japanese hospital system was also an opportunity for domestic producers (like Shimadzu) to develop suitable equipment. Next, Chapter 2 focuses on the users of this new technology—medical doctors—and shows how a new category of specialists (radiologists) emerged and took control of the use of X-ray technology at hospitals. Subsequently, Chapter 3 analyzes the relations between the producers of health equipment and medical doctors, drawing on a survey of patents for support. The chapter discusses the impact of joint research and development activities on launches of new devices and the competitiveness of the manufacturers. Chapter 4 then shifts the attention toward hospitals. It demonstrates the way X-ray technology gradually diffused through the Japanese healthcare system and the impact that it had on hospital management—being both an investment and a source of growing revenues.

However, the managerial changes resulting from the adoption of new medical technology precipitated the need to regulate the organization of the whole healthcare system in order to ensure access to healthcare and reduce price competition between hospitals (Chapter 5). Finally, the conclusion offers a general summary of the process by which medicine evolved into a business.

NOTES

1. http://stats.oecd.org/ (accessed 25 April 2017).
2. Deloitte, *2017 Global Health Care Outlook*, p. 5 and data of the World Health Organization, http://apps.who.int/nha/database/ViewData/ Indicators/en (accessed 25 April 2017).
3. Thomasson, "Economic History and the Healthcare Industry", p. 178.
4. Michel and Vallade, «Une Analyse de long terme des dépenses sociales».
5. Among hundreds of articles, see for example Zweifel, Felder and Meiers, "Ageing of Population and Health Care Expenditure"; Geue et al. "Population Ageing and Healthcare Expenditure Projections".
6. Newhouse, "Medical Care Costs".
7. Sherman, Goodman and Miron, *The Economics of Health and Health Care*.
8. Gelijns and Rosenberg, "The Dynamics of Technological Change in Medicine".
9. Slade and Anderson, "The Relationship between Per Capita Income and Diffusion of Medical Technologies".
10. Getzen, "Population Aging and the Growth of Health Expenditures", p. 104.
11. Fuchs, "The Supply of Surgeons and the Demand for Operations".
12. Webster, *Health, Technology and Society*, p. 4.
13. Rossiter and Wilensky, "Identification of Physician-Induced Demand".
14. Porter and Olmsted, *Redefining Health Care*.
15. Rosen, "Disease and Social Criticism".
16. Foucault, *Naissance de la Clinique*, and *Surveiller et punir*.
17. Huisman and Harkley, *Locating Medical History*; Cooter and Pickstone, *Companion to Medicine in the Twentieth Century*.
18. Gorsky and Sheard, *Financing Medicine*; Stevens, "Sweet Charity; State Aid to Hospitals in Pennsylvania, 1870–1910"; Cherry, "Beyond National Health Insurance"; Wishart, "Class Difference and the Reformation of Ontario Public Hospitals, 1900–1935"; Cherry, "Accountability, Entitlement, and Control Issues and Voluntary Hospital Funding c1860–1939"; and Cherry, "Before the National Health Service".

19. Faure, *Les cliniques privées*; Domin, *Une histoire économique de l'hôpital.*
20. Craig, "The Role of Records and of Record-Keeping in the Development of the Modern Hospital"; Shumsky, "The Municipal Clinic of San Francisco"; Goebel, "American Medicine and the 'Organizational Synthesis'"; Sturdy, "The Political Economy of Scientific Medicine"; Rosner, *A Once Charitable Enterprise*; and Reverby, "Stealing the Golden Eggs".
21. Howell, *Technology in the Hospital.*
22. Rosenberg, "Inward Vision and Outward Glance"; Lynaugh, *The Community Hospitals of Kansas City*; Lane, *A Social History of Medicine*; Grandshaw, "'Fame and Fortune by Means of Bricks and Mortar'"; Labisch and Spree, *Krankenhaus-Report 19. Jahrhundert*; Labisch and Spree, *«Einem jeden Kranken in einem Hospitale sein eigenes Bett»*; Donzé, *Bâtir, gérer, soigner*; and Mohan, *Planning, Markets and Hospitals.*
23. Fye, *Caring for the Heart.*
24. Stevens, *Medical Practice in Modern England.*
25. Weisz, *Divide and Conquer.*
26. Donzé, *L'ombre de César.*
27. Starr, *The Social Transformation of American Medicine.*
28. Schafer, *The Business of Private Medical Practice.*
29. Ueyama, "Capital, Profession and Medical Technology".
30. Brown and Webster, *New Medical Technologies and Society*; Webster, *Health, Technology and Society*; and Keating and Cambrosio, *Biomedixal Platforms.*
31. Stanton, *Innovations in Health and Medicine*; Schlich and Tröhler, *The Risks of Medical Innovation*; Timmermann and Anderson, *Devices and Designs*; Dommann, *Dursicht, Einsicht, Vorsicht*; Schlich, *Surgery, Science and Industry*; Schlich, *The Origins of Organ Transplantation*; and Neary and Pickstone, *Surgeons, Manufacturers and Patients.*
32. Blume, *Insight and Industry.*
33. Pickstone, *Ways of Knowing.*
34. Stanton, "Making Sense of Technologies in Medicine", p. 448.
35. Galambos and Sewell, *Networks of Innovation*; Jones, *The Business of Medicine*; Umemura, *The Japanese Pharmaceutical Industry*; Yongue, "Origins of Innovation in the Japanese Pharmaceutical Industry"; and Takeuchi, "Sengo takokuseki seiyaku kigyo no zainichi keiei".
36. Thomas and Banerjee, *The History of Radiology.*
37. *Nihon ishigaku zasshi*, since 1941.
38. Kira, *Meijiki ni okeru doitsu igaku no juyo to fukyu*; Kim, *Doctors of Empire*; and Donzé, "Studies Abroad by Japanese Doctors".
39. Yamagishi, *War and Health Insurance Policy in Japan and the United States*; Sugiyama, *Senryoki no iryo kaikaku*; and Aldous and Suzuki, *Reforming Public Health in Occupied Japan.*

40. Bartholomew, *The Formation of Science in Japan*; Wittwer and Brown, *Science, Technology, and Medicine in the Modern Japanese Empire*; Frühstück, *Colonizing Sex*; and Aoki, *Kekkaku no shakaishi*.
41. Kim, *Doctors of Empire*.
42. Donzé, "Studies Abroad by Japanese Doctors".
43. Kawakami, *Gendai nihon iryoshi*.
44. Ikai, *Byoin no seiki no riron*.
45. Tsukisawa, "Meiji shotō nihon ni okeru iryō gijutsu no inyu juyō katei".

CHAPTER 2

The Emergence of an Industry

1 Introduction

X-ray device technology first appeared during the second part of the 1890s, following Wilhelm Roentgen's discovery of X-rays in 1895.[1] The technology's application to medicine was not immediate, however: until the development of a new generation of X-ray tubes, the most famous being the Coolidge tube that General Electric (GE) patented in the United States in 1913, radiology devices were not precise enough to be useful tools for medical doctors, particularly in diagnostic usage. The technical characteristics of the Coolidge tube (tungsten filament and vacuum) made it possible to exercise meticulous control over dosage and ray intensity. Thus, users could observe the human body more and more precisely (through radiography) and use rays to cure some forms of cancer and other diseases (through radiotherapy). After some twenty years of research, trials, and improvements, X-ray devices eventually became a stable technology. Production and consumption of the devices entered an industrial phase and experienced dramatic growth after World War I (WWI).

Between 1895 and 1914, the X-ray device industry was largely dominated by multinational enterprises (MNEs) in the field of electric appliances—companies that had the capacity to conduct research on vacuum tubes, a technology that was also used for lamps and radios. That gave a small number of firms sway over the global market of radiological equipment from the early twentieth century onward: GE (USA), Westinghouse (USA), Siemens (Germany), and Philips (Netherlands)

© The Author(s) 2018
P.-Y. Donzé, *Making Medicine a Business*,
https://doi.org/10.1007/978-981-10-8159-0_2

were the dominant players.[2] Some small, specialized companies—most of which were in Germany—managed to remain competitive against these MNEs (Müller; Reiniger, Gebbert & Schall; and Veifa). In some countries, like France and Japan, the particular market conditions allowed domestic firms to develop and grow despite the presence of foreign companies. While X-ray equipment had always been a largely standardized technology since its inception, making it essentially the first global medical technology, the development, manufacture, and distribution of the devices varied from country to country. The specificities of local hospital and medical markets, as well as the conditions of competition, also depended on location. This chapter analyzes the emergence and development of the X-ray equipment industry in Japan—one such specific market environment—through World War II (WWII).

The literature on technology transfer and industrialization in Japan is extremely rich and offers a general analytical framework that makes it possible to better set the case in question here.[3] Addressing the so-called technology of the second industrial revolution, such as electrical appliances, scholars have emphasized two main paths of industrial development. First, the most important was the cooperation with US and German MNEs, which invested in Japan in joint ventures with local partners. Western Electric took a stake in Nippon Electric (NEC, 1899), GE in Tokyo Electric (TE) (1905) and Shibaura Engineering Works (1909), Westinghouse in Mitsubishi Electric (1923), and Siemens in Fuji Electric (1923). Second, some smaller enterprises without foreign capital, like Hitachi (founded in 1910) and Matsushita Electric (Panasonic, 1918), engaged in this industry through the use of local resources, such as universities and technical schools, and cooperated indirectly with foreign companies to develop. Also worth mentioning is the important role played by the state, which adopted an industrial and economic policy favorable to the sector through custom protectionism and other measures.[4]

The industry of X-ray equipment fits in line with this general context, except that it did not benefit from custom protectionism. The import tax on medical equipment was at a fixed 20% of the value in 1911 and remained at that level until WWII.[5] The market for X-ray devices was thus competitive. Apart from this specificity, there were also foreign MNEs and small domestic specialized companies, as was the case for the electric appliance industry in general. Consequently, one must consider the various strategies that these different actors adopted regarding innovation and product development to keep competitive. The major research questions for this chapter are as follows: What kind of devices did these enterprises manufacture and sell? Where did their knowledge and technology come from? What was the basis of their (lack of) competitiveness? What kind of equipment did they develop? Who were their customers?

To answer these questions, this chapter proposes a twofold approach that incorporates industry history and business history. An ideal survey would involve first looking at the general dynamic of the industry at the macroeconomic level and then focusing on some representative enterprises as case studies. However, X-ray devices are a specialized industry for which the statistical sources that researchers normally utilize in studying Japanese industries (production and foreign trade) are unavailable. The only documents that provide quantitative information on the industry are factory censuses by the Ministry of Commerce and Industry.[6]

These censuses include a general "medical devices" (*iryo kikai*) category, which also notes the specialty of each factory. Several indicate "X-ray equipment" or "X-ray tubes." These factories specialized in the production of these goods, but the classification does not mean that other factories—simply mentioned as "medical devices" makers—did not manufacture such products. This was, for example, the case of the company Goto Fuundo, a Japanese partner of Siemens, which appeared in the 1935 census as specializing in "medical devices" at its plant based in Saitama, which produced X-ray devices and other goods. Likewise, the Kawasaki plant of TE was listed among "medical device" producers in 1922 but was absent from the list in 1929 (obviously as it produced mostly other goods), only to reappear in 1935. Finally, Shimadzu appeared in this category only in 1935, although it had manufactured X-ray equipment—in small quantities—from the 1910s to the mid-1920s.

Consequently, Table 1 is no more than a rough estimation of specialized X-ray device-making plants. The resources shed light on several characteristics of the industry, however.

First, most of the companies developed during the early 1930s. The first censuses (1902, 1919, and 1918) did not mention any factories that specialized in making X-ray devices or tubes. Their number went from three in 1922 to two in 1929 and then nine in 1935. The 1920s thus appears to be the decade during which the industry emerged, while the 1930s was a period of high growth of production in Japan. This dynamic

Table 1   X-ray device-manufacturing factories in Japan, 1922–1935 (Source *Kojo tsuran*, 1922–1935)

Company	Foundation	Location	1922	1929	1935
Tokyo Igaku Denki KK	1917	Tokyo	X		
Tokyo Electric KK, Kawasaki plant	1913	Kawasaki	X		X
Okura Denkyu	1918	Kanazawa	X		
Osaka Roentgen	1926	Osaka		X	X
Marunaka Electric KK	1928	Kobe		X	X
Dainihon Roentgen KK	1920	Osaka			X
Shibuya Roentgen	1932	Tokyo			X
Yoshida Tekkojo	1914	Kyoto			X
Morita Shoten	1923	Kyoto			X
Morikawa Seisakujo	1916	Tokyo			X
Shimadzu Seisakujo KK	1875	Kyoto			X

Note The targets of the censuses were factories with at least 5 employees (1929 and 1935) or at least 10 employees (1922)

is evident in medical instrument and device sales catalogues, which mention the producers of available X-ray equipment. The 1934 edition of the most important medical catalogue in Japan listed a total of eight enterprises, five of which were in the 1935 census (Osaka Roentgen, Shimadzu, TE, Dainihon Roentgen, and Morikawa Seisakujo); the other three were sellers, not producers, in Japan (Siemens, Goto Fuundo, and Kubota Seisakujo).[7]

Second, most were small factories, except for TE and Shimadzu. The 1922 census only gives some data about the number of employees. This shows that, besides TE's Kawasaki plant, which employed 2003 workers—nearly half of whom were women—at the time, the two factories mentioned were small artisanal workshops: Tokyo Igaku had 36 employees, all men, and Okura Denkyu 10, five of whom were women. Although the available resources give no information on the number of employees for the following years, most of the companies were small. In 1935, only four of the nine were joint stock companies.

Third, these factories were close to markets: they were either in large cities (Tokyo, Osaka, Kyoto, or Kobe) or in cities with an established medical tradition (Kanazawa). The factories targeted mass markets of medical doctors rather than smaller locales with renowned universities. This mass market-orientation was a characteristic of the overall medical instrument and device industry in Japan.[8]

There was also a large variety of companies: companies with foreign capital, medium-sized Japanese companies (Shimadzu), and domestic artisanal workshops. Key points for discussion, then, include the evolution of relations between these companies and the specificities of their relations to domestic markets. The business history approach that I employ aims at delineating the respective competitive advantages of these various companies, their product development strategies, and their relations to customers.

This chapter comprises three chronological sections (1895–1914, 1914–1930, and 1930–1945). Each corresponds to a particular type of industrial organization.

2   The Beginnings: A Market Dominated by Siemens (1895–1914)

Up until WWI, the Japanese market of X-ray machines for medical use consisted solely of imports—the lone exceptions were a few machines that Shimadzu Works, a manufacturer of scientific instruments, assembled with imported parts from 1908 onward.[9] Due to the lack of foreign trade statistics for these machines, there is no reliable way to determine the various market shares of individual countries. However, a qualitative approach uncovers a virtual monopoly on the part of German manufacturers, mainly Siemens & Halske, Reiniger, Gebbert & Schall AG (RGS), and Veifa. The annals in Goto Goro's book on Japanese radiology (1969) do not mention the acquisition of non-German foreign X-ray machines prior to 1914, most of which were from Siemens.[10]

Falling in line with what most German multinationals were doing on a global scale, Siemens gave priority to an export strategy rather than direct investments up to WWII. However, the company did relocate part of its production local political conditions or competition with other firms dictated change, especially in Central and Eastern Europe. Akira Kudo has examined this phenomenon in the case of Japan.[11] The presence of Siemens in Japan goes back to 1861, with the gift of a telegraph to the Emperor upon the occasion of the signing of the treaty between Germany and Japan.[12] In the 1870s, the German firm delivered several electrical devices and appliances to the Army, the Government administration, and private companies. First, Siemens exported its products through trading companies, subsequently arranging for representation in Japan by sending Hermann Kessler into open an office in Tokyo (1887).[13] The company was officially registered under the name of Siemens Schuckert Electric Co. in 1905 (thereafter Siemens Japan). Although it favored exports and did not make any direct investments in production, Siemens played a key role in technology transfer to Japan through the German and Japanese engineers who installed and maintained its equipment. In 1898, Siemens Japan had eight employees, six of whom were Japanese.[14]

One of the first radiology devices installed in Japan was a machine that the Japanese Imperial Army ordered from Siemens in December 1898 for its school of medicine.[15] The Army placed its first order with Siemens Japan in 1901, requesting "a great many Siemens-Roentgen apparatuses."[16] In any case, the Army and the Navy were the first customers of the German firm at the beginning of the twentieth century. Japanese officers, impressed by the portable X-ray machines that the German Army had used during the Boxer War, decided to acquire some.[17] In 1904, with Japan's war against Russia escalating, the Imperial Army ordered some new X-ray equipment from Siemens to equip its garrison hospitals in Hiroshima and Matsuyama.[18] After the war, the Army and the Navy decided to install Siemens X-ray machines at all their hospitals (1906).[19]

As the volume of orders rose, Siemens Japan adopted a strategy to develop this business actively, notably in civilian medical circles. It launched work on new machines in 1909 and, two years later, opened a separate division for medical devices that employed four individuals—all Japanese citizens, including a doctor[20]—to help formulate a communication policy that would enhance recognition for Siemens Japan products among civilian doctors. By 1903, Siemens had already wowed the public with a demonstration of its X-ray machine at the Fifth National Industrial Exhibition of Osaka.[21] The core goal of that move was, above all, to stress the technological superiority of Siemens as a whole. The opening of a medical division in 1911 had a more practical aim: increasing sales of X-ray machines and penetrating the private medicine market. Keeping with this objective, a Siemens engineer displayed some devices at a conference of the Japanese Medical Society (*Nihon igakkai*) in 1910.[22] This strategy of diversification toward the private sector was successful. In the years leading up to WWI, Siemens not only continued its shipments to the Army but also extended its activities targeting universities and some of the most renowned private hospitals (Hayashi

Hospital, Juzen Hospital, Ogata Hospital, and Tamura Hospital, for example).[23] In 1913, Siemens delivered scores of X-ray machines to different recipients like the Navy and several prefectural hospitals (in Aichi, Gifu, Hiroshima, and Yamaguchi)—benchmark medical institutions in their regions.

The virtual monopoly that German manufacturers, particularly Siemens, had over the Japanese market for X-ray machines arose out of two factors: the relative weakness of American and British manufacturers up to 1914 and the fascination of the Japanese scientific and medical world with German medicine. At the time, Germany and the other German-speaking countries (Austria and part of Switzerland) were the favorite destinations for Japanese doctors training abroad in the late nineteenth century.[24] When the University of Tokyo instituted its Faculty of Medicine in 1871, the chair positions went first to German doctors and, in the next generation, to Japanese doctors who had done their training at the University of Berlin and elsewhere in Germany.[25] Of special note is the case of Julius Scriba (1848–1905), a professor of surgery at the University of Tokyo who trained many Japanese surgeons. In February 1898, Scriba brought back an X-ray machine from Germany and set it up in his department.[26] The social networks of medicine appeared to have formed a pivotal channel for the supply of X-ray equipment in Japan in the years leading up to 1914.

3 Political and Technological Breakdown: Toward a Competitive Market (1914–1930)

The First World War was a breakdown on both the political and technological levels, ending Siemens' hegemony over the market for X-ray machines in Japan. On the one hand, the war interrupted economic relations with Germany in the X-ray machine market and many other sectors of the economy.[27] Not only did imports of German goods halt overnight, but the Japanese authorities also seized the holdings of German companies—especially patents. In the case of X-ray machines, the abrupt disappearance of German firms, which had totally controlled the market until 1914, made it possible for rival companies to make forays into the arena. This was notably the case with other foreign manufacturers, such as the American company Victor X-Ray Corporation, which shared close ties with GE. Moreover, the shifting conditions for competitiveness on the Japanese market went together with a major technological breakthrough in the United States: the development of the Coolidge X-ray tube at the GE laboratory (1913).[28]

The political and technological shakeup of the 1910s led Japanese importers and distributors to launch non-German X-ray machines and sometimes attempt to engage in production. The trading house Iwayashi Iwamoto Tokichi marketed X-ray machines made by Watson (a British firm) and Victor (an American firm), for example, delivering around ten machines to hospitals in 1915.[29] In addition, the company set up a radiology division that Tokyo Medical Electric Co. (*Tokyo igaku denki*), founded in 1916, would eventually absorb after the war.[30] The company Goto Fuundo, which went on to partner with Siemens in the mid-1920s, redirected its sourcing from Germany to France, the United States, and the United Kingdom.[31] Moreover, Shimadzu, TE Medical Care (*Tokyo iryo denki*), Akiyama, and other domestic manufacturers began producing their own devices. These Japanese producers also took advantage of the absence of German manufacturers to export their goods during the war, mainly to Russia, India, China, and Australia.[32] In the first half of the 1920s, numerous small companies brought machines onto the market. By 1923, the list of companies marketing X-ray devices included Shimadzu, Dainihon Roentgen, Okura Roentgen, Morikawa Works, Akiyama Works, and Goto Fuundo, not to mention the distributors of foreign machines.[33]

The main feature of the years 1914–1930 was a transition that saw the dominant forces in the Japanese market for X-ray devices go from Siemens to Shimadzu, a domestic company, while GE and its subsidiary TE focused on the manufacture of tubes. There is no statistical evidence to determine precisely when this shift happened, as Shimadzu's sales of X-ray devices are unknown prior to 1935, but the evolution of the sales of Siemens' agent in Japan reveals a decline during the second part of the 1920s. Moreover, qualitative documents (correspondence and reports, etc.) illuminate this change. The following section tackles the reasons why Siemens lost its competitiveness against a local player despite the German firm's technological advantage.

3.1   The Decline of Siemens

By the early 1920s, when Siemens was planning its return to Japan, the structure of the country's X-ray machine market had changed radically. Although Siemens' main rivals on the global scale, namely GE and Westinghouse Electric, passed on the opportunity to engage in this business despite a favorable commercial flow between 1914 and 1918, some local newcomers had emerged and established themselves as dominant actors—especially Shimadzu, which benefited from GE technology and adopted a particularly active strategy in promoting its machines within medical circles. The new, international competitiveness of the market led Siemens to restructure this division both on a global scale and in Japan.

3.1.1 The New Organization of Siemens

The German X-ray machine industry underwent a broad concentration wave in the 1920s, which benefited Siemens.[34] This rationalization of the means of production—a result of the financial difficulties that many manufacturers faced after WWI—enabled this sector of German industry to recover its prewar competitiveness. The main merger that occurred during this period was Siemens & Halske's takeover of the company Reiniger, Gebbert & Schall AG (RGS) in 1924. Founded in Erlangen in 1886 to manufacture electrical devices for medical applications, RGS eventually embarked on the production of X-ray machines for Wilhelm Roentgen in 1896.[35] After becoming a joint stock company in 1906, RGS pursued a growth strategy that centered on the acquisition of small rival firms like Veifa Weke (1916), a Frankfurt-based manufacturer of X-ray machines. RGS subsequently set up a holding company, Industrieunternehmungen AG (Inag), in 1921. Bringing together some twenty small and medium-sized firms that were involved in the production of medical appliances and materials, including X-ray machine manufacturers RGS, Veifa, Sanitas, and Polyphos, this new holding company aimed at centralizing distribution in hopes of leveling the field with big enterprises like Siemens. The strategy was not financially viable, however, resulting in the takeover of RGS and Inag by Siemens & Halske (S&H) in 1924. Siemens then founded a common sales company for X-ray devices, Siemens-Reiniger-Veifa GmbH (SRV, 1925), but the group's different production units were still largely autonomous. The consolidation process went further during the crisis of the 1930s. S&H management decided in 1932 to merge RGS, SRV, and Phoenix-Röntgenröhren-Fabriken AG, an Inag-controlled X-ray tube maker, into Siemens-Reiniger-Werke (SRW), a new company based in Erlangen. The company also transferred most of the production of electro-medical equipment at S&H's Berlin plant to Erlangen.[36]

This rationalization effort in Germany in 1924 also provided an opportunity to restructure the import and distribution of X-ray equipment in Japan. For Siemens, this type of business occupied a lower rung on the priority ladder than other key sectors like telecommunication and energy. In a report on business opportunities in Japan from November 1919, R. Momotani, a Siemens Japan employee, paid relatively little attention to X-ray machines and tubes.[37] When S&H and the *zaibatsu* Furukawa created the joint venture Fuji Electric in 1923, they also organized a medical division with six employees.[38] However, Fuji Electric's corporate history indicates that the company only imported products—production was not part of its activities.[39] Still, the division exhibited growth during the months following the Great Kanto Earthquake (which occurred on September 1, 1923). Many hospitals and clinics used the post-disaster reconstruction effort as an opportunity to reorganize themselves into modern medical institutions. Between September 1923 and June 1926, Siemens delivered a total of 101 X-ray machines, 20 X-ray tubes, and 32 various medical devices, including electrocardiograms and diathermy devices, to medical establishments in the Tokyo area and other locations.[40] Despite these deliveries, however, Siemens' exports of electro-medical goods to Japan were in decline: they dropped from a value of 566,500 DM in 1924 to a value of 476,800 DM in 1926.[41]

Fuji Electric's medical division was headed from 1924 onward by Otto Kresta, a German engineer sent by S&H. A Ph.D. in physics and a specialist in X-ray devices, Kresta played a key role in the reactivation and development of Siemens' medical networks.[42] One way that Kresta made an impact was by participating actively in Japan Roentgen Association (*Nihon rentogen gakkai*) events from 1924 onward. The only foreigner to attend these gatherings regularly up until WWII, Kresta gave papers in German on X-ray machines, their operation, and their use, then publishing his research with the journal of the Association (*Japan Roentgen Association Review*; *Nihon rentogen gakkai zasshi*). The objective of this involvement was to strengthen the scientific presence of the firm within the medical world and also make its own new machines known. After 1926, Kresta continued his efforts at Goto Fuundo, the medical goods trading company with which SRW had signed an agreement (Table 2).

3.1.2 The Agreement with Goto Fuundo (1926)

In reaction to its declining sales and the emergence of Shimadzu, SRW entered into an alliance with Goto Fuundo, a small trading firm specializing in the sale and the distribution of drugs and medical goods, in

Table 2 Papers presented by Otto Kresta at the Japan Roentgen Association, 1924–1929 (*Source* Goto, *Nihon hoshasen igaku shiko*)

Title	Date
Technology of deep therapy devices	1924
X-rays and their application	1924
Protection against radiation from X-ray machines	1926
New trends in the X-ray field	1929
The Japanese climate and the processing of Roentgen machines	1929

Note No more conferences are mentioned after 1929

1926. Established in Tokyo in 1886 by Setuzo Goto, a young graduate of the Faculty of Pharmacology at the University of Tokyo (1883), this company originally manufactured and distributed medicine. Later, it diversified into the trade and then the production of medical instruments and machines.[43] This transition from pharmaceuticals into mechanics, which most certainly induced a technological paradigm shift, was not exceptional; several other cases capture similar progressions. One example was the Osaka-based company Shiraimatsu, a drug-trading house that originated in 1716 and eventually converted to mechanics and the production of equipment for hospitals in the 1870s.[44] Another similar case was that of Sankyo, which first specialized in the import and distribution of drugs. In 1908, it opened a division for importing and trading in medical devices mostly from Germany.[45] This transfer toward new activities obviously owes a great deal to the specificity of the medical market, which formed during the Edo period, and these firms' control of distribution channels, which facilitated the flow of new products.

Goto Fuundo followed a comparable path, along which medical instruments and appliances—particularly X-ray machines—quickly assumed an important role alongside drugs. Indeed, the company did abandon its business in medicines despite the growth of the appliances division. According to the 1928 edition of an industrial directory, Goto operated a drug factory in the Nakano Ward of Tokyo as well as several sale subsidiaries throughout Japan, including one in Doshomachi, Osaka—a long-standing hub in the drugs sector.[46] This pharmaceuticals-oriented infrastructure appears again in the 1936 edition of the directory.[47] Among the five members of the board of directors of this family firm was Shinzo Fukuhara, the son of the founder of the cosmetics company Shiseido: a business that largely used the same sales and distribution channels as the pharmaceutical industry.

Besides establishing his company's presence in the medicine business, Setuzo Goto soon launched into the import and distribution of surgical instruments and equipment for hospitals. He regularly published a trading catalog (the tenth edition of which came out in 1906).[48] The foreign machines available from Goto's firm included some X-ray machines, as well. In September 1900, he delivered one to the Faculty of Medicine at Sendai Second High School.[49] Three years later, Setuzo Goto's tour of Europe, which most likely took him to Germany, marked a decisive step.[50] That same year, he imported some parts for X-ray machines from the German company Hirschman (1903).[51] In 1908, he obtained exclusive rights for importing and distributing X-ray machines from the firms Hirschman and RGS to Japan.[52] He also began to do business with Siemens, from which he ordered several medical appliances—including six X-ray tubes and a complete set of radiology equipment (orthoscopes)—in 1912.[53] Finally, Goto Fuundo was quick to adopt an active communication strategy targeting medical circles; in April 1908, for example, it organized a demonstration highlighting the practical use of X-ray machines at a meeting of the Japanese Digestive Organs Diseases Association (*Nihon shokakibyo gakkai*).[54]

In order to maintain and repair the medical appliances and X-ray machines that it sold to the hospitals and clinics, Goto Fuundo had to internalize some technical know-how that eventually helped it launch into production. In 1915, the company hired Motomu Watanabe, an engineer who had graduated that same year from the Electric Department of Tokyo Industrial College (Tokyo Institute of Technology since 1929).[55] In 1921, he went on a business trip to Europe together with the Dr. Koichi Fujinami, a pioneer of radiology in Japan and a professor at Keio University (see Chapter 2).[56] Watanabe subsequently served on the board of directors until after the war.[57] A second engineer, Kosaku Kawamura, joined the company around 1917. He graduated from the same department as Watanabe[58] and became chief engineer at Goto Fuundo around 1921.[59] Finally, Goto Fuundo tried to start producing X-ray machines in 1918, a decision that clearly stemmed from the opportunity opened up by the wartime interruption of imports from Germany. That year also saw Goto Fuundo found a subsidiary, TE Industry (*Tokyo denki kogyo*), whose purpose was to manufacture electrical appliances—particularly X-ray machines.[60] Top-flight researchers played key roles in that effort: while the new firm's technical direction was under the control of Iwayama, an engineering graduate,[61] Goto Fuundo hired Professor Fujinami and Uichi Torikata, who held a Ph.D. in electrical engineering from the University of Tokyo and was at the time director of the Electrotechnical Laboratory of the Ministry of Communication, as consultants. Despite amassing an impressive array of knowledge resources, however, this new firm appears to have quickly given up its activities. The main directories listing industrial companies in the country in 1919 makes no mention of Goto Fuundo.[62] The company underwent a restructuring in 1919 and took the form of a joint stock company with a capital of 550,000 yen.[63] The objectives of this new enterprise were the "manufacturing of […] surgical, chemical, physical, bacteriological, and optical apparatuses and instruments, as well as other general electrical apparatuses and instruments,"[64] in addition to the traditional activities that Goto had engaged in (the manufacture and sale of drugs, the trade of various medical materials, and the business of hospital equipment). Goto Fuundo apparently took over TE Industry's medical instrument and machine workshop in 1919, evidenced by a 1936 directory that mentioned the existence of a Goto Fuundo-affiliated mechanics workshop.[65]

Despite these difficulties, Goto Fuundo stood as a major dealer in medical appliances in the 1920s: it signed many exclusive import and distribution contracts with various foreign (mainly German) medical equipment manufacturers like Mayer & Rotzler (1923), Veifa-Werke (1924), Phoenix (1924), and RGS (1924), all of which were part of the Inag holdings.[66] In return, Inag received 50,000 yen (9.1%) of Goto Fuundo's capital, a share that went to Siemens after it took over Inag. Other similar contracts were signed with Siemens (1926), Adam Schneider (a German manufacturer of devices for dentists; 1928), and Schaerer (a Swiss producer of hospital equipment; 1928).[67] For all these firms, the goal of signing agreements with Goto Fuundo was gaining access to the Japanese medical market. The contract with Mayer & Rotzler, for example, explicitly specified that "Goto engages to make a generous advertisement for Mayer's products, adapted to the territory covered by the agreement. Goto especially undertakes to provide, as need be, catalogues in the Japanese and Chinese languages to doctors and draw their attention to the innovations through appropriate leaflets, advertisements, and publications in key journals, as well as giving thought to a well-equipped, appropriate space for sale and demonstration."[68] Agreements with other firms bore similar clauses; the contracts with RGS and Phoenix also stipulated the organization of semiannual "Roentgen courses."[69]

For Siemens, the takeover of Reiniger, Gebbert & Schall AG (RGS) led to the restructuring of the distribution of medical goods on the Japanese market and the conclusion of an exclusivity contract with Goto Fuundo, which evidently possessed better networks with medical circles than Fuji Electric. In 1926, Goto Fuundo signed two contracts: one with Siemens Reiniger Veifa (SRV), giving it exclusive rights to distribute SRV's products on the Japanese market, and one with Fuji Electric, pertaining to the sale of potential Fuji Electric medical appliances in Japan.[70] The 1926 contract between SRV and Goto Fuundo was renewed in 1931 and then again in 1934 for four years.[71] In this context, Goto Fuundo hired Otto Kresta, who had been head of the medical division of Fuji Electric from 1923 onwards, in 1926.[72] Kresta became a board member and played a key role as a technical consultant until WWII.[73]

The commercial and financial consequences of this agreement were disappointing for SRW, however, as it did not give the company enough to overcome the competitiveness of Shimadzu or keep a dwindling market share from shrinking further. While the 1926 contract stipulated a guarantee on annual orders totaling at least 250,000 yen,[74] the actual transactions reached that level only three times through 1933, including a year before the signing of the contract (see Fig. 1). Between 1926 and 1931, Goto Fuundo's orders from SRW only averaged 229,701 yen. The 30% devaluation of the Japanese yen in December 1931 then made German products more expensive and precipitated a drop in orders, which plummeted from a value of 95,550 yen in 1932 to a value of 35,500 yen in 1933. Still, SRW remained competitive with other foreign MNEs. According to an internal document from SRW, the German firm exported X-ray machines to Japan to the tune of 77,000 marks in 1933—an amount that topped the value of the official German foreign trade statistics (76,000 marks). Siemens obviously had no German rival in Japan, and American exports of X-ray machines amounted to a paltry 7100 marks in 1933.[75] However, SRW's real competition emerged on the domestic market in the early 1930s as TE and Shimadzu began to dig stronger footholds in the field. Goto Fuundo's position in the medical device market had indeed started to recede in the first half of the 1930s, with its dividend rate tapering off from 10% in 1927 to at least 7% in 1930, 5% in 1931, and 4% in 1935.[76]

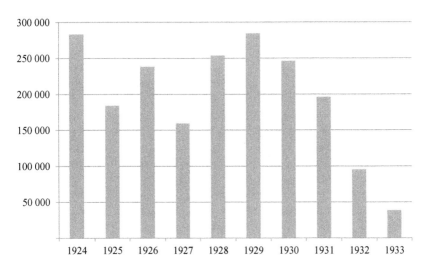

Fig. 1 Sales from SRV–SRW to Goto Fuundo, 1924–1933 (in yen) (*Source* MAE, 770-2, Unser Export nach Japan und unsere zukünftigen Aussichten, 20 October 1934. *Note* Data for the years prior to 1927 is unavailable)

3.2 Tokyo Electric and the Production of X-ray Tubes in Japan

Although it had established itself as a key player in the X-ray industry through the release of the Coolidge tube, GE did not compete directly with Siemens and other manufacturers of full equipment during the 1920s. GE's subsidiary in Japan for light electrical appliances was TE, a small company whose roots stretch back to 1890. GE took a stake in TE in 1905, and TE later merged with Shibaura Works in 1939 to form Toshiba. TE benefited from GE's technology in launching electrical appliances in Japan but also carried out R&D in its own laboratory, making it one of the major players in the industry.

In the field of X-ray technology, TE followed the lead of its parent company and focused on tube manufacturing. The acquisition of knowledge for developing and manufacturing tubes came from GE, of course, but also from cooperation with local doctors who were involved in radiological development: Fujinami, for example, began working as a consultant for TE in 1914.[77] Based on the experience it acquired from GE, TE's engineering force developed a special tube for Japanese market—the "Giba tube"—in 1915. TE then obtained a patent in Japan for Coolidge tubes (no. 34,628) in 1919 and proceeded to intensify its X-ray R&D efforts during the 1920s. The company launched *Rentogen geppo*, a monthly technical journal, in 1921 as a channel for introducing new innovations to medical doctors.[78] Published under different names until WWII, the journal contributed to a broader awareness of TE's tubes within medical circles.[79]

Yet, like GE in the United States and throughout the world, TE did not engage in the business of full equipment until 1930—instead, it produced tubes and sold them to other partners.[80] In 1917, it had exclusive sale contracts with two companies: Shimadzu and Goto Fuundo.[81] Five years later, Shimadzu succeeded in signing a new contract that ensured its tube supply (1922).[82] This connection was essential for Shimadzu to market high-quality equipment and challenge Siemens in Japan, as tube technology represents the most important component of overall product quality.

The sales of medical instruments by TE show a fast growth in the early 1920s (see Fig. 2), with an unusually high level in 1925–1927. The most likely reasons are the strong demand for X-ray devices following the post-Kanto Earthquake reconstruction of hospitals and the growing development of production by Shimadzu. However, as Shimadzu gained

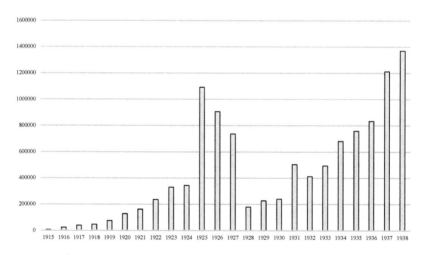

Fig. 2 Sales of medical instruments by Tokyo Electric, in yen, 1915–1938 (*Source* Created based on *Tokyo shibaura denki kabushiki kaisha 85 nenshi*, p. 938)

control over the production of X-ray tubes in the early 1930s, the sudden drop of TE's sales in 1927 remains a mystery. Another cause of the decrease may be the emergence of many domestic copies of tubes, a phenomenon that appears during the second part of the 1920s. Indeed, the success of TE and the importance of tubes led a few small domestic companies, such as Kanezawa Medical Appliances and Shibuya Roentgen, to manufacture lower-quality copies.[83] According to trade catalogues, tubes produced in Japan were valued at about half the price of tubes imported from the United States; clearly, there was a place on the market for low-quality goods. For example, in 1926, a "U type" X-ray tube cost 450,000 yen when imported from the United States but only 250,000 yen when produced in Japan.[84]

While TE was thus not a direct competitor with Siemens in the Japanese market, it was an active supporter behind the emergence and growth of Shimadzu—the local enterprise that would reach the pinnacle of the industry in Japan during the first part of the 1920s.

3.3   A Successful Newcomer: Shimadzu

Shimadzu Corporation (*Shimadzu seisakujo*) was founded in Kyoto in 1875 by Genzo Shimadzu (1839–1894) as a workshop that specialized in the manufacture of scientific instruments aimed primarily at schools.[85] The school-oriented market for this type of industrial activity resulted from a change in education policy, with the widespread adoption of a Western-style educational system cultivating new needs. In venturing into this field, Genzo Shimadzu benefitted not only from his know-how in traditional craftsmanship, which he had developed over several years working at his father's workshop for manufacturing Buddhist worship objects, but also from the support of a chemical and physics research institute (*Kyoto seimikyoku*) that the authorities of Kyoto Prefecture had created in 1870.[86] This external backing, particularly through a German engineer who taught there, enabled Shimadzu to embark on the production of a whole series of new instruments and devices for schools.

However, it was mostly the company's second-generation owner, Genzo II Shimadzu (1869–1951), who turned the family workshop into an industrial firm with a diversified range of activity in fields like medicine. Two years after taking over the management of the firm in the wake of his father's death, Genzo II took the first X-ray in Japan (1896).[87] This achievement was possible thanks to the young owner's collaboration with physicist Hanichi Muraoka (1853–1929). From 1878 and 1881, Muraoka studied physics at the University of Strasbourg, where he obtained a Ph.D. and met then-associate professor Wilhelm Roentgen. After returning to Japan, Muraoka held several academic positions, including that of physics teacher at Kyoto Third High School from 1893 onward.[88] Producing the first Japanese X-ray image was undoubtedly both a scientific and promotional success for Shimadzu, who continued his efforts in the field by developing the first X-ray machine for teaching in 1897.[89] Subsequently, the company designed these types of devices for its traditional market (schools) to provide resources for physics education.[90] It then took around ten more years for the devices to shift from scientific apparatuses to medical appliances: Shimadzu did not produce its first X-ray machines for medical practice until the end of the 1900s, a time when Siemens dominated the market.

The political and technological breakdown of the mid-1910s was the opportunity that led Shimadzu to cross the threshold into the production of X-ray equipment. The company marketed its first mass-produced X-ray machine for medical purposes (the A model) in 1915[91] and secured its tube supply through a contract with TE two years later.

For more than fifteen years, spanning from WWI to the beginning of the 1930s, Shimadzu thus took advantage of favorable conditions to establish itself as the largest X-ray machine producer in Japan. As there are no available resources on the gross sales of Shimadzu's X-ray machine division prior to 1935, it is difficult to gauge the firm's growing competitiveness relative to Siemens. According to Shimadzu's corporate history, X-ray device sales amounted to only one or two machines a year at the beginning of the 1910s. That number rose to about 100 machines and a value of 700,000 yen in 1924 to 250 machines and an estimated value of 1.7 million yen in 1926. By 1934, the sales volume had reached 2500 machines (for an unknown value).[92] In comparison, exports of SRW X-ray machines to Japan came out to monetary values of less than 300,000 yen in both 1924 and 1926.[93] In the first part of the 1920s, then, Siemens fell behind a domestic competitor that had internalized know-how and adopted an active marketing strategy toward accessing a growing medical market.

3.3.1 Shimadzu's R&D Policy

Producing X-ray machines that could compete with appliances imported from Germany required Shimadzu to internalize certain technological skills, a process that relied on collaborations with Kyoto University and other external research centers. By hiring engineers who were graduates of technical colleges and universities and subcontracting portions of its research activities to outside institutions, Shimadzu was able to reap the rewards of advanced technologies that enabled the development of new kinds of X-ray equipment. This internalization of scientific and technical knowledge paid off in the early 1930s, when TE jumped into the production of complete X-ray devices.

Reliance on outside scientists was not merely a strategy specific to the X-ray machine division but rather a general characteristic of the way that Shimadzu went about its business. The company recruited scientists as consultants for various products in the 1900s, for example. In 1911, seven scientists (including one doctor) worked together in this type of arrangement,[94] and years later, a collaborative relationship with Dr. Shichiro Hida allowed Genzo Shimadzu to obtain his first patent for an X-ray machine.[95] A graduate of the University of Tokyo (1898), Hida made a career as a surgeon in the Army and then set out as a private practitioner. In addition to being one of Japan's pioneering forces in radiology and the use of X-ray machines in surgical applications,[96] Hida was also among the 43 founders of the joint-stock Shimadzu Corporation in 1917.

In the 1920s, Shimadzu beefed up its organizational R&D capabilities by hiring engineers to lead the development of new X-ray devices. The first such engineer, Shunichi Fukuda, was a professor of physics at Kumamoto Industrial High School (*Kumamoto koto kogyo gakko*) when Shimadzu hired him away from his post (1920).[97] Up until his death in 1930, Fukuda supervised the creation of new equipment, especially the launch of the first Japan-built radiotherapy machine (the Jupiter model) in 1922[98] and a device designed for the dentist market in 1928. Despite these in-house developments, however, Shimadzu counted on outside suppliers for special parts like tubes and depended on foreign firms for other specific parts. During his business trip to Europe in 1920, Tsunesaburo Shimadzu—brother to Genzo II and member of the firm's board of directors–signed agreements with two producers of parts for X-ray equipment: CAF-Kahlbaum AG (Germany) for X-ray screens and Gebrüder Miller GmbH (Austria) for X-ray spectrometers.[99] Given these conditions, the Shimadzu subsidiary that opened in Berlin in 1922 and remained operational until 1932 may have been tasked with obtaining parts or technical assistance for the production of X-ray machines from

German companies.[100] Shimadzu had particularly close business dealings with S&H, whose X-ray counters Shimadzu imported to Japan at the end of the 1920s.[101] Up until 1930, then, Shimadzu was an assembler of X-ray equipment—a highly developed one, of course—but dependent on the outside for technology. That heavy reliance on external sources was also evident in the company's patenting activity, which secured just four patents in the field of radiology during the 1920s—or roughly 7% of the total radiology patent registrations in Japan over that span.[102]

3.3.2 Making Its Machines Known

Together with the development of its technological competencies, Shimadzu actively worked to spread awareness of its X-ray machines throughout the medical community during the interwar period. The strategy was an intersection of scientific information on the utilization and usefulness of X-ray machines and pure advertising for its own products. At the roots of these dual dimensions were two key realities: the newness of X-ray equipment made it necessary to inform users of its proper use, on the one hand, and the intense market competition—which involved multinational firms such as Siemens and GE—put Shimadzu in a position where it had to make a stronger name for itself. The objective of the policy was thus to encourage the consumption of X-ray equipment, ideally Shimadzu-made products.

The early communication policy was initially consistent with a company producing scientific instruments for education, which was Shimadzu's traditional market: until 1908, Shimadzu's X-ray machines were aimed at schools rather than doctors. Siemens' quasi-monopolistic domination of the market in Japan surely delayed Shimadzu's diversification into the medical sector. For some ten years, Shimadzu evidently viewed its X-ray machines as scientific instruments suited to use in physics classes. Soon after his company produced the first X-ray equipment for teaching in 1897, Genzo II made public presentations at conferences in the Kansai region (Kyoto, Osaka, and Kobe).[103] At a nationwide meeting of secondary school directors in Kyoto in 1908, for example, he demonstrated how his appliances worked.[104] When his X-ray machines hit the medical field after WWI, Shimadzu pursued and developed a three-pronged communication policy envisioned establishing networks in the medical world, organizing scientific events, and setting up schools for radiology technicians.

First of all, Shimadzu forged ties with medical circles through relationships with doctors. This element of the communication strategy
appears to have been a key element of Shimadzu's blueprint for expanding into the medical field in the 1910s. When the firm became a joint-
stock company in 1917, it comprised 43 founders, 12 of whom were
doctors (see Table 3). This proximity between doctors and engineers
may appear to fall in line with the approach to medical device development that would eventually become commonplace in Europe during the
1950s and 1960s,[105] but Shimadzu's relationships with doctors were
different: the presence of doctors within the Shimadzu ranks did not
reflect a shared desire to work together on developing X-ray machines.
Except for surgeon Shichiro Hida, the "idea man" behind Shimadzu's

Table 3 Founding doctors of Shimadzu Corporation, 1917 (Source *Shimadzu
Seisakujo shi*, p. 36, *Dainihon hakashi roku*, Izumi, *Nihon kingendai igaku jinmei
jiten*, and *Kaiin shimei roku*)

Name	Career
Shichiro Hida (1872–?)	Army surgeon; director of Hida Hospital, Tokyo (circa 1910)
Otojiro Kitagawa (1864–1922)	Director of Wakayama Prefectural Hospital (1890); director of Koseikwan Hospital, Nagoya (1891); president of the Medical Society of Nagoya
Futo Kusunoki (1876–?)	Professor at Aichi Medical College, Nagoya (1912); private practitioner in Nagoya (1916)
Tokutaro Nakahara (1871–1926)	Vice-director of Rakusando Hospital, Tokyo (1900); director of Nakahara Hospital, Tokyo (1912); director of Nippon Medical College, Tokyo (1918)
Nao Nakarai	Unknown
Kaname Nanba (1873–1929)	Director of Nogeyama Hospital, Yokohama (1903), and then of Nanba Hospital, Yokohama (1916)
Masakayo Ogata (1864–1919)	Director of the Ogata Obstetrical-Gynecological Hospital, Osaka (1893); member of the Osaka Municipal Assembly
Tsunesaburo Sakura (1855–1921)	Army surgeon; director of Daikan Hospital, Korea
Kinya Sato (1864–1920)	Vice-director of Koseikwan Hospital, Nagoya (1891)
Koichi Shibata	Unknown
Kunimatsu Takeda	Unknown
Michishige Takayasu (1872–?)	Director of Takayasu Hospital, Osaka (circa 1899); director of the Osaka Charity Hospital; president of the Physicians' Association of Osaka

first X-ray device for medical practice (1915) and co-founder of the Tokyo-based firm Hida Electric Industry (1915),[106] none of these doctors were engaged in the development of radiology or medical devices. Not one—not even Hida—held any patents in the field of radiology.[107] Rather than serving as sources of know-how, these doctors functioned as key resources for the firm's commercial opportunities. The nine doctors with documented careers have similar profiles. All were part of the group of "nameless practitioners" who transformed the Japanese medical system during the Meiji period.[108] Alongside the great medical figures at the Universities of Tokyo and Kyoto who captured the interest of scholars, there was also a stratum of specialized medical elite who stayed largely in the shadows of history but nonetheless played a key role in the modernization of Japanese medicine: private practitioners who had trained abroad on their own. A stay at a Western university, essentially in a German-speaking country, was viewed as a long-term investment. In the extremely competitive Japanese hospital market—there were 808 hospitals in 1910, 88.9% of which were private[109]—German training provided a valuable edge, as only a small minority of doctors benefited from this kind of background.[110]

The doctors who helped turned Shimadzu into a joint-stock company in 1917 all belonged to this group of "nameless practitioners." They enjoyed excellent training: apart from Sakura, all held doctoral degrees from the University of Tokyo or the University of Kyoto—the best medical schools in the country. Seven of them also did training in Europe, mainly in German and Austrian faculties. These foreign-educated doctors paid for their studies at their own expense, making their long-term career investments, except for Kusunoki and Sakura. When Shimadzu Corporation got its start in 1917, the founding doctors were running their own private hospitals, and several were engaged in professional associations. The career of Masakyo Ogata exemplifies these various characteristics. Born in 1864 as the son of a doctor, he studied medicine at the University of Tokyo before paying his own way through training in Germany and Austria, where he specialized in obstetrics and gynecology (1888–1892). Upon his return to Japan, he joined his father's hospital in Osaka and took over the management of the institution. After obtaining his Ph.D. in medicine from the University of Tokyo in 1905, Ogata became a prominent figure in Osaka in the early twentieth century. Not only was he the president of the Osaka Physicians' Association, president of the Osaka Midwifery

Association, and vice-president of the Dai-Nihon Physicians' Association, he also served as director of the Osaka Charity Hospital's College of Medicine and a member of the Osaka Municipal Assembly. In between all these responsibilities, he also ran a medical laboratory in the city.[111] Like Ogata, the doctors who joined Shimadzu were entrepreneurs who helped turn medicine into a business. For these private practitioners, new technologies such as X-ray machines were destined to both improve their respective medical practices and strengthen their positions in the medical market. This was probably their main interest when they came on board and laid the foundation for Shimadzu in 1917. As for the firm itself, the purpose of collaborating with these doctors was obvious: it allowed the company to access networks facilitating the sale and distribution of new devices, which the company would then launch in the market.

Shimadzu's involvement in the medical world went beyond including doctors among its shareholders, though. It also developed an active communication policy that focused mainly on organizing and participating in scientific events (see Chapter 2).

4   NEW COMPETITIVE CONDITIONS (1930–1945)

The approaching expiration of GE's patent on the Coolidge X-ray tube in the mid-1930s (1934 in the case of Japan) and the fast-growing demand for radiological equipment had a deep impact on the conditions of competitiveness in the X-ray industry throughout the world.[112] With the doors to the industry opening, the market for X-ray tubes saw the arrival of several newcomers—including Shimadzu (1934) and Kawanishi Machine (1935)—and several other small companies that produced low-quality copies of these tubes.[113]

As it lost its advantage, GE shifted from the production of tubes to the manufacture and sale of complete X-ray equipment. In the United States, Victor X-Ray Corporation, a Chicago-based manufacturer of medical devices that GE had invested in 1920 and fully acquired in 1926, became GE X-Ray Corporation and engaged actively in X-ray device business on a global scale (1930).[114] In Japan, TE established itself as the most important challenger to Shimadzu. Siemens, meanwhile, attempted to recover its competitiveness by bolstering ties with Goto Fuundo, but its limitations in transferring technology and production to Japan prevented a comeback.

4.1   A New Manufacturer of X-Ray Equipment: Tokyo Electric

The Japanese market for X-ray machines changed radically in the 1930s when GE's patent for the Coolidge tube expired (July 1934).[115] Until then, the activities of Tokyo Electric (TE; GE's subsidiary in Japan) in the business of radiology had only gone as far as importing and then manufacturing tubes under a 1922 agreement with Shimadzu, the main Japanese manufacturer of X-ray machines.[116] Anticipating the end of their monopoly, GE and TE had begun to produce complete installations in the 1930s with the launch of the "Giba 75" machine (1932), a standardized X-ray machine that would ensure market success for TE.[117]

Developed specifically for the Japanese market, the Giba 75 was simple, small, and cheap. The public—especially medical doctors—got most of its exposure to the new device through an article in TE's sales subsidiary journal in 1932. The article presented the device as an improvement on a Victor-developed device from the United States, a piece of equipment that had enjoyed widespread use "since [being] launched on the market, by general clinics and hospitals as a common X-ray device, and by large hospitals as an additional device."[118] Two years later, Kishi Iwao, an engineer in TE's R&D center, explained in the same journal that X-ray machines are not works of art—and that meant that price, not design, was of chief importance. From that perspective, then, mass-production was the optimal way to deliver good quality at inexpensive prices. Alluding to the benefits of mass-production, Iwao also said that the new plant for medical equipment that had opened that year had been inspired by Ford facilities.[119] In 1930, TE also founded Nippon Medical Electric (*Nihon iryo denki*), a sales company charged with the task of marketing the machines imported from GE and produced in Japan by TE.[120]

The launch of the Giga 75 enabled TE to enter a new period of fast growth. Figure 2 (p. 30) shows that the sales of medical instruments went from 410,422 yen in 1932 to 1.4 million yen in 1938. Although this amounts to about one-third of Shimadzu's sales, the net total was far larger than that of Siemens. Consequently, GE—through its subsidiary TE—established itself as the second-largest player in the Japanese market after its engagement in the business of complete equipment.

4.2   The Domination of Shimadzu

Competition in the X-ray equipment intensified in the 1930s when TE launched into production of complete X-ray machines and Siemens embarked on a joint venture to manufacture complete X-ray machines in Japan (Goto Fuundo Manufacturing (GFM), 1933).[121] Shimadzu reacted to the stiffer competition by strengthening its organizational capabilities. After the death of lead development engineer Fukuda in 1930, the responsibility of managing Shimadzu's X-ray machine division went to Sekito Kikuchi, a graduate of the Faculty of Sciences at Tohoku University.[122] After completing his studies, he taught in a technical college at Hamamatsu before returning to Tohoku University, where he worked as a researcher and obtained his Ph.D. in 1930.[123] Shimadzu also hired other engineers to work under Kikuchi, including Koji Nakabori.[124] Immediately after graduating from the Department of Electrical Engineering in the Faculty of Engineering at Kyoto University in 1935, Nakabori entered Shimadzu and then spent his entire career there as a researcher. He obtained his Ph.D. from Kyoto University in 1956 and became a member of the Shimadzu board of directors in 1963.[125]

In addition to promoting this strategy of employing engineers with university degrees, Shimadzu also cooperated with outside institutions in conducting R&D on Coolidge tubes.[126] In 1932, the company commissioned the Aoyagi Research Laboratory, which was headed by a Kyoto University professor who specialized in research on vacuum tubes, to work on the topic.[127] That same year, Shimadzu also subcontracted some R&D to the Japan Quartz Industry (*Nihon sekiei kogyo*), an Osaka-based firm that received Shimadzu funding. In 1934, Japan Quartz Industry produced a prototype of a Coolidge tube based on a model from the German company Müller and delivered the results to Shimadzu.[128] Using that prototype, Shimadzu began in-house production of the tubes in 1940.[129]

Shimadzu's technological development in the first part of the 1930s allowed the firm to amass a growing number of patents: over the course of the decade, it completed 23 registrations—or 21.7% of all the patents registered in Japan for X-ray equipment during that period. As a result, Shimadzu became one of the main players in this new industry. The company also appears to have been very active on the product-marketing front, as well, launching 19 new appliances during the 1930s.[130]

After the war against China began in 1937, Shimadzu was, like other Japanese enterprises, instructed to shift toward war production. While the share of the company's X-ray machine division relatively to total sales did decline during the war (going from 19.2% of gross sales in 1935 to 17.8% in 1940 and 8.8% in 1944), however, its value continued to increase. It rose from 1.7 million yen in 1935 to 4.7 million yen in 1940 and 6.2 million yen in 1944.[131]

The Japanese Army was Shimadzu's main customer, ordering X-ray appliances in bulk for the medical support teams servicing Army troops and hospitals.[132] This specific demand for simple, light, and easily transportable devices also spurred R&D at Shimadzu. The company registered total of 20 new patents from 1937 to 1943 (19.0% of the total). One particularly key innovation was an indirect radiography machine, which Shimadzu rolled out in 1938 and the Army adopted for the enlistment of soldiers two years later. This context also explains the development of an X-ray automobile machine for collective radiographies.[133]

4.3   The Efforts of Siemens

For Siemens, the issue was not the technology but rather the market. At a very early stage, it controlled its supply of Coolidge-type high vacuum X-ray tubes. Even though its rival Allgemeine Elektrizitätsgesellschaft (AEG) had obtained manufacturing rights for the GE patent in the European market shortly before WWI broke out, Siemens held some patents in Germany for the tungsten anti-cathodes integral to the production of Coolidge X-ray tubes. The two German multinationals thus signed an agreement permitting AEG to use the Siemens patents in exchange for producing a determined quantity of X-ray tubes for Siemens.[134] Until the end of the 1920s, Siemens had no problems procuring tubes. Two independent manufacturers also emerged as producers and global exporters of high-quality X-ray tubes: C.H.F. Müller and Phoenix Röntgenröhrenfabriken AG. Müller was eventually taken over by the Dutch multinational enterprise Philips in 1927,[135] while Phoenix was acquired by SRW in 1932. Founded in 1918, Phoenix primarily supplied Veifa with X-ray tubes and then essentially became an exclusive Siemens supplier after 1925.[136] The takeover in 1932 reflected Siemens' desire to secure its supply of X-ray tubes.

In reaction to GE's arrival on the X-ray machine market, SRW tried to establish an international cartel with other European firms (AEG, Philips, Müller, and Elema-Schönander) for a share of the world market.[137] Under this agreement, Japan joined Latin America, Sweden, Norway, Italy, Spain, Yugoslavia, and Switzerland as the markets assigned primarily to Siemens. According to a document dated 1934, Siemens and Philips shared the Japanese market at a relative proportion of 62%

to 38%.[138] Philips and Müller could thus export to Japan, but their actions did not receive priority: Siemens business took precedence in Japan, where the company encountered only American and domestic competitors.

4.3.1 The Establishment of Goto Fuundo Manufacturing (1932–1934)

In June 1932, SRW signed a contract with Goto Fuundo to set up a joint venture in Japan. The new company, Goto Fuundo Manufacturing (GFM), received the approval of the German management in November 1933.[139] SRW continued to support the development of Goto Fuundo by participating in various capital increases (in July 1938, February 1939, and September 1939)[140] and granting a loan of 50,000 yen (in April 1937).[141]

According to its statutes, the objective of the new company (GFM) was "to produce electro-medical apparatuses, light therapeutic apparatuses, and Roentgen apparatuses for medical purposes" except "high-vacuum or gas discharge tubes."[142] The capital of the new enterprise amounted to 400,000 yen, which SRW and Goto Fuundo shared equally. Instead of paying cash contributions, SRW received its shares in exchange for the free provision of licenses and know-how. SRW began giving GMF the necessary patents and blueprints for its devices as well as access to engineers, who provided practical assistance.[143] GFM obtained the exclusive and free license for the production of SRW's X-ray machines in Japan. Goto Fuundo, meanwhile, obtained its shares by offering the use of its factory and contributing a certain amount of cash. GFM was registered at the Goto Fuundo address and naturally took over the Goto Fuundo production facilities.

The GFM administration drew heavily on Japanese managers linked to Goto Fuundo. Its board of directors comprised three members, with two designated by Goto Fuundo and one by SRW. Company leadership also included an SRW-appointed Japanese citizen inspector.[144] Goto Fuundo was in charge of GFM management and paid a minimum dividend of 6%, guaranteeing Siemens royalties of 10% on sales and minimum annual orders of 300,000 yen instead of 200,000 yen.[145]

However, SRW was not only looking for an agreement that could ensure good financial results—its principal concern was to control technology transfer, particularly potential GFM-driven innovations and possible cooperative arrangements with other firms. The 1932 agreement that established the joint venture included a long article on innovation, which stipulated that "inventions and other propositions for improvements proceeding from the supervisors or employees shall be communicated by the Factory to SRW immediately and no later than the time when the protection rights for such inventions or improvements are applied for in Japan. SRW retains the exclusive authority to utilize such inventions and improvements and acquire protection rights outside Japan."[146] Moreover, the document stated that the "Factory shall not acquire the rights to other inventions or protection rights without the express consent of SRW in each case. Should SRW provide its express consent, it will advise the Factory on the acquisition. The Factory shall do its best to help SRW acquire these rights for utilization outside Japan under conditions that provide advantages equivalent to or greater than those in Japan. SRW shall determine whether or not to accept the conditions at its own discretion."[147]

SRW's prudent approach is also evident in its stance on the transfer of production, which the company limited as much as possible. The GFM production site was the workshop that Goto Fuundo had operated in the Tokyo area since 1919, a facility where the company produced spare parts for X-ray machines and other medical devices.[148] Destroyed during the Kanto Great Earthquake in 1923, the factory was moved to Urawa Ward (Saitama City) in 1927. The site worked on the production of "general medical apparatuses such as incubators, mechanical disinfection apparatuses, centrifugal precipitators, water sterilizers, electric transformers, diaplasis treatment apparatuses, and all kind of Roentgen equipment."[149] After 1934, this factory not only served as the production center for SRW products in Japan but also functioned as the location where Goto Fuundo continued to manufacture appliances and instruments on its own—and that dual-purpose arrangement created an ambiguous situation that led to problems between Goto Fuundo and Siemens after WWII. When Otto Kresta came to Berlin in December 1933, he spoke with two SRW representatives about launching a production program in Japan at a value of 100,000 marks and a limited volume of machines (30 small X-ray machines, 10 Heliophos, 20 diathermy machines, and various other appliances).[150] The discussions underscored the exacting restrictions that SRW wanted to place on the transfer of production, with the company only willing to shift production for machines whose import to Japan was no longer competitive. These smaller devices, which were meant for the Army, the Navy, and private hospitals, demonstrated high-growth potential due to increasing demand but relatively little market opposition as imported products were too expensive—high exchange rates and the cost of foreign curren-cies after the devaluation, combined with the cheap labor in Japan, made imports impractical. Company leaders thus decided to assemble these machines at the GFM factory with some parts produced in-house and others imported from Germany. However, negotiations with TE and GE delayed the launch of production for about a year.

At the same time that this production program was starting to get off the ground in Japan, SRW management began negotiations with TE in early 1934. The director of TE, Yamaguchi, approached Siemens in the spring of 1934 on the occasion of a trip to Berlin and proposed the idea of his firm taking over the production of SRW medical devices in Japan.[151] Kresta recommended the management team in Germany to found a new joint venture with TE and Goto Fuundo, endow it with capital of 2.7 million yen, and split the funding between TE (44.4%), which would be in charge of production, Goto Fuundo (29.7%), which would be responsible for marketing, and SRW (25.9%), which would supply patents and brands.[152] However, Yamaguchi set some condi-tions on the agreement: he wanted to centralize all the production at TE's factory and transfer Goto Fuundo's workshop there.[153] The part-ners rejected these conditions, though. On the one hand, SRW claimed a negotiation with GE on the global scale and an agreement between both multinationals. On the other hand, Goto Fuundo balked at giving up its production facilities.[154] The potential partners' inability to reach a satis-factory agreement finally led SRW to pursue a plan that would transfer production to Japan through GFM.

4.3.2 The Growth of Production in Japan (1935–1940)

The licensed production of SRW machines really got underway in 1935. According to a document detailing GFM manufacturing by product origin from 1933 to 1937, no production took place in Japan in 1933 and 1934 (see Fig. 3). Once SRW made the decision to produce X-ray machines in Japan, however, the transfer moved quickly, just as a similar effort at Fuji Electric had since the mid-1920s.[155] The value of prod-ucts imported from Germany and sold by Goto Fuundo declined steadily from 1934 onwards, dropping from 419,000 yen in 1934 to 174,000 yen in 1937, while the value of in-house production skyrocketed from a mere 52,000 yen in 1935 to 270,000 yen in 1937. In relative terms, the share of domestic production went from 12.8% in 1935 to 43.8% in 1936 and 60.8% in 1937.

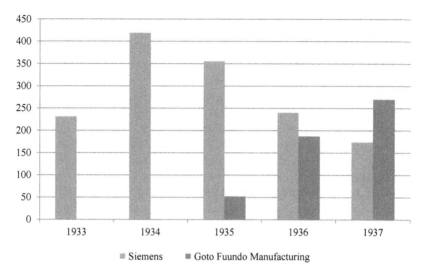

Fig. 3 Gross sales of Goto Fuundo by product origin, 1933–1937 (in thousands of yen) (*Source* MAE, unmarked folder, Gegenwärtiger Stand des SRW-Geschäfts in Japan, 4 January 1939. *Note* There are no figures for the years after 1937)

As manufacturing in Japan grew, so did the range of machines subject to the transfer of production to GFM. The evolution of the production programs between 1935 and 1938 sheds light on this phenomenon (see Table 4). GFM produced little more than orthoscopes in 1935, but the subsequent years saw the production diversify significantly: the program expanded to include not only different kinds of X-ray machines but also diathermy devices. The transfer of production was thus accompanied by a real technology transfer; general stagnation in the total volume of parts from SRW after 1934 also attests to the passage of technology from SRW to GFM. The value of the parts that GFM received was at 35,800 RM in 1935, dropped to 22,600 RM in 1936, and then came back up to 33,000 RM in 1937.[156] Growth in production scale did not mean that GFM was necessarily more dependent on SRW but rather reflected the internalization of some resources.

Despite the production and collaborative arrangements Japan, SRW and Goto Fuundo registered only a very small number of patents in the country. From 1900 to 1945, the differences in patent registrations

Table 4 Number and types of machines produced by GFM, 1935–1938 (*Source* MAE, unmarked folder, Gegenwärtiger Stand des SRW-Geschäfts in Japan, 4 January 1939)

	1935	1936	1937 (Second semester)	1938 (First semester)
Ultratherm (diathermy device)	–	17	18	15
Heliolex 300 mA 60 kV (X-ray machine)	–	–	–	3
Heliodor Duplex (surgery appliance)	–	4	–	–
Tuto Heliophos (X-ray machine)	1	5	2	3
Orthoscope (X-ray machine)	22	17	–	4
Pantoscope (X-ray machine)	–	1	6	5
Tele-Pleoscope (X-ray machine)	–	1	–	2
Tele-Pantoscope (X-ray machine)	–	4	7	4

were striking: rivals Shimadzu (37 patents registered in the field of X-ray machines during that time frame) and TE (71 patents) made frenzied use of legal protection for their technologies in Japan, SRW registered only six (all between 1926 and 1933), and its partner Goto Fuundo only two (one in 1927 and one in 1939).[157] This is a rather surprising piece of the SRW story, especially considering that Siemens was a regular user of the patent system in other cases.[158] With SRW relatively inactive on the patent front, competitors were thus able to copy most of SRW's X-ray machines in Japan within the scope of the law. For SRW, this strategy embodied the technological competitiveness Siemens enjoyed in the field of X-ray machines and stemmed from a desire to dominate the market by virtue of product excellence: as it transferred the production and assembly of consistently top-quality X-ray machines to GFM, SRW thus aimed to prevent domestic companies that did not have the necessary organizational capabilities from copying the devices. According to a report by the Tripartite Commission dated 1954, this was a deliberate strategy on the part of SRW: "It might have been the intention of SRW to keep Goto Factory in possession of devices that were always new and up-to-date as a precautionary measure to prevent competing companies from imitating devices."[159] Statements by Goto Fuundo's board of directors runs along the same lines. In a February 1954 letter to the Ministry of Finance, the board wrote: "Our company could manufacture and sell the newest

SRW-type apparatuses by copying the devices that we had imported as goods from SRW under the terms of the sales agreement. Our company took pride in the novelty and superiority of our products as compared with the articles of other manufacturers. This was acknowledged by all those involved in this line of business, whereby our company was placed in a position to compete with any other manufacturer at a margin sufficient to pay for the license fee."[160] Despite the development of its technological facilities, GFM still depended on SRW for some parts of the production process, probably with regard to practical know-how and tacit knowledge.[161] It tried to register some patents for copies of SRW machines in Japan but never succeeded: "applications have always been rejected on the grounds that the corresponding equipment was widely known to the public."[162] From 1945 onward, Goto Fuundo never succeeded in developing its own machines without the support of SRW.

A look at gross sales for GFM from 1936 to 1945 shows two distinct phases in the development of the firm (see Fig. 4). First, the years 1936–1940 are characterized by the transfer of production and technology

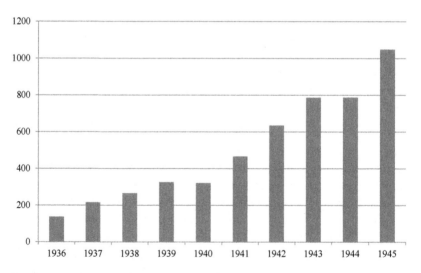

Fig. 4   GFM gross sales, 1936–1945 (in thousands of yen) (*Source* SCAP, CPC 41474, Siemens Reiniger Werke, Cost Accounting, no date. *Note* The values are different from these given in the SRW document used for Fig. 3, but the trends and the order of magnitude are similar)

from SRW. Gross sales rose from 137,000 yen in 1936 to 326,000 yen in 1939, and the stagnation in 1940 resulted quite obviously from the severance of commercial relations with SRW due to the war in Europe: the last delivery of X-ray machines and parts from Germany indeed occurred in September 1940.[163] These four years of cooperation with SRW sharpened the competitive edge of Goto Fuundo, which was marketing GFM production. While its dividend rate dropped between 1930 and 1934, Goto Fuundo came out of those years on an upward swing (5% in 1937, 7% in 1938, and 8% in 1940).[164] In comparison with Shimadzu (its main rival on the Japanese market), however, GFM experienced limited growth. While Shimadzu saw the gross sales of its X-ray machines division increase from 1.7 million yen to 2.5 million yen in 1937,[165] Goto Fuundo's sales of SRW products only inched up from 407,000 yen to 444,000 yen over the same period.[166] These numbers apparently include SRW products (those imported from Germany and manufactured by GFM) only, however; Goto Fuundo's overall gross sales—which would have also covered products made in-house and goods supplied by firms other than SRW—were surely higher, but there are no supporting documents. Still, for SRW, which distributed all its production in Japan through Goto Fuundo, this comparison with Shimadzu reveals a reality in the Japanese X-ray machine market that was completely different to what had been in place before the First World War: between 1914 and 1935, SRW's position in the market declined from a virtual monopoly holder to a second-rank competitor.

For Goto Fuundo, the termination of commercial relations with SRW in 1940 did not put an end to the firm's growth, which continued during the war thanks to strong demand for X-ray equipment from the Army and Navy. GFM gross sales increased steadily despite the cut-off in the supply of German parts and machines, peaking at one million yen in 1945. The value of Goto Fuundo gross sales during these years is unknown, but the firm continued to pay a dividend of 8%—a testament to good business conditions.[167] This positive development could not reverse the balance of power with Shimadzu, however: gross sales for Shimadzu's X-ray machines division amounted to 6.7 million yen in 1943 and 6.2 million yen in 1944.[168]

4.4   The Proliferation of Small Assembly Manufacturers

The growing demand of X-ray devices also spurred the emergence and development of numerous small, independent assembly makers.

Dainihon Roentgen, founded in 1919 by engineer Keizo Muro, a Kyoto University graduate who worked in Shimadzu's medical instrument division, is a rare—and probably non-representative—example of a spin-off process.[169] Most of these new companies were the business projects of mechanics who had experience working for medical doctors and relied on external suppliers for tubes and other high-tech parts. They marketed cheap, low-quality equipment that had no trouble finding customers in a highly competitive hospital market.

From 1935 to 1938, Eisuke Watanuki, a medical doctor at the Electric Research Center of the Ministry of Communications (*Tsushinsho denki shikenjo*), analyzed X-ray devices and other electro-medical instruments made by 23 companies in Japan. In the report he published in 1939, he emphasized that the lack of organization in the industry precluded any standards and allowed for a multitude of equipment on the market—all with slightly different technical criteria. Therefore, it was hard for the community of medical doctors to make proper use of such machines. The dogged competition between these small assembly makers also precipitated the launch of lower-quality goods, as price was more important than quality or security.[170]

Instituting standards was thus a major issue for the X-ray device industry during the second part of the 1930s, especially given the ongoing proliferation of assembly manufacturers. From 1938 to 1940, medical journals featured several papers stressing the need to improve the quality of parts and the rationalization of work in order to achieve mass-production.[171]

5   CONCLUSION

The X-ray equipment industry in Japan during the first part of the twentieth century evolved in a three-phase process that featured growing competition but a relatively stable, limited number of enterprises. From 1895 to 1914, the German MNE Siemens exerted control over the market thanks not only to its technological superiority but also to the excellent reputation of German science in Japanese medical circles. However, Siemens refrained from producing in Japan and instead focused on exporting small lots of large, high-quality equipment to institutional customers (Army, Navy, universities, and large hospitals). The second phase started during WWI and lasted until the early 1930s. The period was marked by the decline of Siemens, which was unable to recover its former dominant position in Japan after 1918 despite signing an agreement with Goto Fuundo, a local distributor of medical instruments and devices, in 1926. The market grew rapidly, fueling the emergence and development of Shimadzu, a domestic firm without any foreign capital. A contract with TE, GE's Japanese subsidiary, for the supply of Coolidge X-ray tubes supported Shimadzu in the 1920s and helped give the firm what it needed to compete against Siemens through the development of cheap, high-quality goods. Finally, the industry entered its third phase in the early 1930s when TE got into the business of complete X-ray equipment—not just tubes. Following Shimadzu's example, TE launched simple, cheap, high-quality, mass-produced equipment for the domestic market. However, Shimadzu was able to maintain its leadership position and acquire the necessary knowledge for developing and producing tubes cooperative links with private research institutes. Siemens, meanwhile, lost all of its competitiveness—not even the eventual foundation of a joint venture with Goto Fuundo to assemble and produce some devices in Japan could get the company back to its previous levels of success.

The dynamic of the Japanese X-ray equipment industry thus hinged on the evolution among the three main actors in the business (Siemens, Shimadzu, and TE). The dominant trend was the constant decline of Siemens, a company that remained the world's most competitive X-ray manufacturer until WWII. Internal documents from Siemens estimated its share of world exports at 36% between 1936 and 1938.[172] What explains the world leader's dramatic failure in Japan, then?

To answer this question, one has to consider the issue of adapting technology to specific environments. Japanese historians like Tetsuro Nakaoka have emphasized that imported technologies run the risk of failing if unless the parties involved adapt it to natural conditions: this is the fate that befell the blast furnace in Kamaishi and cotton spinning factories in Osaka during the early Meiji period.[173] Adapting technology and products to local social and economic conditions was also essential.[174] In the world of X-ray equipment, however, Siemens is a remarkable case—a company that never adapted its technology and goods to local conditions in Japan or anywhere else in the world.[175] The Siemens business model revolved around producing superior, high-cost products at its German plants, with the idea being to stay at the top of the industry through the excellence of its products. This strategy was simply unfeasible in Japan due to a medical market structure that bore very little resemblance to those of Siemens' main markets in Western Europe. Companies that aligned more closely to the domestic market, particularly Shimadzu but also TE, succeeded in developing devices that were suitable for local doctors—equipment that was smaller, simpler, and cheaper. The following chapters analyze the ways in which these firms cooperated with doctors and internalized the knowledge it took to develop such products, using a survey of patents to illuminate the course of events (Chapter 3). Before that, however, it is crucial to discuss radiologists and establish a better understanding of who these medical doctors were and what their needs entailed (Chapter 2).

NOTES

1. About radiology in general, see Holtzmann Kevles, *Naked to the Bone*.
2. Chandler, *Scale and Scope*, pp. 218–219 and 579; Boersma, "Structural Ways to Embed a Research Laboratory into the Company"; and Donzé and Wubs, "Global Competition and Cooperation in the Electronics Industry".
3. Rosenberg, "Economic Development and the Transfer of Technology"; Jeremy, *International Technology Transfer*; Jeremy, *The Transfer of International Technology*; and Donzé and Nishimura, *Organizing Global Technology Flows*.
4. Odagiri and Goto, *Technology and Industrial Development in Japan*.
5. *Nihon kanzei*, pp. 166–167.
6. *Kojo tsuran*, 1922, 1929 and 1935.
7. *Tokyo ika kikai dogyo kumiai mokuroku*, pp. 409–450.
8. Donzé, "The Beginnings of the Japanese Medical Instruments Industry".
9. Goto, *Nihon hoshasen igaku shiko*, vol. 1, p. 64.
10. Ibidem.
11. Kudo, *Japanese–German Business Relations*.
12. Siemens K.K., *100 Jahre Siemens in Japan*; Takenaka, "Business Activities of Siemens in Japan"; and Siemens Corporate Archives, Berlin (thereafter SCA), 7912, *Chronology of Siemens-Schuckert D.K.K., Tokyo*, 1944.
13. Siemens K.K., *100 Jahre Siemens in Japan*, p. 17.
14. SCA, 7912, *Chronology of Siemens-Schuckert D.K.K., Tokyo*, 1944, p. 5.
15. Goto, *Nihon hoshasen igaku shiko*, vol. 1, p. 22.
16. SCA, 7912, *Chronology of Siemens-Schuckert D.K.K., Tokyo*, 1944, p. 6.
17. Ibidem.
18. Ibidem, p. 7.
19. Goto, *Nihon hoshasen igaku shiko*, vol. 1, p. 55.

20. Ibidem, p. 69.
21. SCA, 7912, *Chronology of Siemens-Schuckert D.K.K., Tokyo*, 1944, p. 7.
22. Goto, *Nihon hoshasen igaku shiko*, vol. 1, p. 75.
23. Siemens Medical Archives (thereafter MAE), unmarked folder, *Die Tätigkeit des Haus Siemens in Japan auf das Gebiet der elektromedizinischen Technik*, 31 May 1958.
24. Donzé, "Studies Abroad by Japanese Doctor"; Kim, *Doctors of Empire*.
25. *Tokyo daigaku igakubu hyakunen shi*, pp. 123–134.
26. Goto, *Nihon hoshasen igaku shiko*, vol. 1, p. 22.
27. On the relationships between Japan and Germany, see Kudo, Tajima and Pauer, *Japan and Germany*.
28. Siemens, *History of the House of Siemens*, vol. 2, pp. 79–80. On the Coolidge tube, see Arns, "The High-Vacuum X-Ray Tube".
29. Goto, *Nihon hoshasen igaku shiko*, vol. 1, p. 126.
30. Ibidem, p. 160.
31. Ibidem, p. 126.
32. SCA, 15 Ln 376, R. Momotani, *Future Prospects in Japan with Special Consideration of the Siemens & Halske business*, November 1919.
33. Goto, *Nihon hoshasen igaku shiko*, vol. 1, pp. 223–224.
34. Siemens Georg, *History of the House of Siemens*, vol. 2, pp. 81–85; SCA, 7912, *Chronology of Siemens-Schuckert D.K.K., Tokyo*, 1944, p. 4.
35. Siemens Georg, *History of the House of Siemens*, vol. 1, p. 280.
36. Feldenkirchen, *Siemens, 1918–1945*, pp. 312–313.
37. SCA, 15 Ln 376, R. Momotani, *Future prospects...*, op. cit.
38. SCA, 7912, *Chronology of Siemens-Schuckert D.K.K., Tokyo*, 1944, p. 2.
39. *Fuji denki shahsi*, p. 281.
40. MAE, unmarked folder, *Die Tätigkeit des Haus Siemens in Japan auf das Gebiet der elektromedizinischen Technik*, 31 May 1958.
41. SCA, statistics on turnover.
42. Momotani, *Nihon ni okeru shimensu*, p. 42.
43. Goto, *Nihon hoshasen igaku shiko*, vol. 1, p. 42.
44. *130 nen no ayumi*.
45. Yamashita, *Iyaku wo kindaika shita kenkyu to senryaku*, p. 145.
46. *Nihon kogyo yokan*, 1928, p. 105.
47. Ibidem, 1936, p. 127.
48. Goto, 1906.
49. Goto, *Nihon hoshasen igaku shiko*, vol. 1, p. 30.
50. Ibidem, p. 42.
51. Ibidem.
52. Ibidem, p. 64.
53. SCA, 7912, Lieferübersichten, 8 June 1935.
54. Goto, *Nihon hoshasen igaku shiko*, vol. 1, p. 64.

55. Ibidem, p. 128.
56. Ibidem, p. 194.
57. He was still a member of the Board in 1950. Goto Fuundo, *Eigyo hokok-usho*, 1950.
58. *Nikkan kogyo shimbun*, 1934, p. 201.
59. Goto, *Nihon hoshasen igaku shiko*, vol. 1, p. 194.
60. Ibidem, p. 160.
61. Ibidem.
62. This company was for example not cited in the 1919 and following editions of the *Nihon kogyo yokan*.
63. Goto, *Nihon hoshasen igaku shiko*, vol. 1, p. 170.
64. MAE, unmarked folder, *Statutes of S. Goto Fu-undo Co. Ltd.*, not dated (probably 1919).
65. *Nihon kogyo yokan*, 1936, p. 127.
66. MAE, unmarked folder, Contracts between Goto Fuundo and various foreign firms.
67. Ibidem.
68. MAE, unmarked folder, Contract between Goto Fuundo and Mayer & Rotzler (art. 3), 18 August 1923.
69. MAE, unmarked folder, Contracts between Goto Fuundo and various foreign firms.
70. SCA, 7912, *Vertretung des UB Med und seiner Vorgänger in Japan, 1887–1979*, 1979, p. 4.
71. MAE, 770-2, Contracts between SRW and Goto Fuundo, 12 November 1931 and 1 January 1934.
72. Momotani, *Nihon ni okeru shimensu*, pp. 53–54.
73. National Diet Library, Tokyo (NDL), Archives of the Supreme Commander of the Allied Powers (thereafter SCAP), CPC 41470, Memo, 2 October 1946.
74. MAE, unmarked folder, Contract between SRW and Goto Fuundo, 1926.
75. MAE, unmarked folder, Gegenwärtiger Stand des SRW-Geschäfts in Japan, 4 January 1939.
76. MAE, 174, Dividendenzahlungen von Goto.
77. Goto, *Nihon hoshasen igaku shiko*, vol. 1, p. 113.
78. *Rentogen geppo*, 1921–1922.
79. *Matsuda irigaku jippo*, 1926–1930; *Iryo denki jippo*, 1931–1940.
80. *Tokyo shibaura denki kabushiki kaisha 85 nenshi*, p. 474.
81. *Ika kikai shinpo*, vol. 1, p. 4.
82. *Shimadzu seisakujo shi*, p. 45; Goto, *Nihon hoshasen igaku shiko*, vol. 1, p. 179 quotes 1920.
83. Goto, *Nihon hoshasen igaku shiko*, vols. 1 and 2.

84. *Tokyo ika kikai dogyo kumiai mokuroku*, p. 323.
85. *Shimadzu seisakujo shi*, p. 1.
86. Ibidem, 2.
87. Ibidem, 16.
88. Ibidem.
89. Goto, *Nihon hoshasen igaku shiko*, vol. 1, p. 18.
90. *Shimadzu seisakujo shi*, p. 353.
91. Goto, *Nihon hoshasen igaku shiko*, vol. 1, p. 126.
92. *Shimadzu seisakujo shi*, p. 356.
93. MAE, 770-2, *Unser Export nach Japan und unsere zukünftigen Aussichten*, 20 October 1934.
94. *Shimadzu seisakujo shi*, p. 27.
95. Database of the Industrial Property Digital Library, www.ipdl.inpit.go.jp/homepg.ipdl (accessed in February and March 2010).
96. *Dainihon hakushi*, vol. 2, pp. 255–256 and Goto *Nihon hoshasen igaku shiko*, vol. 2, p. 118.
97. *Shimadzu seisakujo shi*, p. 45.
98. Ibidem, p. 354.
99. Ibidem, p. 47.
100. Ibidem, p. 48.
101. Goto, *Nihon hoshasen igaku shiko*, vol. 1, p. 22.
102. Database of the Industrial Property Digital Library, www.ipdl.inpit.go.jp/homepg.ipdl (accessed in February and March 2010), *Tokkyo bunrui betsu somokuroku.*
103. Goto, *Nihon hoshasen igaku shiko*, vol. 1, p. 18.
104. Ibidem, p. 64.
105. Schlich, *Surgery, Science and Industry* and Anderson, Neary and Pickstone, *Surgeons, Manufacturers and Patients.*
106. It produced notably some X-ray tubes. Goto *Nihon hoshasen igaku shiko*, vol. 1, p. 127.
107. Database of the Industrial Property Digital Library, www.ipdl.inpit.go.jp/homepg.ipdl (accessed in February and March 2010).
108. Donzé, "The Beginnings of the Japanese Medical Instruments Industry".
109. *Historical Statistics of Japan*, vol. 5, pp. 170–171.
110. Donzé, "The Beginnings of the Japanese Medical Instruments Industry".
111. *Dainihon hakushi*, vol. 2, pp. 78–79.
112. Donzé and Wubs, "Global Competition and Cooperation in the Electronics Industry".
113. *Kobe kogyo sha shi*, p. 112.
114. Janssen and Medford, *Envision: A History of the GE Healthcare*, pp. 24–25.

115. *Shimadzu seisakujo shi*, p. 378.
116. Ibidem, p. 45 and Goto, *Nihon hoshasen igaku shiko*, vol. 1, p. 179 cites 1920.
117. *Tokyo shibaura denki kabushiki kaisha 85 nenshi*, p. 708.
118. "Kokusan giba 75 gata rentogen sochi", *Iryo denki shinpo*, vol. 2, no. 3, 1932, p. 5.
119. Iwao Kishi, "X-sen sochi seiyojo no kanken", *Iryo denki shinpo*, vol. 4, no. 3, 1934, pp. 1–4.
120. *21 seiki he no kakehashi*, p. 8.
121. MAE, Agreement between S. Goto Fuundo Ltd., Tokyo, and Siemens-Reiniger-Werke AG, Berlin, 30 June 1932–25 November 1933, not marked.
122. Matsushita, *Kindai nihon*, vol. 6, pp. 229–230.
123. Goto, *Nihon hoshasen igaku shiko*, vol. 2, p. 114.
124. Ibidem, p. 312.
125. Yamada, "Nakabori Kouji".
126. *Shimadzu seisakujo shi*, p. 79.
127. *Dainihon hakushi*, vol. 5, pp. 108–109.
128. *Shimadzu seisakujo shi*, p. 378. In fact, the tubes of the firm Müller were made at that time by the Dutch company Philips, to which Müller belonged since 1927. Boersma, "Tensions within an Industrial Research Laboratory", p. 82.
129. *Shimadzu seisakujo shi*, p. 80.
130. Ibidem, p. 79.
131. NDL, Archives of the GHQ, USB-12, M1654-7, Interview with Shimadzu Manufacturing Co. Ltd, 26 October 1945. The exchange rate of 100 yen was about 30 US dollars in 1934. Miwa and Hara (ed.) 2007, p. 115.
132. *Shimadzu seisakujo shi*, p. 86.
133. Ibidem, pp. 78–79.
134. Siemens, *History of the House of Siemens*, vol. 2, p. 80.
135. Boersma, "Tensions within an Industrial Research Laboratory", p. 82.
136. Siemens, *History of the House of Siemens*, vol. 2, p. 85.
137. MAE, 753, Verträge auf dem Arbeitsgebiet der Siemens-Reiniger-Werke AG. This document is undated but more recent than 1932, as its maps represent Manchukuo, which was founded then. Except the United States, Canada, Mexico, the United Kingdom and France, this agreement covers the entire world.
138. MAE, 770-2, letter received from an anonymous correspondent in Berlin by Otto Kresta, 28 July 1934.
139. MAE, unmarked folder, Agreement between Goto Fuundo and SRW, 30 June 1932–25 November 1933. The agreement was signed in 1932 in Japan and countersigned in Germany in 1933.

140. MAE, 174, various financial statistics on Goto, 1935–1943.
141. MAE, 174, Verzinsung des Darlehns, 1935–1944.
142. MAE, unmarked folder, Agreement between Goto Fuundo and SRW, 30 June 1932–25 November 1933, art. 3.
143. Ibidem, art. 4.
144. Ibidem, art. 12.
145. Ibidem, art. 11.
146. Ibidem, art. 16.
147. Ibidem, art. 16.
148. SCAP, CPC 41476, Letter from Goto Fuundo to an unknown recipient, 13 June 1949.
149. Ibidem.
150. MAE, unmarked folder, Protokoll über eine Besprechung – Fabrikation in Japan, 7 December 1933.
151. MAE, 770-2, Letter from Sehmer (SRW Berlin) to Otto Kresta, 9 May 1934.
152. Ibidem, Letter from unknown correspondent (Berlin) to Otto Kresta, 28 July 1934.
153. Ibidem, Letter from Otto Kresta to SRW, 28 July 1934.
154. Ibidem, Letter from unknown correspondent to SRW, 28 August 1934.
155. Udagawa 1987, p. 25. See also Watanabe 1984.
156. Ibidem.
157. Database of the Industrial Property Digital Library, www.ipdl.inpit. go.jp/homepg.ipdl (accessed in February and March 2010) and Japan Patent Office 1958.
158. Boch, *Patentschutz und Innovation.*
159. SCAP, CPC 34029, Disposition of vested interests formerly owned by Siemens Reiniger Werk AG under licence agreement with K.K. Goto Fuundo, 5 March 1954.
160. SCAP, CPC 34029, Letter from Goto Fuundo to the Minister of Finance, 5 February 1954.
161. This can also be observed in the chemical industry, for example. Kudo, *Japanese–German Business Relations.*
162. SCAP, CPC 41476, Letter from Goto Fuundo to an unknown recipient, 13 June 1949.
163. SCAP, CPC 34029, Letter from Goto Fuundo to the Minister of Finance, 5 February 1954.
164. MAE, 174, Dividendenzahlungen von Goto, 1927–1943.
165. SCAP, USB-12, M1654-7, Interview with Shimadzu Manufacturing Co. Ltd., 26 October 1945.
166. MAE, unmarked folder, Gegenwärtiger Stand des SRW-Geschäfts in Japan, 4 January 1939.

167. MAE, 174, Dividendenzahlungen von Goto, 1927–1943.
168. SCAP, USB-12, M1654-7, Interview with Shimadzu Manufacturing Co. Ltd., 26 October 1945.
169. *Nihon jinmei daijiten.*
170. Watanuki, "Ika denkiki ni kansuru chosa".
171. See for example Seki, "Rentogen sochi no kikaku tosei ni kanshite".
172. SMA 7615 4-2-05, Vortrag des Herrn Direktor Dr. Sehmer anlässlich der Bilanz- und Aufsichtsratssitzung, 15 November 1950.
173. Nakaoka, *Nihon kindai gijutsu no keisei.*
174. Miyamoto and Kasuya, "Soron", p. 38.
175. Donzé, "Multinational Enterprises and the Globalization of Medicine".

CHAPTER 3

The Birth of a New Medical Discipline

1 Introduction

Born in July 1890 to a family of medical doctors in Mie Prefecture, Yoshikazu Segi graduated from the Aichi Medical College in Nagoya in June 1915, just a few days before he turned 25.[1] Segi had several career choices. According to Shuhei Ikai, most of the graduates of medical colleges in the 1910s engaged in private practice (*kaigyo-i*) even if hospitals, medical schools, and the army offered them positions.[2] However, the private-practice market tended to become increasingly competitive—especially in large cities—as more and more young doctors graduated from the prestigious imperial universities of Tokyo, Kyoto, and Kyushu. At the end of the nineteenth century, young medical school graduates generally trained to work in public offices (medical schools, prefecture hospitals, army, and the bureaucracy); in the early twentieth century, however, they began to pursue private medical practice in greater numbers, making the medical market extremely competitive.

For Segi and many other graduates of medical colleges, specialized knowledge became vital to establishing a profitable position in the medical market. Segi decided to come to Tokyo and, in August 1916, entered the department of radiology at Juntendo Hospital. By that time, the institution had been operating under the direction of Koichi Fujinami—a young celebrity of the Japanese medical world and one of the promoters of radiology in Japan—for several years. The radiology department at Juntendo Hospital was a kind of incubator of talented radiologists

© The Author(s) 2018   57
P.-Y. Donzé, *Making Medicine a Business*,
https://doi.org/10.1007/978-981-10-8159-0_3

and numerous medical graduates from all around Japan flocked to the institution to study radiology under Fujinami. Segi was one of them. He spent around three years in the department before joining the University of Tokyo in October 1919 and pursuing research on the use of X-rays to cure tuberculosis under the supervision of professors Atsuro Mitamura and Matao Nagayo. In 1922, he moved to Kyoto University and specialized in orthopedic surgery and radiology. The following year, he became an inaugural member of the Japanese Society of Radiology (*Nihon rentogen gakkai*). In 1925, he obtained his Ph.D., returned to Tokyo, and opened a private clinic specializing in radiology—one of the first of its kind in the city. Until his death in 1974, he continued his career as medical practitioner, researcher, and organizer of the profession. He was appointed honorary advisor of the Japanese Society of X-Ray Technicians in 1971.

This apparently ordinary career of a Japanese medical radiologist during the first part of the twentieth century sheds light on some essential characteristics of the medical system and organization of medical specialties in Japan. Segi never took any particular exam, nor did he obtain any official certification to be recognized as a "radiologist." These conditions were not specific to the field of radiology itself but rather common to all of medical specialties in Japan. The specialization of medicine is indeed not the direct consequence of the adoption of anatomical pathology as a theoretical paradigm or of technological progress, which would have led doctors to focus on the study of a specific organ, as classical and positivist historiography tends to suggest.[3] In his seminal work, George Rosen has emphasized that specialization must be understood in its economic and social context[4]: Medical specialization is a social construction and has taken various forms in different countries.

In his works on the professionalization of medical specialists in the United States, Germany, France, and the United Kingdom, George Weisz illuminated the impact of academic, political, and social contexts on the ways in which medical specialization has emerged and developed into an organized system.[5] He especially emphasized the essential issue of using certification to regulate specialized practices and thereby set the official boundaries of the specialties and demarcate each field from others. Moreover, medical specialization grew into a global movement, with doctors training overseas and international congresses assembling delegations from countries around the world.[6] However, each country had a different way of defining boundaries.

In this context, medical societies and state governments were major actors. In some countries, like Germany and the United States, professional associations of doctors took charge of the regulation and certification of specialties during the 1920s.[7] These groups wanted to avoid the intervention of the state and thus formulated their own internal measures to delimit specialties, especially in terms of what training "specialists" would receive. In France, however, specialization took place through state intervention and within a prolonged legal process, and full implementation did not occur until 1947. As Rosemary Stevens has argued, in the United Kingdom, the certification of specialties did not result from the demand of doctors, who were traditionally general practitioners (GP). The impetus for certification protocols was health insurers' requests for a better definition of "specialties" in the 1930s.[8]

In Japan, meanwhile, there was a de facto specialization of the training of doctors and hospital organization. The Imperial University of Tokyo thus introduced a system, comprising specialized chairs in the Faculty of Medicine and specialized clinics in the University Hospital, in 1893.[9] However, neither the state nor professional associations regulated the different medical specialties. The 1906 law on medical doctors (*ishiho*) did not mention anything about the differentiation of specialties, either, which meant that the doctors had full reign over such decisions.[10] The system of medical specialties in Japan developed freely, then, with all practitioners theoretically able to declare themselves specialists in any discipline. Medical associations existed but did not set up restrictive training programs or confer official degrees. In all, the system had a very liberal quality.

In 1940, two years after the founding of the Japanese Ministry of Health, the state proposed moves that would strengthen its presence and action within the broader context of healthcare system reform. In addition to devising several other measures, the state wanted to redefine the training of medical doctors and introduce an official certification program for the training of specialists.[11] Despite opposition from doctors, the government adopted the law on national health (*kokumin iryoho*) in 1942. However, tangible measures affecting doctor training did not go into practice until the end of the war. Later, in 1956, the Ministry of Health tried again to regulate medical specialties, but the project that the Ministry submitted to the Diet in 1957 gave rise to such strong opposition among medical associations that the government effectively abandoned the idea in 1963 and the state granted medical associations the responsibility to regulate specialties.[12] Consequently, the process of regulating medical specialties (*senmon-i seido*) took a considerable amount of time to fall into place: The first associations to adopt official certification were the societies of anesthesia (1962), radiology (1966), and neurosurgery (1966). It was only in 1981 that Japan saw the creation of an organization in charge of supervising and coordinating the certification-related activities for the various medical societies: the Japanese Board of Medical Specialties (*nihon senmon isei hyoka nintei kiko*).[13]

Despite this lack of a definitive legal framework, however, medical specialties had been defined by the structure of social relations surrounding the university hospitals of Tokyo, Kyoto, and Kyushu since the end of the nineteenth century. Belonging to a network of "specialists" was indeed a major issue in cultivating a professional career. Literature in the social sciences has emphasized that today, medical careers in Japan depend on the insertion into networks (*i-kyoku*), whose centers are the largest faculties of medicine in the country.[14] Young graduates who find places in *i-kyoku* can access positions in a wide range of "associated hospitals" (*kanren byoin*), where the decisions of university professors largely dictate employment. Mori and Goto even compared this system to the Japanese manufacturing industry, where there is a complementarity and dependency relationship between large enterprises (or, in terms of the medical field, faculties of medicine and university hospitals) and small- and medium-size enterprises (associated hospitals).[15] In 1962, for example, the Faculty of Medicine at Keio University had a total of 41 associated hospitals in its group.[16] It gave many job opportunities to Keio graduates. This system has grown even stronger since the turn of the century, as internships have been compulsory for obtaining the status of medical doctor since 2004.[17]

Although this system formed after World War II (WWII), one can see a very similar pattern developing during the first part of the twentieth century.[18] The lack of official certification for medical specialties at the time was balanced by the need for integration into the social networks that essentially controlled young doctors' access to prestigious positions and influential careers. Segi's entrance into the Japanese Society of Radiology signified the social recognition of his ability to be a radiologist. The statutes of this society were relatively vague on the criteria for membership, as well, only mentioning that members had to accept the objective of the society as defined in Article 2: "the progress of academic research and the diffusion of knowledge related to radiology and to physiotherapy."[19]

This chapter examines the process by which radiology emerged as an autonomous field in a free-market, unregulated context. The primary focus is on the careers of the medical doctors who helped structure the field, ranging from the first doctors who exhibited an interest in X-ray technology during the 1890s and 1900s to the next generations of practitioners who made radiology a recognized specialty. Looking beyond these individual trajectories, the overarching analysis explores the institutional context (academic societies and professional training) and the external actors (technicians in radiology and manufacturers of medical devices) who drove the autonomy of radiology.

2   THE FIRST INTERESTS IN APPLYING X-RAY TECHNOLOGY TO MEDICINE

As was the case in Western countries, nothing predestined doctors in Japan to take control of radiology as a medical technology and make it a specialty.[20] At the end of the 1890s and during the subsequent decade, the first experiences with using X-ray machines belonged not only to doctors but also to physicists and photographers. One of the first pieces of radiological equipment in Japan was imported from Germany in October 1897 by Konishiroku (Konica since 1987), which was then a small, Tokyo-based company that specialized in the manufacture of cameras.[21] Likewise, the first X-ray machines produced by the Kyoto-based firm Shimadzu were developed for teaching physics.[22]

Still, there were some differences in the Western and Japanese experiences with X-ray technology. Unlike the situation in Europe and the United States, where physicists—or even photographers—were relatively common sights in the first X-ray rooms at large hospitals, X-ray usage in Japan was under the dominant influence of doctors since hospitals first installed the devices.[23] This distinction essentially arises out of the geographical distance between Japan and Western countries and the major roles that doctors played in the introduction and diffusion of new expertise and technologies in Japan.[24] These doctors were not only Japanese nationals, however; some German doctors employed by the Japanese authorities in the 1870s and 1880s to train the first generations of professors in the Faculty of Medicine at the University of Tokyo were actively engaged in this transfer.[25] Julius Scriba, professor of surgery at the University of Tokyo from 1881 to 1887 and then 1889 to 1901, was one of the first to realize the medical use of X-ray machines.[26] Besides Konica, most of the importers of radiological equipment were doctors.

The Japanese and European cases both show that during this period, surgeons expressed a special interest in X-ray technology for its potential contributions to preoperative diagnosis. Two men, one with a military background and one from the University of Tokyo, played a major role in establishing the medical applications of X-ray technology. Both came from the same generation of practitioners, trained in medicine in Germany during the 1890s, specialized in surgery, and furthered the modernization of the Japanese hospital system.

The first was Eijiro Haga (1864–1953),[27] who was a pivotal force in publicizing the effects of X-rays and their possible applications in medicine. Haga was active in three main arenas. First, the army became one of the largest buyers of radiological equipment during his leadership stint. Haga was the director of the School of Medicine of the Army (*rikugun guni gakko*), where he set up a Siemens X-ray machine in December 1898 at his own expense and proceeded to order two others soon after.[28] In 1905, he also installed portable radiological equipment in the Second Field Hospital for use at the rear of the battlefield during Japan's war against Russia.[29]

Second, Haga published several scientific articles in medical reviews in order to inform his colleagues about the possibilities that the new technology offered. Although Haga never had the intention of building a new and autonomous field of medicine, he worked to propel the general development of medical knowledge. Notable works by Haga include two articles that were cowritten with Kanehiro Takaki and published in the review of the Japanese society of surgery (*nihon geka gakkai kaishi*) in 1903. In these joint articles, the authors tackled the use of radiological pictures for some cases of fracture and bone deformation.[30]

Third, Haga worked hard to training a staff that would be capable of using radiology equipment properly—an effort that targeted not only military doctors, who learned how to use the technology from Haga, but also junior technicians. Military nurses learned the manipulation of X-ray machines and became technical assistants to doctors. After they went back to civilian life, some of them pursued their careers at large public hospitals.

The second doctor to promote the use of radiology in Japan in the 1900s was Yoshinori Tashiro (1864–1938),[31] a general-purpose surgeon representative of this discipline as it existed in countries under German influence at that time. His influence on the development of radiology did not result from his academic works in this field but rather tied back to his interest in X-rays as a supporting technology for surgery. Tashiro also played a key role as an organizer of the first meetings and joint research groups that led to the creation of a structured academic society. Tashiro graduated from the University of Tokyo in 1889 and immediately enrolled in the department of surgery to study under Professor Scriba. He left school two years later to work at his family's private hospital before eventually coming back to the University of Tokyo in 1896 to study bacteriology. In 1900, the Ministry of Education chose Tashiro to study surgery and pathology at Freiburg University in Germany. Upon his return to Japan in 1904, Tashiro became an assistant professor of surgery at the University of Tokyo and specialized in orthopedic surgery—a field in which X-ray technology was particularly useful. His works on using radiography to observe rachitic malformations in children in Toyama Prefecture, published in 1906, had a significant impact on the Japanese medical world.[32] In 1907, he also equipped his department with an X-ray machine.[33] In addition to pursuing his work at the University of Tokyo, Tashiro became director and head of surgery at the newly founded Mitsui Philanthropic Hospital (*mitsui jizen byoin*, today Mistui Memorial Hospital) in 1908.

2.1 *Setting up the First Joint Research Groups*

The first expression of a collective will to make radiology the object of joint research came in 1913, with the organization of two groups—one in Osaka and one in Tokyo. The most important was the Research Group on Radiology (*rentogen gaku kenkyukai*), which Professor Tashiro founded in Tokyo in September 1913.[34] Although it is unclear exactly what activities the first incarnation of the group—a gathering of nine doctors, all of whom were University of Tokyo graduates (see Table 1)—engaged in prior to 1917 and 1918, the profiles of the founding members suggest that their activities may have been extensions of Tashiro's works, namely the study of the possible application of X-rays to surgery and other various fields of medicine. Raku Naito is an excellent example.

Table 1 Founding members of the Research Group on Radiology, 1913 (*Source* Goto, *Nihon hoshasen igaku shiko*, vol. 1, p. 92, *Dainihon hakashi roku*, Izumi, *Nihon kingendai igaku jinmei jiten*, and *Kaiin shimei roku*)

Name	Birth date	Professional career
Yoshinori Tashiro	1864	Professor at the University of Tokyo, department of orthopedic surgery; promoter of the modernization of hospital surgery in Japan
Tokutaro Nakahara	1871	Graduate of the University of Tokyo (1900); doctor at Rakusando Hospital, Tokyo
Shichiro Hida	1872	Graduate of the University of Tokyo (1898); doctor and head of radiology at the School of Medicine of the Army
Miki Kobayashi	?	Graduate of the University of Tokyo (1902); doctor at the School of Medicine of the Navy
Kaiichi Kaneko	1883	Graduate of the University of Tokyo (1908); doctor at the University of Tokyo, department of orthopedic surgery
Raku Naito	?	Graduate of the University of Tokyo; head of the surgery department at Tokiwa Hospital, Tokyo
Fumie Soshi	?	Doctor in the department of dermatology at the Red Cross Hospital, Tokyo
Koichi Fujinami	1880	Graduate of the University of Tokyo; head of the department of radiology at Juntendo Hospital, Tokyo
Mori Bokuno	?	Doctor at the University of Tokyo, department of surgery of prof. Kondo

Appointed in 1911 to head up the surgery department at Tokiwa Hospital (Tokyo), the health center created by Japan Railways after the nationalization of Japan's railways in 1906,[35] Naito produced only one publication on record: a first-aid leaflet that was published in 1914 and created for the employees of railway companies to employ in the case of an accident.[36] Given this background, Naito was obviously a general-purpose surgeon like Tashiro. Another member was Tokutaro Nakahara, a surgeon who specialized in orthopedic surgery during the interwar years and became president of Nippon Medical School in 1926.[37] Kaiichi Kaneko followed a similar path: He studied under the supervision of Tashiro, became an orthopedic surgeon, and assumed leadership of the department of his specialty at Rakusando Hospital (Tokyo) after haven been a professor at Tokyo Women's Medical School.[38] None of these doctors—save for Shichiro Hida and Koichi Fujinami, whose careers I cover below—engaged in radiology as a specific emerging field.

The other group was Association R.R. (Roentgen-Radium), which formed in December 1913 in Osaka. The group was smaller than its Tokyo counterpart was and must have conducted relatively low-profile activities, considering that the records of official business go no further than the organization's foundation. The founding members were four doctors: Masakiyo Ogata, a gynecologist–obstetrician, graduate of the University of Tokyo, and director of a private hospital in Osaka; Konoshin Sakurane, a surgeon who graduated from the University of Tokyo and specialized in dermatology, eventually becoming the first professor in dermatology at Osaka University[39]; Juichi Matsumoto, an urologist who trained in Germany; and Kenkichi Horiuchi, a former classmate of Ogata and later a driver of the ENT discipline in Japan. This second group, too, basically comprised doctors who saw radiology as a supporting technology for their own specialties; the only exception was Ogata, who was an active participant in radiology-related societies during the interwar years.

The first radiology-centered research groups organized just before World War I (WWI) did not signify a real step toward the birth of a new medical discipline; essentially, they expressed the collective wills of some doctors to collaborate on improving and developing applications of a new technology for their own practices. However, the network that these groups helped forge—especially in Tokyo—would later be a basis for the foundation of a structured academic society at the beginning of the 1920s. At an individual level, these groups also included several doctors who would eventually establish themselves as the leaders and promoters of a new medical field: Fujinami, Hida, and Ogata. In November 1914, these three men, together with two professors of the University of Tokyo (Tashiro and his colleague Keizo Dohi, professor of dermatology), launched an academic review dedicated to the application of physics to medicine: the *Journal of Iatrophysics Medical Treatments*,[40] which published 12 volumes through 1921.

Not all the members of the research groups had the same impact on the construction of radiology as a medical specialty. Two individuals seem to have had a key influence. In the mid-1960s, the Japanese medical community reached a kind of consensus: that the two main promoters of radiology in the country had been Fujinami in Tokyo and East Japan and Urano in Kansai and West Japan (*higashi ni fujinami, nishi ni urano*).[41] The following pages thus introduce these two figures, outlining their careers, actions, and influence on the development of radiology as a distinct medical field.

2.1.1 The Career of Fujinami

Scholars believe Koichi Fujinami (1880–1942) to be the first medical doctor to specialize in radiology in Japan.[42] Nothing in his training marked the path to such a career, however. For example, he had no particular interest in surgery and studied a wide variety of specialties until he was in his early thirties. Born in Nagoya to a family of doctors, he started his studies at Okayama Special School of Medicine (*Okayama igaku senmon gakko*), where he had a special interest for pathology—a discipline in which his brother Akira pursued a brilliant career at Kyoto University. He continued his training at the University of Tokyo, where he became an assistant in dermatology in 1907 and later in the research center for infectious diseases (*densenbyo kenkyujo*).

In 1909, the Japanese authorities sent Fujinami to Vienna University in order to learn a new discipline: radiology. Vienna General Hospital (*Allgemeines Krankenhaus*) was at that time one of the most advanced hospitals in the division of clinical medicine, especially surgery, and also in the development of radiology as a new specialty, with Robert Kienboeck and Guido Holzknecht leading the way.[43] Fujinami's specific objective was to acquire the necessary knowledge and know-how to transfer this discipline to Japan. He stayed in Austria for four years and used his time to develop a thorough familiarity with X-rays.[44] When he came back to Japan in 1912, he pursued his career in the discipline and established himself as the chief radiologist in the country. Juntendo Hospital appointed Fujinami head of the department of radiology, one of the many Japanese firsts in Fujinami's storied career, and obtained a Ph.D. from the University of Tokyo in 1915. In 1920, he was scouted out by Keio University to serve as the radiology department chair in the new Faculty of Medicine, the first of its kind at a private university. Fujinami continued working in various capacities at Keio until his death in 1942.

Fujinami began by raising the profile of radiology in larger circles of medical doctors. He gave several papers on the use of X-rays in specific fields of medicine, including articles for the national conferences of the Japanese Society of Dermatology (1912–1914), the Japanese Medical Association (1912), the Japanese Association of Medical Doctors of Railway Companies (1923), the Japanese Society of Gastroenterology (1924), the Japanese Society for Tuberculosis (1924), and many regional and local meetings of these societies. Fujinami also gave numerous public conferences and talks at hospitals, such as Juntendo (1912–1913) and the Tokyo Kenbikyo-in (1917).[45] These papers usually appeared in academic journals.

Targeting all medical doctors, Fujinami also published several books on radiology. One of the most prominent works was *Radiology* (*Rentogen gaku*). Edited by Fujinami and released in 1914, the book was a collaborative project uniting people from various backgrounds: a doctor in physics (Shin Moronuki), a doctor in engineering (Keizo Muro, a Shimadzu employee who founded the company Dainihon Roentgen in 1919), a technician from the Ministry of Posts and Communications (Noboru Marumo) and an engineer from Tokyo Electric (Tetsuya Fuji, head of the R&D center for X-ray machines). Aiming to explain the theoretical and practical basis of radiology to medical doctors, the work was a big success and went through at least seven editions through 1934.[46] Notable titles among Fujinami's other books include *Radium-therapy* (*Rajiumu ryoho*, 1913), *X-ray diagnosis of internal organs* (*Naizo rentogen shindangaku*, 1916; coauthored with Dr. Renpei Fukumitsu), and the Japanese translation of a book on radiotherapy (*Rentogen ryoho*, 1914), which was originally published by German radiotherapy proponent Dr. H.E. Schmidt (Berlin). Through his editorial activities, Fujinami diffused knowledge about the various applications of X-rays (both diagnostic and therapeutic) in Japan.

Finally, Fujinami had close relationships with several radiological equipment manufacturers since the 1910s. He had particularly strong work connections with Tokyo Electric, playing a role in developing the company's first X-ray tubes during WWI. Fujinami was also in attendance at public lectures offered by Tokyo Electric since 1918 (see below).[47] In 1918, he became a technical advisor at Tokyo Electric Industry (*Tokyo denki kogyo*), a small company founded that year.[48] Despite his proximity to the manufacturing community, however, Fujinami was not an entrepreneur—he never created any company nor registered any patent in his name.

Fujinami's impact on the construction of a new medical specialty did not result only from his efforts to inform his colleagues about the field of radiology, however. He was also instrumental as an organizer of the discipline itself and as a trainer of a new generation of medical doctors. In 1920, Fujinami published a paper titled "The situation of radiology progress in our country" in *Ikai jiho*, a general medical journal. The paper presented his plan to launch a new autonomous medical specialty.[49] He began to deplore that the increasing number of X-ray devices in hospitals, which had been become more and more prevalent since 1910, did not go together with a change in medical practice. Due to doctors' lack of interest, X-ray equipment was "purely decorative, without any utility."[50] He criticized "the immense disregard and ignorance of doctors in our country for radiology"[51] and argued that it was necessary to transmit knowledge in physics and electricity to young practitioners so that they could understand how to use of the machines.

Determined to spark changes, Fujinami proposed three levels of intervention to strengthen the diffusion of radiology. Controlling the access to and manipulation of X-ray equipment was a major necessity, first of all, with the idea being to limit X-ray operations to doctor-trained technicians and doctor-supervised nurses. Access to radiological units also needed to be reserved to doctors specializing in the field and forbidden to other practitioners. Regulating the use of X-ray technology in hospital settings and the medical system was a key issue for organizing the new specialty. The exclusive ability to understand and master the use of radiological equipment gave a professional legitimacy to the title of "radiologist."

Second, Fujinami called for the design of new training programs for medical doctors supervising hospital radiology departments—and that made his department at Juntendo Hospital an incubator for radiologists from 1912 to 1919. Doctors throughout Japan went as far as leaving their positions to come to Juntendo for a few months, sometimes even a few years, to learn radiology from Fujinami. That was the case for Yoshikazu Segi, whose story appeared at the beginning of this chapter, and Saiichi Koike, a Kanazawa Special School of Medicine graduate (1911) who practiced in Ishikawa Prefecture before going to Juntendo—a training program that allowed him to open and take charge of a new department of physical medicine at the Kanazawa Prefecture Hospital (1916). Shinobu Terasaki, from Nagasaki Prefectural Hospital, followed a very similar path. After a stint at Fujinami's department in 1915, he organized a center for electro-medical care at his home hospital.[52]

Okayama Prefecture Hospital's Shigeo Furuya also trained at Juntendo in 1916 and proceeded to pursue his career in the field: first as radiology department director at Kokura-kinen Hospital in Fukuoka (1920) then as a director of Chikko Hospital, and finally as an independent practitioner in Osaka (1933).[53] Furuya was a dedicated researcher in his specialty of radiotherapy, a field in which he published one of the first textbooks in Japanese: *New Theory on Radiotherapy* (1925), which featured a preface by Fujinami.[54] Four years later, he obtained a Ph.D. from Keio University.

Fujinami's training system had no institutional organization, however, which made it impossible for him to meet all the needs of the Japanese medical system alone. When he published his article in *Ikai jiho*, there was only a smattering of short-term learning opportunities available: one or two annual conferences at the Tokyo Izumibashi Jizen Hospital and at various special schools of medicine, the courses offered by Tokyo Electric, and another course at Kyoto Medical University.[55] Fujinami was the first to provide a real training for radiologists. In the 1920s, a new generation of medical students would begin to make the discipline of radiology their professional specialty of choice.

Third, Fujinami regretted that the activities of radiology were "not gathered in a unified organization."[56] The relevant research fell into specific categories, and the medical community saw radiology as more of a supporting technology for other fields than a specialty. The School of Medicine of the Army engaged seriously in research on radiology, for example, but especially in relation with surgery. Fujinami proposed the creation of an autonomous academic society, similar to those in the West, so that members could join forces in advancing radiology as a discipline. In the years following the publication of "The situation of radiology progress in our country," he pushed hard to accomplish this objective and became one of the major figures of the Japanese Society of Radiology (*Nihon rentogen gakkai*, see below). In order to promote research in radiology, he also founded *Keio series in radiology* (*Keio rentogen-gaku sosho*) in 1926. The new journal was short-lived, however, only producing releases for several years before disappearing completely in 1930. From then on, Fujinami published his work through general radiology journals established throughout the country.

2.1.2 *The Career of Urano*

Considered the main promoter of radiology in Kansai and Western Japan, Tamonji Urano (1886–1954) belongs, like Fujinami, to the generation of doctors trained in German-speaking countries before WWI.[57] Unlike his colleague from Keio, however, he became a major player in the development of radiology not because of his academic career but rather thanks to his activities as a hospital doctor, his cooperation with equipment manufacturers, and his work as an educator.

Urano was born in 1886 in Nagano Prefecture and educated at Chiba Medical College, from which he graduated in 1906. He then worked for several years in the departments of surgery at Chiba and Niigata Prefecture Hospitals before leaving for Germany in June 1912 to study radiology at Munich University, where he obtained his Ph.D. In January 1913, he joined the team of Dr. Holzknecht at Vienna University Hospital. However, the outbreak of war in Europe put an abrupt end to his training. He came back to Japan in 1914 and served as the head of the radiology department at Okayama Prefecture Hospital and an assistant professor at Okayama Medical College (1915), where he was among the pioneers of radiology educators in Japan. Okayama Medical College was also where Urano met professor of internal medicine Junjiro Shimasono, who had graduated from the University of Tokyo, trained in Germany, and quickly secured a professorship at Kyoto University (1916). Urano continued his research under Shimasono and obtained a Ph.D. from Kyoto University in 1922. From 1919 to 1922, Urano acted as the first head of the new X-Ray Central Office (*Chuo rentogen shitsu*) at Kyoto University Hospital.[58]

While he was teaching in Okayama and then working in Kyoto, Urano started a career as a hospital radiologist. In 1916, he became head of the new radiology department at Osaka's Kaisei Hospital, an institution that had been founded in 1900 and recently been rebuilt and equipped with modern technology after a fire (1915).[59] He remained in his position at Kaisei until 1933, helping solidify the institution's reputation as a major spot for the development of radiology in Osaka. Urano organized some public lectures (1917) and, from 1924 onward, regional meetings of the Japanese Radiology Society.[60] His involvement in nurturing the field of radiology in the hospital context led his peers to elect him president of the Japanese Radiology Society in 1932. Finally, in 1933, he left his position at Kaisei Hospital, opened his own private clinic of radiology in Osaka (*Urano rentogen-ka-iin*), and ran the institution until his death in 1953.

Moreover, Urano actively trained radiologists and technicians in radiology. During his time at Kyoto University, he organized courses for all doctors (1919 and 1921).[61] Later, he did the same for the Association of Osaka's doctors (1923), and in 1930, he became a lecturer in radiology at Osaka Medical College (*Osaka koto ika senmon gakko*). His most important contribution, however, was his involvement in helping Shimadzu open a training center for X-ray technicians in Kyoto in 1927 (see below). Urano taught at the center until 1945, also serving as its director from 1930 to 1935. He also authored a radiology textbook, published by Shimadzu, in 1919.[62]

Urano's close ties with Shimadzu extended beyond teaching: he also held shares in this firm since its transformation into a joint-stock company in 1917.[63] Research and development was another area where Urano assisted Shimadzu, which registered a patent for one of Urano's X-ray tubes in 1933 (no. 101,414). A 1967 medical journal entry on Urano's activities at Kyoto University included a picture of the subject wearing a necktie featuring Shimadzu's family crest.[64]

2.2   The Foundation of an Academic Society

The creation of an academic society was a major step in the construction of a new field of research and a new medical specialty, effecting an institutionalization that gave its members visibility within the medical world and enabled them to distinguish and establish themselves as "specialists." The key was to assemble all the personalities that represented promoters of the discipline: university professors, hospital directors, and medical college teachers.

In Japan, the first specialized academic societies formed soon after the opening of the University of Tokyo; the proliferation of these groups reflects the creation of new chairs. National societies gradually sprouted up in the fields of anatomy (1893), pediatrics (1896), ophthalmology (1897), surgery (1898), and dermatology (1901), among others,[65] with each specialty organizing its own session at the annual conference of the Japanese Association of Medical Sciences (*Nihon igaku-kai*) since its foundation in 1902. The number of sessions went from 8 in 1902 to 33 in 1943.[66]

The launch of an academic society of radiology had its roots in the research group that surgery professor Tashiro formed in 1912. Among the five doctors who met in November 1922 in Tokyo to found a society of radiology, four were former members of this group (Tashiro, Fujinami, Hida, and Kaneko), and the fifth was Kaichiro Manabe, who had also graduated from the University of Tokyo but had been in Germany in 1912. The new radiology society in the early 1920s was more structured than the informal research group that originated ten years earlier. The objective of the group was to establish an organization and build a nationwide membership and scope of activity. The association was named the "Japanese Society of Radiology" ("Japanese Roentgen Society" in Japanese, *Nihon rentogen gakkai*), a tribute to Wilhelm Roentgen—the discoverer of the X-ray, who had died two months earlier.[67]

The constitutive assembly took place on April 4, 1923, at the University of Tokyo. With Tashiro presiding, the gathering drew more than 500 persons who, after having heard talks from Manabe (the principal promoter of radiotherapy in Japan), Shoji Nishikawa (a physicist specialized in the industrial applications of radiology), and a representative of Tokyo Electric (who presented about Coolidge X-ray tubes), officially became the founding members of the society.[68] Not all the members were doctors; the society's statutes laid the groundwork welcoming nondoctors to the fold after the acceptance of the association's council. For example, Genkichi Shimadzu, a board member at Shimadzu and representative of the company in Tokyo, gave a toast at the party at the end of the day.[69]

The governance of the academic society followed the classic model and bore a strong resemblance to those of the various professional associations that existed throughout Japan at that time: a president, a board of 6 managers (kanjikai), and a council of 42 members (hyogikai). Tashiro assumed the presidency of the group and chose six individuals to form the board (see Table 2),[70] which revealed two defining characteristics. First, the society bore a striking resemblance to research group that originated in 1912: Four of its members (Tashiro, Hida, Kaneko, and Fujinami) were on the new board in 1923. Second, the board included specialists in radiology (Hida, Fujinami, and Manabe) as well as surgeons using X-rays as a supporting technology for their own activities (Tashiro, Kaneko, Kitayama, and Iwasaki). Most members specialized in orthopedic surgery—a field in which radiology was particularly useful in diagnostic applications.

The 42-member council had the same twofold structure: Few of the member doctors engaged in radiology as a specialty, and most were practitioners from other disciplines who used X-ray technology in their work. When the society formed, the council included only nine members who held positions as radiologists—the same number of surgeons on the council. Given its makeup, the Japanese Society of Radiology thus followed a much more scientific than professional goal. Instead of attempting to gather a tight cadre of the first radiology specialists, the society aimed to support the development of research pertaining to the use of radiology for diagnostic and therapeutic purposes. The order of the day was to develop knowledge of X-ray technology and diffuse it among medical doctors (Table 3).

The *Journal of the Japanese Society of Radiology* (*Nihon rentogen gakkai zasshi*), published since July 1923, conveyed this essentially scientific

Table 2 Founding board of managers of the Japanese Society of Radiology, 1923 (*Source* Goto, *Nihon hoshasen igaku shiko*, vol. 1, p. 220, *Dainihon hakashi roku*, Izumi, *Nihon kingendai igaku jinmei jiten*, and *Kaiin shimei roku*)

Name	Birth date	Professional career
Yoshinori Tashiro	1864	Professor at the University of Tokyo, department of orthopedic surgery; promoter of hospital surgery in Japan
Shichiro Hida	1872	Doctor at the School of Medicine of the Army, in charge of radiology; graduate of the University of Tokyo (1908)
Kaiichi Kaneko	1883	Doctor at the University of Tokyo, department of orthopedic surgery; graduate of the University of Tokyo (1908)
Koichi Fujinami	1880	Doctor at Juntendo Hospital, department of radiology; graduate of the University of Tokyo
Kuniyuki Katayama	1884	Doctor specializing in orthopedic surgery; professor at Jikkei School of Medicine, Tokyo; graduate of the University of Tokyo
Koshiro Iwasaki	?	Head of the departments of surgery and radiology at Kojimachi Saiseikai Hospital, Tokyo; graduate of the University of Tokyo
Kaiichiro Manabe	1878	Professor of internal medicine and promoter of radiotherapy at the University of Tokyo; graduate of the University of Tokyo

objective clearly. The journal featured articles by specialists from various medical fields (surgery, internal medicine, orthopedics, etc.) who demonstrated the possible applications of X-ray technology in their own practices. Several players in the medical equipment industry, particularly Tokyo Electric and Shimadzu, participated regularly in society activities, using academic conferences to showcase innovations that their firms had developed and highlighting potential contributions to medical practice.

The Japanese Society of Radiology grew quickly during its first decade in existence. The number of society members is not exactly certain, but the Goto's chronicle of the group notes the number of participants at general assemblies for some years: The total went from 51 during the first assembly in 1923 to 520 members in 1933.[71] Beginning in 1924, the society organized regional sections in Tokyo and in Kansai to facilitate the organization of regular workshops in hospitals and universities in the corresponding areas.

Table 3 Founding members of the council of the Japanese Society of Radiology, 1923 (*Source* See Table 2)

Name	Professional career
Ryokichi Inada	Professor of internal medicine at Kyoto University
Koshiro Iwasaki	Head of the departments of surgery and radiology at Kojimachi Saiseikai Hospital, Tokyo
Benzo Hata	Professor of surgery at Hokkaido University
Hajime Hayashi	Independent orthopedist and surgeon in Tokyo
Keizo Dohi	Professor of dermatology at the University of Tokyo
Kikuo Otsuki	Surgeon at the University of Tokyo
Masao Sumita	Professor of orthopedic surgery at Kyoto University
Juemon Ogata	Professor of obstetrics at Osaka Medical College
Kanaichi Kawamura	Professor of surgery at Kyoto Prefectural University of Medicine
Keizo Katsunuma	Professor of internal medicine at Aichi Medical College
Sanyu Katsura	Unidentified
Kaiichi Kaneko	Head of the department of radiology at Mitsui Jizen Hospital, Tokyo
Kinuyuki Katayama	Professor of surgery at Jikkei School of Medicine, Tokyo
Michimaru Takahashi	Director of the Navy School of Medicine
Hoshiro Sho	Director of Gumzan Charity Hospital
Tokutaro Nakahara	Professor at Nippon Medical School
Atsuchi Nagamachi	Independent surgeon and radiologist in Tokyo
Kichiya Saigo	Director of Red Cross Hospital, Tokyo
Shunji Uemura	Unidentified
Motae Yamada	Director of Nagasaki Medical College
Iwao Matsuo	Professor of internal medicine at Kyoto University
Maiichiro Manabe	Professor of internal medicine (radiotherapy) at the University of Tokyo
Shotaro Yamagawa	Professor of internal medicine at Tohoku University
Toshikazu Mashimo	Professor of internal medicine at Kyoto University
Koichi Fujinami	Professor of radiology at Keio University, Tokyo
Kura Kondo	Unidentified
Kobayashi	Unidentified
Shigeru Koike	Doctor specializing in respiratory diseases at Kyoundo Hospital, Tokyo
Saiichi Koike	Head of the department of radiology at Kanazawa Prefectural Hospital
Kametoshi Obata	Professor of surgery at Osaka City Medical College
Eiji Arima	Professor of internal medicine at Hokkaido University
Keigi Sawada	Professor of internal medicine at Niigata Medical College
Kunio Sato	Professor of dermatology at Chiba Medical College

(continued)

Table 3 (continued)

Name	Professional career
Taiga Saito	Assistant professor of radiology at Kyoto University
Tamonji Urano	Head of the department of radiology at Kaisei Hospital, Osaka
Tokuei Kimura	Assistant professor of internal medicine at the University of Tokyo
Ichiro Kitamura	Professor of dentistry at Aichi Medical College
Yosai Shimodaira	Head of the department of surgery at Ishikawa Prefectural Hospital
Kotaro Jimbo	Unidentified
Shichiro Hida	Doctor and radiologist at Hida Hospital, Tokyo
Sadanobu Seo	Professor of surgery at Chiba Medical College
Terasuke Onodera	Professor of internal medicine at Kyoto University

Note In grey, the nine members who held positions as radiologists

The final important point meriting mention here is the foundation of other research groups in radiology—especially regional associations—during the 1920s. The Chubu Radiology Association (*Chubu rentogen kyokai*), for example, formed in the Nagoya region and published a journal from 1928 and 1930.[72] In 1929, a similar association was founded in Tohoku region.[73] In December 1923, the Japanese Society of Medical Instrumentation (*Nihon ika kikai gakkai*) also set up a section devoted to the development of electro-medical instruments (*denki bukai*).[74] The group started out with 11 members, including representatives from the industry (Tokyo Electric, Shimadzu, Matsumoto, Okura Roentgen, etc.), medical doctors (among whom were professor of surgery Kondo and the ubiquitous Fujinami), and a technician from the Office of Hygiene of the Ministry of Interior. There are no surviving records of the activities of the group, but its undertakings also focused on practical, academic issues rather than professional pursuits.

3   The Implementation of a Training System

In addition to organizing an academic society, implementing a training system specific to radiology was a major challenge in the process of constructing a new medical discipline. In most of the Western countries that George Weisz examined, these two issues were intimately linked; the medical professional associations played crucial parts in the accreditation of new specialties, a process in which professional training was essential.

In Japan, however, the creation of pathways occurred outside the boundaries academic societies, which focused only on research activities. However, the doctors engaged in the organization of radiology training programs were also the major promoters of the Japanese Society of Radiology. The formation of a network of professional training programs for specialists in radiology must be understood within the context of professional training for doctors in pre-WWII Japan.[75] Official diplomas did not specify medical specialties, and the two only official, Ministry of Education-approved designations that faculties of medicine offered were "medical doctor" and "dentist." Doctors honed their individual specialties through an informal framework, selecting specific fields during their academic studies and postgraduation internships at university hospitals. For young doctors, taking an interest in finding a specialty, practicing a specialty, and researching a specialty in hospital departments and the laboratories of established doctors allowed them to acquire scientific knowledge and access the social networks that laid the foundations for their future professional careers. Young doctors were welcomed into specialized academic societies and appointed to positions at big private hospitals in major cities and major prefectural hospitals.

During the interwar years, therefore, most radiologist training took place in the Japanese university community. This process gradually developed through three main phases: an informal period (the 1910s), a period that saw the institutionalization of training and the domination of Keio University (the 1920s), and a period where the number of academic chairs escalated rapidly (the 1930s).

3.1   The First Attempts to Train Radiologists

During the 1910s, numerous professors and doctors who used radiology for their own clinical practices began to organize courses that were open to all their fellow practitioners. The courses, which were particularly popular at the University of Tokyo from 1915 onward, taught the use of X-ray machines and showed their possible applications in various fields of medicine.[76] Courses were also organized in other large cities throughout the country, and the major promoters of radiology—Fujinami, Hida, and Urano among them—were often in attendance. These three doctors participated in a one-week course at the Nagoya Kyoritsu Hospital in 1919, for example.[77] Additionally, some doctors also gave courses at the private hospitals where they worked: Kuniyuki Katayama at Mitsui Jizen

Hospital (Tokyo) offered courses between 1919 and 1923, while Koji Mizuguchi at Ogata Hospital (Osaka) presented a public lecture titled "Gynecological diagnostic and radiology" in 1916.[78] Hida, meanwhile, gave a public course at his private hospital in Tokyo in 1921. Miyahara spoke about the contributions of radiology to the struggle against pulmonary tuberculosis in 1923 at the Research Center on Tuberculosis.[79]

These conferences and public lectures had a twofold objective. First, they attempted to disseminate practical knowledge among a larger audience of doctors—especially physicians who had not graduated from an imperial university. Second, they served to establish radiology as a new specialty in the medical field, as well. The doctors who offered these public courses were the chief promoters of the use of X-rays—clear leaders of the field and the first "specialists" in Japan. For the private hospitals that organized and hosted these conferences, meanwhile, the presentations represented an excellent opportunity to strengthen their image as technological leaders in an extremely competitive hospital market.

However, the training of doctors in radiology during the 1910s was not yet the domain of faculties of medicine. There was no chair of radiology in Japan, first of all. Training proceeded at the small handful of hospitals that had "specialists" like Fujinami and Urano on staff, and the courses targeted doctors who already held university or medical college degrees. Hospitals created some internships in the departments of these two radiologists (Fujinami and Urano), giving doctors opportunities to acquire knowledge that would be useful for their practices. The department of radiology of Juntendo Hospital (Tokyo), under the direction of Fujinami (who led the department from 1912 to 1919), became a veritable mecca for professionals hoping to learn radiology in Japan.

3.2   The Formal Structuring of Training Programs and the Integral Role of Keio University

Keio University, a private institution, became the first university to open a chair of radiology in 1920. This precocity emerges from the general context of the university's move to create a faculty of medicine in 1917, a manifestation of the institution's ambition to become a center of excellence for research and teaching in medicine and compete head to head with the University of Tokyo.[80] Funded by the imperial house and the Mitsui zaibatsu, the faculty at Keio functioned under the directorship of world-famous bacteriologist Shibasaburo Kitasato, who had left the Institute for Infectious Diseases after its takeover by the University of Tokyo and founded his own research center: The Kitasato Institute (1914).[81] Keio recruited and hired away excellent doctors in all disciplines.[82]

Fujinami was no exception, assuming a professorship at Keio in July 1920 and thereby becoming the first chair of radiology in Japan.[83] In 1923, Fujinami rounded out his team by employing Yutaro Sakurai, a young researcher from the Faculty of Medicine at Kyoto University, as an appointed lecturer. At the same time, Fujinami hired two nondoctors to give special lectures: Torao Iwayama, a Ph.D. in engineering who presided over classes on the use of X-ray equipment, and Tamio Furusawa, a Ph.D. in physics who took charge of classes focusing on the measurement of rays.[84]

Fujinami occupied the Keio chair until his death in 1942 and, under his leadership, Keio University became one of the major training centers for radiologists after the imperial universities of Tokyo, Kyoto, and Kyushu. Through 1945, a total of 76 radiologists had studied at Keio—in other words, 11% of all the Japanese doctors who finished their university curricula with work on radiology walked the Keio halls.[85] While Keio may have trailed the prestigious imperial universities in terms of pure presence, the upstart faculty elicited concrete reactions: The imperial universities, first in Kyushu and then in Tokyo, implemented processes for institutionalizing radiology as a specialty and establishing new chairs.

3.3   The Proliferation of Chairs of Radiology

The lateness of the institutionalization of radiology at imperial universities reflects the control that established professors in other chairs, like those in orthopedic surgery or internal medicine, had over the technology. The creation of chairs of radiology took place in different contexts, but it implied everywhere a loss of power for the professors who used to control X-ray equipment. Some faculties (those in Kyushu, Osaka, and Tokyo) recruited young, promising doctors and sent them to Germany, while others (Kyoto, for example) were late in institutionalizing radiology despite the presence of talented researchers.

Kyushu University, founded in Fukuoka in 1911, opened a chair of radiology in 1929 and appointed Professor Yoshisada Nakajima to fill the position. Himself a graduate of Kyushu University, Nakajima began an internship in the department of internal medicine of his alma mater and eventually developed an interest in radiology. After becoming head of X-ray equipment in the department in 1915, he secured a position as lecturer in 1923 and started giving special classes on radiology.[86] Nakajima later went to Austria and Germany, where he trained in radiology from 1925 to 1927 and actually spent time studying under Professor Holzknecht in Vienna. When he came back to Japan, he was appointed assistant professor and head of the center of radiology at Kyushu University Hospital—a post that became a chair two years later.[87] Nakajima taught radiology for twenty years and made his university a leading center of radiologist training in interwar Japan. By 1945, a total of 92 doctors (13.6% of all radiologists in Japan) had done their graduate theses in radiology at Kyushu University—a total that trailed only that of the University of Tokyo.

The Faculty of Medicine at Osaka University opened a chair of radiology two years after its counterpart Kyushu upon becoming an imperial university in 1931. Rather than being a pure, original creation, however, the chair at Osaka University grew out of an education program that had existing for some time. Osaka University itself was the product of a merger uniting various special schools; one of the parties to the unification was Osaka University of Medicine (*Osaka ika daigaku*), whose roots stretched back to 1838.[88] The professor of radiology appointed in 1931, Masamichi Nagahashi, was a graduate of that school (1915) and refined his specialty in radiology during a stay at Cambridge University (1920–1923), whose University Hospital had incidentally been the first UK institution to offer a diploma for doctors specializing in radiology (1919).[89] Appointed professor two years after his return to Osaka, Nagahashi forged a reputation as a leader in radiology and in 1927 published a book on the various applications of X-rays in clinical medicine.[90] Essentially, the mode of institutionalization adhered closely to the processes that the examples of Keio and Kyushu exemplify: new universities using new medical technology like radiology to reinforce their positions in the academic arena.

In contrast, the autonomization of chairs of radiology occurred at a later stage in the two oldest and most prestigious faculties of medicine in Japan: the programs at the Tokyo and Kyoto imperial universities. At the University of Tokyo, the first course of radiology was given in 1925 by Kenji Takaki, a professor of orthopedic surgery and disciple of Tashiro.[91] The core goal was not so much to train specialists but rather to educate future surgeons in the use of X-ray equipment. Two years later, however, the Faculty of Medicine decided to offer a special radiology course under the control of a specialist in the new field—not an existing chair. The institution poached a 28-year-old doctor named Masanori Nakaizumi. A 1919 graduate of the University of Tokyo Nakaizumi was pursuing a research career at Riken (*Rikagaku kenkyujo*), an institution that was established with private funding and 1917 and eventually became the most important research and development (R&D) center in Japan, where he explored the possibilities of applying X-rays to medicine. He was appointed lecturer in radiology in 1927 and assigned to the radiology center of the second department of surgery. However, he made soon after a long training stay in Germany, Austria, and the United States (1927–1931), during which he was promoted to assistant professor (1928).[92] While he was abroad, the Faculty of Medicine built a clinic of radiology—complete with Siemens' most modern machines.[93] The new clinic admitted its first patients in 1932 and began handling radiological tasks for all the departments of Tokyo University Hospital in 1933. Finally, in 1934, the University of Tokyo officially instituted a chair of radiology and promoted Nakaizumi to professor. In the transition into his new post, Nakaizumi hired an assistant professor and three assistants.[94] The department of radiology, meanwhile, gradually took control of X-ray technology throughout the hospital. In addition to putting together a training course for doctors from other departments on the operation of radiological equipment (1937), the organization also gained began managing all purchases of medico-electrical equipment for the whole hospital (1940).[95]

At Kyoto University, the first chair of radiology did not appear until the end of WWII.[96] A Center of Radiology (*Chuo rentogen shitsu*) had been opened in 1919 at Kyoto University Hospital and was headed successfully by doctors Tamonji Urano (1919–1922), Taiga Saigo (1922–1924), and finally Takayoshi Iwai (1924–1945). Exactly what position this center held within the Kyoto University structure is unclear; obviously, though, the facility was a service center for other departments. Center leaders were carrying out research but the facility's development was stifled by the absence of a chair and of any possible future career in the field of radiology. That stagnation may be the main reason why Urano and Saito, who were lecturers and never promoted to higher functions, left Kyoto University and pursued their careers elsewhere. After obtaining his Ph.D., Urano found employment at private hospitals in 1922. Saito, on the other hand, established himself in Kyoto as an independent doctor, continued his work as a radiologist, and assumed the presidency of the Japanese Society of Radiology in 1932.[97] Iwai was an assistant professor in 1923 and conducted research on the use of X-rays in treating tuberculosis. He later rose to the rank of professor at the Research Center on Tuberculosis at Kyoto University in 1941 and, for some time, concurrently continued to direct the Center of Radiology.[98] In the end, the Center leadership position was transformed into a chair of physical treatment (*rigakuteki shinryo*) in 1944 and renamed the chair of radiology in 1949. The chair was entrusted to Itsuma Suetsugu, a doctor who held his degree from Kyoto University (1925) and specialized afterward in radiology at Keio University under the supervision of Fujinami. His next stop was the Nagasaki University of Medicine, where he became a lecturer in charge of radiology and physical treatments in 1926. After spending fifteen years building his career in Nagasaki, along with heading to Europe for training from 1928 to 1930, Suetsugu was recruited by Kyoto University in 1941 and named the first professor of radiology in 1945.[99]

As for private universities, the basic pattern was to set up chairs of radiology and entrust them to doctors responsible for the X-ray equipment in the hospitals affiliated with their respective faculties of medicine. Educational efforts were extensions of clinical services. This was the case at Nihon University, for example, which created a chair of radiology a few years after opening a faculty of medicine (1925). At first, the institution appointed a doctor to oversee the radiology department of the hospital (1927); the next leader was Seiichiro Seki, a lecturer in radiology (1928). However, Seki left the position after one year and became head of the radiology department at Yokohama City Juzen Hospital. In Seki's wake, Nihon University proceeded to offer the chair of radiology to Kanesada Abe, a doctor with a background in orthopedic surgery at the University of Tokyo (1929). Maintaining the post until 1946, Abe served concurrently as the director of the radiology departments at two Nihon University-affiliated hospitals (Surugadai Hospital and Itabashi Hospital).[100]

The two private universities of medicine in Tokyo followed a similar path. In 1930, Tokyo Jikei Medical School hired Sukehiro Higuchi, who had been an assistant in the department of internal medicine at Kyushu University. Jikei administrators appointed Higuchi assistant professor and head of the department of radiology, later promoting him to professor in

1932.[101] The other institution, Nippon Medical School, opened a chair of radiology later on. Its hospital had employed Kazuo Saito, a doctor specializing in orthopedic surgery, as the director of the center of radiology since 1931. As the school instituted a number of chairs, however, administrators appointed Saito professor of orthopedic surgery in 1935 and handed the chair of radiology to Sobei Takahashi, a young specialist.[102]

The last area to examine is the development of radiology education at the colleges of medicine—which often had connections to prefectural hospitals—and other public medical schools. Even if there were not always actual chairs of radiology at these institutions, school officials had been recruiting specialists in radiology since the late 1920s. These specialists helped spread their expertise in X-ray technology among new generations of students: Examples of specialists that fell into this category include Goro Goto, professor of radiology at Kyoto Prefecture Medical College (hired in 1928), Ryunosuke Motojima, professor of surgery and radiology at Tokyo Medical College (1931), Kaisuke Kameda, assistant professor at Kumamoto Medical College (1931), and Sannosuke Tarusawa, associate professor at Iwate Medical College (1936).[103]

3.4   A Quantitative Overview of Graduates in Radiology

Although the lack of any official diplomas to validate recognized, standardized training prevented the Ministry of Education from gathering any census data on radiologists in the years prior to WWII, one can infer the number of radiologists using Goto's annals of radiology in Japan. For each year, he gave the names of students who completed their graduation work on a radiology-related subject—one can assume these students to be "specialists" in the field.[104] Figure 1 tracks the numbers of specialists from 1913 to 1945 and shows the percentage of these specialists who trained at the top five universities (Tokyo, Kyoto, Kyushu, Osaka, and Keio). The first graduation work in a radiology-related field appeared in 1913, when University of Tokyo student Shaku Kikkoji submitted a paper that dealt with the clinical use of radium.[105] Until 1919, there were only nine students to work on radiology, among whom eight did their studies at the University of Tokyo and one at Kyoto.

The general evolution evident in this figure uncovers three main points. First, the second part of the 1920s witnessed a major turning point where the number of graduates began to skyrocket. While there

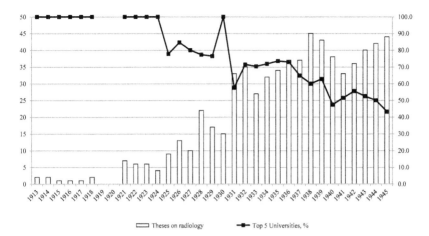

Fig. 1 Japanese doctors who completed their graduation work on radiology, 1913–1945 (*Source* Created by the author on the basis of information published by Goto, *Nihon hoshasen igaku shiko*)

were only 4.6 graduates per year on average from 1920 to 1924, there were 14.2 from 1925 to 1929, and 39 from 1935 to 1945. The burgeoning numbers of young doctors deciding to specialize in radiology was not the direct consequence of new chairs opening up in the discipline, then, but actually had their origins in the years prior to the creation of the new academic posts. Most of these doctors completed their graduate work in various departments that used X-rays as a supporting technology, such as orthopedic surgery and internal medicine.

Second, the five leading faculties of medicine (Tokyo, Kyoto, Kyushu, Osaka, and Keio) played a key role in the training of radiologists. Over the entire period, these universities accounted for 64.7% of all radiologists. Instituting a chair of radiology at an early stage provided no tangible advantage in terms of graduate count, however. The University of Tokyo, which benefited from unrivaled prestige, had the highest rate (19.4%), and Kyoto University, which was very late in opening a chair, occupied the third rank (11.9%) behind Kyushu (13.6%) but slightly ahead of Keio (11.3%) and Osaka (8.3%). Thus, autonomizing chairs of radiology was not essential to training more students but rather connected more strongly to the status of the discipline within the medical field and to professional matters (see below).

Third, the proportion of doctors graduating from the top five universities dropped substantially with the development of private schools in Tokyo and public medical schools throughout the country. While the "big five" had a monopoly on the training of radiologists until 1924, their share shrank during the second part of the 1920s and averaged 74.1% from 1930 to 1935. The decrease continued and intensified from the mid-1930s on, eventually falling to just 43.5% in 1945. These numbers reflect how radiology training for medical doctors had spread throughout Japan.

4   Using X-ray Machines Properly: The Role of Manufacturers

Academic research and professional training were just two of the factors that enabled the first generations of doctors to make use of radiology. As Fujinami emphasized in 1920, a good knowledge of the function and manipulation of X-ray machines was a necessary condition to the proper use of the technology in medical practice.[106] However, this technical aspect of the professionalization process was particular in that a new segment of actors intervened: the manufacturers of radiological equipment.

The enterprises that produced and distributed X-ray equipment were not mere suppliers of new technology. This role was, of course, essential to the rise of radiology as a new medical specialty; as tools for meeting the needs of doctors, efficient, high-quality machines were important in driving their spread throughout Japanese society. Despite being responsible for this industrial dimension (which Chapter 1 addresses in detail), however, the manufacturers of radiological equipment did not assume a purely passive, accommodating relationship with doctors. On the contrary, they adopted early communication strategies targeting doctors and aiming at giving them knowledge of how to use their devices and promoting a widespread, basic understanding of X-rays. For these companies, there were two core objectives in play: increasing the overall consumption of radiological equipment across the country and enlarging their own market shares. One consequence of their involvement was to strengthen the idea of radiology's technical specificity and thereby support its autonomization as a specialty.

Their overall strategy included various concrete actions, few of which were specific to certain firms. There were two major ways to get involved: participating in the activities of medical academic societies, particularly in radiology, and setting up training courses for doctors.

4.1   Participating in Medical Academic Societies

As early as the 1910s, manufacturers had started establishing a presence in the scientific pursuits of doctors. Siemens, which then enjoyed a quasi-monopoly over the Japanese market of X-ray devices, was the first company to send a representative to join the annual conference of a medical society. In 1910, a Siemens engineer attended the annual conference of the Japanese Society of Internal Medicine (*naika gakkai*) and exhibited various electro-medical and radiological devices during a break in the proceedings.[107] During the 1920s, Otto Kresta, the German engineer and head of Siemens' medical division in Japan, participated regularly in the meetings of the Japanese Society of Medical Instrumentation (*Nihon ika kikai gakkai*), whose president was University of Tokyo professor Tashiro. The society's journal eventually published a paper Kresta, which outlined the recent developments of X-ray equipment in Germany, in 1925.[108]

Siemens' most important competitors in Japan adopted a similar strategy. Tokyo Electric made its first presentation through Tatsutaro Miyahara, a doctor at the University of Tokyo and promoter of radiology applications. In 1915, he gave two papers at the annual conference of the Japanese Dermatological Association (*Nihon hifuka gakkai*) on the improvement of X-ray tubes by Tokyo Electric.[109] The following year, Tokyo Electric engineer Tetsuya Fujii published an article on X-ray tubes in the first Japanese academic journal dedicated to the application of physics in medicine—the *Journal of Iatrophysics Medical Treatments*.[110] Later, in 1923, a representative of Tokyo Electric attended the founding assembly of the Japanese Society of Radiology and demonstrated the use of Coolidge tubes and other devices.[111]

Shimadzu, meanwhile, made active forays into medical circles at the beginning of the 1920s through an engineer named Shunichi Fukuda. He published a paper titled "About X-Rays" in the journal of the Japanese Society of Medical Instrumentation in 1923, two years before Kresta did the same.[112] In the long, introductory article, which was addressed to a public that was unfamiliar radiology, the author explained what X-rays were, how radiological equipment worked, and what the possible applications in the medical field were. The following year, Fukuda participated in the second general assembly of the Japanese Society of Radiology and gave a presentation called "About equipment used to generate X-rays."[113]

The activities of the main X-ray device manufacturers in the 1910s thus helped define the boundaries of radiology as an autonomous medical field. Radiologists gradually became X-ray practitioners, mastering the use of radiological equipment and their proper medical applications. Joint R&D projects between these companies and doctors continued to grow during the 1920s; over the course of the next decade, the presence of manufacturer engineers at conferences of radiology societies was common. These deepening levels of cooperation between manufacturers and doctors are also evident in an analysis of medical device patent registrations from the interwar period (see Chapter 3).

4.2   Contributing to Professional Training

Organizing public lectures was the second line of the X-ray machine manufacturers' communication strategy, another effort that contributed to the autonomization of radiology as a field. Since the end of the 1910s, Tokyo Electric and Shimadzu had begun setting up intensive courses for all doctors. They invited the most prominent, recognized specialists in radiology at that time, like Fujinami and Urano, to explain the benefits of using the technology for medical purposes.

Tokyo Electric was the first to launch this type of initiative by organizing a series of conferences on medical radiology, "Lectures of Tokyo Electric on Radiology" (*Tokyo denki KK rentogen koshukai*), in May 1918. The main speaker was Fujinami, who was then at Juntendo Hospital. The conferences also drew several engineers—probably staff members from Tokyo Electric like Tetsuya Fujii, head of the company's R&D center on radiology.[114] Although there are no available details on what kind of impact this first experience made, the end effect was obviously a positive one: Tokyo Electric again put together a course in October of the same year and continued the series without interruption until 1929. The next year, the company Japan Electric Medicine (*Nihon iryo denki KK*), Tokyo Electric's new subsidiary in charge of medical device marketing and sales, pursued these courses and organized them until the end of WWII.[115] The change in sponsor highlights the idea that, for device manufacturers, transmitting knowledge to doctors was a marketing business.

Shimadzu followed in Tokyo Electric's footsteps in the aftermath of WWI. In 1921, it ran its first one-week course (*koshukai*) introducing the principles of X-ray machines and their possible applications to medicine. Designed to present new models to doctors and their assistants and explain their proper use, these yearly courses became increasingly popular—attendance grew from 22 participants in 1921 to 80 in 1922 and 113 in 1924.[116] The talks delivered during this course were also published by Shimadzu from 1923 on under the title "Lectures on radiology" (*rentogen gaku kogishu*). This course was subsequently taken over and continued in 1940 by the Japanese Medical Radiology Society (*Nihon igaku hoshasen gakkai*).[117]

The content of the first one-week course in 1921 shed light on the collaboration between Shimadzu, Kyoto University, and some private practitioners (see Table 4). Besides Fukuda, the head of the X-ray machine division at Shimadzu, four professors (three from Kyoto University and one from Kyoto Third High School) and three practitioners (including

Table 4 Content of the first one-week course, June 1921 (*Source* Goto, *Nihon hoshasen igaku shiko*, vol. 1, pp. 191–192)

Lecturer	Title
Sonosuke Mori, professor of physics at Kyoto Third High School	On the nature of radiological tubes and X-rays On the techniques to become proficient at taking X-ray pictures
Tamonji Urano, doctor, head of the radiology department at Osaka Kaisei Hospital and lecturer at Kyoto University	On the application of the techniques to make X-ray diagnoses for specific ailment On the application of the techniques to conduct X-ray therapy for specific ailments
Shunichi Fukuda, physician at Shimadzu	The concept of electricity and the principles of the X-ray machine
Eiji Aoyagi, professor of electrical engineering at Kyoto University	Belief and science
Matayoshi Ishino, professor of physics at Kyoto University	On the structure of materials and X-rays
Matsuo Iwao, professor of medicine at Kyoto University	Internal medicine through X-rays
Nobuo Hayashi, doctor in private practice in Nagoya and Chiba Prefecture	Diagnostics (clinical lesson)
Kazuhiko Tanaka, radiologist at Osaka University Hospital	Photographs (practical lesson)

Urano) gave lectures. Fujinami and Urano did not oppose each other in their relations with manufacturers: Fujinami began participating in Shimadzu courses, as well, in 1922.

The success of Shimadzu's course led the company to organized more specialized conferences. It gave one for dentists in 1923 and later set up local courses in peripheral regions more than a decade later, including sessions in Kyushu (1937) and Hokkaido (1939). Finally, the enterprise organized a Roentgen Festival (*rentogensai*) in February 1924 to mark the first anniversary of Wilhelm Roentgen's death, gathering more than 200 participants in Kyoto for a series of scientific presentations.[118] Similar events have taken place every year since then, a practice that still exists today.

Although Tokyo Electric and Shimadzu largely dominated the offerings of public lectures, some smaller companies tried to make their presence felt. Tokyo Medical Electric (*Tokyo igaku denki KK*), for example, gave courses between 1919 and 1921.[119] The absence of Siemens and Goto Fuundo, its medical device distributor in Japan, in the lecture market is telling—expresses the focus of the German multinational on purely technological matters.

5   Useful Allies: X-ray Technicians

From very early on, radiologists drew on the support of junior technical staff in charge of the manipulation of radiography and radiotherapy equipment, as well as the management of X-ray laboratories as soon as they were created. X-ray technicians played a key role in the development of radiology as a medical specialty and as a supporting technology for other specialties. Their importance came not so much from their mastery of particular know-how but rather out of their subordinate function in the service of doctors. Technicians had the requisite knowledge for using X-ray equipment correctly, of course, but that expertise was not enough to make them major actors. There was a strong vertical division of labor in radiological departments between technicians, who took pictures, and doctors, who interpreted them.[120] This specialization made it possible for X-ray laboratories to rationalize work and establish the right conditions for mass production, thus making radiology a technology with a profound, unique impact on the transformation of medicine into a profitable business.[121] Although "radiographers [were] often portrayed as passive technicians,"[122] they furthered development of radiology as a specialty.

Literature on the history of medicine reveals only a secondary interest in this junior technician community. Even in his seminal book detailing the impact of medical technology on hospital development, Joel Howell did not analyze the emergence of this profession.[123] However, one can make some general observations about the characteristics of junior technicians in Western communities. First, X-ray technicians in Europe and the United States were largely female. Nurses—either laypeople or members of the clergy—constituted the majority of this specialist force, even with armies working to train men in the profession.[124] In the United States, the first association of X-ray technicians, founded in 1920, included numerous women in its governing bodies.[125]

The answers as to why religious nurses occupied these functions in most European hospitals in the interwar period, both in Catholic and Protestant regions, go back to the low costs of employing clergy members and their reputations for a disciplined, obedient mindset.[126] The doctor-favoring divisions of labor and hierarchical relations that appeared almost from the get-go in radiological departments necessitated the inclusion of technicians, a process that was facilitated by the employment of "X-ray sisters"—or "Roentgenschwestern," as they were called in German-speaking areas.[127]

One important point to note is the absence of any absence of specific, certified technician training Radiologists helped hold back the professionalization of the profession by imparting the necessary practical knowledge to their technicians, which thus enabled the doctors to maintain control over the group.[128] In United Kingdom, the first non-religious X-ray technicians formed an association in 1920, organized their own training courses, and began conferring their certifications in 1922.[129] This case is an exception to the norm in Western countries, however, and the relative importance of this association within the community of British X-ray technicians is unknown.

From a comparative perspective, then, Japan is a rather special case. X-ray technicians were mostly men, a reality that owed a great deal to the minimal influence of religious congregations in the country. Unlike the conditions in Western countries, training programs were also quick to form in Japan. This section explores the reasons behind this particular path.

In 1917, the *News on Medical Instruments* (*Ika kikai shinpo*) journal published a paper by Inji Kitadono titled "The training of technical operation for Roentgen equipment," in which the author emphasized the need to create a training program for junior technicians who worked with doctors and oversaw the use of X-ray machines.[130] According to his estimates, there were about 500 pieces of radiological equipment in use throughout Japan at that time—an infrastructure favorable to the emergence of radiology as a new medical discipline was already in place. However, Kitadono stressed that the development of a specialty would require more than just the existence of equipment; another key component would be staff who knew how to use the devices properly. Radiology technology also had applications in all medical fields as a support tool, notably for diagnostics, which opened up considerable potential for growth. Despite the auspicious conditions and need for staff, there was no professional training available in Japan at the time.

The lack of training programs did not mean that there were no X-ray technicians at hospitals, however. In 1925, several years after Inji's paper appeared, the estimated number of technicians was at around 600 individuals nationwide—slightly fewer than one person per piece of equipment, on average.[131] However, there are no surveys or documents that show precisely what their training background was. Numerous male nurses from the Japanese Army and Navy who were in charge of X-ray equipment pursued their careers at large civil hospitals after their demobilization (mostly at university hospitals, Red Cross hospitals, and prefectural hospitals).[132] Both the Army and the Navy had excellent medical schools, dating back to 1886 and 1897, respectively, where they may have trained male nurses for the use of X-ray devices.[133] For example, the first X-ray technician on record in Hokkaido was Keizaburo Kaizuka, who had worked at Mukko Hospital in Muroran City since at least 1913. He then joined the Navy before getting a job at Sapporo City Hospital, where he worked with Dr. Junji Kaneko.[134]

Faculties of medicine and their affiliated hospitals were a second major training ground for technicians. Professors and doctors educated the staff that they needed in the X-ray departments that they headed, which were often the oldest and largest in the country. Unfortunately, there is very little evidence available to evaluate the overall impact of this pathway on the development of X-ray technicians as a community.

Third, one must stress the influence of medical equipment manufacturers on the institutionalization of X-ray technician training, as well. Indeed, the first school to train this specific type of support staff originated in the private, Kyoto-based company Shimadzu, which worked since 1926 to organize the Training Center for X-Ray Technology

(*Rentogen gijutsu koshujo*).[135] For Shimadzu, this institution corresponded to a clear strategic goal: making the company the premier producer of X-ray equipment in Japan. Competition with Siemens and the numerous small Japanese assembly makers that had emerged was grueling in the mid-1920s. For Shimadzu, training technicians with a strong command of the field was a way to build long-term relations with users.

The center opened in 1927 close to the Shimadzu works in Kyoto and benefited since the beginning from the financial and human resources support of the company. During the first fiscal year (1927–1928), contributions from Shimadzu amounted to more than half of the center's revenues (52.4%).[136] The first director of the center, who stayed in charge until his death in 1930, was Shunichi Fukuda, an electrical engineer who had graduated from Kyushu University and headed up Shimadzu's X-ray R&D department.[137] In 1927, the center's teaching staff of seven instructors included three engineers and one doctor from Shimadzu as well as Kyoto University professor Aoyagi, who did research for the company (see Chapter 1). Shimadzu's influence on the content of the training program was clear (see Table 5).

Shimadzu targeted its course offerings at 20 young male junior high school graduates. The courses, which initially lasted half a year and then expanded to nine months in 1932 and one year in 1935, covered

Table 5 Lecturers at the Kyoto Training Center for X-ray Technology, 1927 (*Source* Goto, *Nihon hoshasen igaku shiko*, vol. 2, p. 28, *Dainihon hakashi roku*, Izumi, *Nihon kingendai igaku jinmei jiten*, and *Kaiin shimei roku*, Shimadzu Corporation, *Eigyo hokokusho*, 1929–1930, list of shareholders)

Name	Career
Shunichi Fukuda, director	Engineer at Shimadzu; head of R&D on X-ray devices
Eiji Aoyagi	Professor of electrical engineering at Kyoto University; founder of the private R&D center Aoyagi
Tamonji Urano	Doctor; head of the radiology department at Kansei Hospital, Osaka; lecturer at Kyoto University; shareholder in Shimadzu
Taiga Saito	Doctor; president of the Japanese Society of Radiology (*Nihon rentogen gakkai*); shareholder in Shimadzu
Shuroku Kurimoto	Engineer at Shimadzu
Kamesaburo Nagasaka	Engineer at Shimadzu
Masahide Ueyama	Engineer at Shimadzu
Keiji Fujimoto	Medical doctor at Shimadzu

the theory of medicine (anatomy and physiology), physics (electricity, mechanics, and mathematics), and practical classes on devices and their operation. During the first years of the program (1927–1931), practical courses represented more than one-third of all study time: 12 weekly classes out of a total of 35.[138] The objective was thus to train a technical staff capable of using X-ray equipment properly.

Corporate strategy was just one of the factors that led Shimadzu to open and develop its school. Since the beginning, the company cooperated closely with medical doctors, especially with the main promoters of radiology in Japan, whose goals aligned with Kitadono's aims. The development of radiology as a medical discipline necessitated the presence of technical assistants at hospitals, which is why doctors worked together with Shimadzu's engineers to manage the training center. Two famous radiologists—both shareholders in Shimadzu—began giving classes in the center's inaugural year (see Table 5): Urano, head of the X-ray department at Kaisei Hospital in Osaka and former lecturer at Kyoto University, and Saito, president of the Japanese Society of Radiology. The influence of doctors on the center remained palpable event after Fukuda's death—Urano (1930–1935), Aoyagi (1935–1944), and Fujimoto (1944–1948) served successive terms as center director.[139]

It is rather difficult to estimate the impact of the Kyoto Training Center for X-Ray Technology prior to the onset of the Pacific War. One the one hand, several sources indicate that the center's popularity declined during the 1930s: The annual average number of graduates went from 39 in 1928–1931 to 17 in 1940–1942 (see Fig. 2). Moreover, a high proportion of students left the school before completing training, even despite a relatively short length of study: 50 students (13.4% of the total) withdrew between 1928 and 1941.[140] The acquisition of basic practical knowledge was clearly enough to get a job in a hospital, given the high demand for qualified technicians. Unfortunately, there are no resources available on where graduates and students took employment, but it was apparently the entire national market, rather than specific local or regional markets.

One the other hand, the center played a valuable role in training the technical staff necessary for developing hospitals and helping radiology emerge as a specialty. Although the available resources do not provide information on where the graduates ended up working prior to WWII, comparing the total number of students (352 for the period from 1928 to 1940) with the number of general hospitals in Japan (3226 in

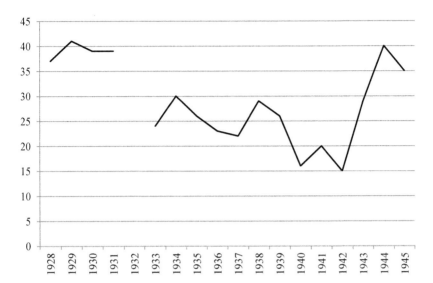

Fig. 2 Number of Kyoto Training Center for X-ray Technology graduates, 1928–1945 (Source *Toseki: soritsu 50 shunen kinenshi*, Kyoto hoshasen gijutsu senmon gakkogakuyukai, 1977, pp. 213–214. *Note* No data exists for 1932 as the lengthening of study time that year meant that no students actually graduated. The data includes students who left the school before graduating)

1940)[141] reveals that the Shimadzu center trained the technical staff for about 10% of all the hospitals in the 1930s—a considerable contribution for one single private school.

The center remained a pioneer until the 1950s, providing an instrumental setting for training X-ray technicians in Japan along the way. Besides the Butsuryo College of Osaka (*Osaka butsuryo senmon gakko*), which was founded in 1933 and ran courses for X-ray technicians from 1935 onward, the Shimadzu center was the only training facility for radiology technicians until 1950.

Whatever training path X-ray technicians followed, though, there was no organized, controlled, or standardized system for professionalization at the national level. Technicians had a dependent relationship with the doctors who trained them for their own needs; they were essential subordinates who provided doctors with reliable, appropriate operations of new technological equipment. In the end, these technical assistants played a vital role in the construction of a new medical specialty.

The beginnings of X-ray technician professional associations exemplified this relation of dependence. The first professional association was founded in Tokyo in 1923 under the name *Keiko-kai* and renamed the Japanese Roentgen Association (*Nihon rentogen kyokai*) in 1925.[142] In 1927, it had 236 members and published a journal, *Keiko*. It also established regional branches in places like Hokkaido (1925), Kyoto (1927), Nagoya (1928), Osaka (1928), and Tohoku (1929).[143] Although the objective of such an association was to obtain the support of the state for training and get its certificates officially recognized, it was medical doctors—not the technicians themselves—who were directly responsible for the creation of the association, which even accepted doctors as members. The association took shape through the efforts of Yoshikazu Segi, a radiologist who had trained under Fujinami and established himself in Tokyo as an independent practitioner.[144] As one of the first doctors to seek professional training for technicians, Segi was instrumental in helping technicians gather into an association first in Tokyo (1923) and then at the national level (1942).

More evidence of technicians' dependency on doctors came with the conflicts between radiologists during the 1930s (see below), which saw the doctors split into two distinct associations in 1934. This division was harmful for the collective awareness of technicians, who followed their bosses into their new respective associations.[145]

In Osaka, X-ray technicians created their own association without doctors in 1936 (Osaka X-Ray Technicians Association, *Osaka hoshasen gijutsusha kai*). Six years later, this association joined a new national association, the Japanese Society of X-Ray Technicians (*Nihon hoshasen gijutsu gakkai*), which gathered technicians from all over[146] the country. The Japanese Medical Science Society (*Nihon igakkai*), which corresponded to the central association of doctors, encouraged the creation of the association. Its main objective was to obtain the legal recognition of X-ray technicians' training from the Diet, which it officially petitioned with the supported of Japanese Medical Radiology Society and the Ministry of Health in 1942.[147] The following year, X-ray technicians from all over the country formed a new association at Kyushu University—without the involvement of any medical doctors—and called their new group the Japanese Society of X-Ray Technicians (*Nihon rentogen gijutsu-in gakkai*), which aimed at "promoting research on technology related to radiology and improving the status of X-ray technicians."[148]

However, war postponed the adoption of such legislation. In 1947, X-ray technicians gathered again in a new organization, the Japanese Association of X-Ray Technicians (*Nihon hoshasen gishi kai*; renamed the *Nihon ekkusu-sen gishi kai* in 1951). The goal of this group was to obtain official certification. This Japan-wide organization was buoyed by the creation of numerous professional associations of X-ray technicians in various prefectures like Ibaraki (1949) and Ishikawa (1951).

Lobbying in favor of a law on professional training, the new national association reached an agreement with the Ministry of Health and associations of doctors in 1951. With that, the Parliament then proceeded to adopt a law on X-ray technicians (*shinryo ekkusu-en gishi ho*) that year. The law introduced the principle of training in special schools and a Ministry of Health-administered official certification framework.[149] It also put X-ray technicians under the control of doctors and required that radiological equipment be installed in hospitals or health centers (*shinryojo*). This was a victory for medical doctors, a step that strengthened the collective power of radiologists.

6   Defending Professional Stakes

While the Japanese Society of Radiology had traditionally limited its activities to academic matters, it ventured into the professional arena in 1932: It opposed the extension of General Electric (GE)'s patent on Coolidge tubes.[150] The innovation in question had a considerable impact on the application of radiology to medicine because it allowed users to control dosage and ray intensity for the first time. Thanks to this patent, GE (an American multinational) and its subsidiaries around the world, including Tokyo Electric in Japan, benefited from an enviable competitive advantage. The group dominated the market of high-quality X-ray tubes, which were sold at expensive prices. The expiration of the patent, which was set to arrive in 1934 in Japan, put GE on precarious ground—other Japanese producers would be able to manufacture copies for cheaper prices when the patent was no longer valid. GE thus tried to obtain an extension of patent protection in Japan.

For radiologists, the issue was obviously to have access to cheap, high-quality products, particularly as a large number of them worked in private clinics or small hospitals with limited financial resources (see Chapter 4). GE's request led to spirited discussions at 1932 and 1933 meetings of the Japanese Society of Radiology, which decided to oppose to it.[151] The Japanese Roentgen Association (X-Ray technicians) and the Japanese Medical Science Society (central medical association) chimed in with their opposition, as well. The three associations made their positions clear to members of the Parliament, which bowed to the pressure and refused the extension.

At the 1932 general assembly, the Japanese Society of Radiology made a second resolution with a very symbolic meaning: It appointed Professor Tashiro honorary president.[152] This choice embodied the shift to a new generation of radiologists who were determined to strengthen the autonomy of their discipline—instead of serving surgeons and other practitioners as mere "assistants," the radiologists now wanted to be fully recognized specialists. Professional stakes became a major issue for specialization. However, the cultivation of this collective awareness was not necessarily a smooth, steady process: The 1930s was a decade of tumultuous conflict among radiologists, with the promoters of autonomization grappling with other doctors who wanted to maintain the traditional relations with other disciplines (subordination). This clash led to the scission of the Japanese Society of Radiology in 1933.

The main actor behind the split was Yoshisada Nakajima, professor of radiology at Kyushu University.[153] The Japanese Society of Radiology held a council meeting on April 1, 1933, in advance of its general assembly. At the meeting, Nakajima expressed his opposition to the appointment of Kaichiro Manabe to the presidency of the society—even though Manabe had been elected with more than an absolute majority.[154] Moreover, Nakajima refused his selection as a member of a four-member committee in charge of defining norms designed to prevent accidents stemming from the use of X-rays. The committee included Manabe, as well as radiology professors Nakaizumi (the University of Tokyo) and Nagahashi (Osaka University). Nakajima criticized the overall stranglehold that the University of Tokyo had on the Japanese Society of Radiology. Although Nakajima had no personal grudge against Manabe himself, he objected to the fact that the organization had elected a professor at the University of Tokyo and a specialist in internal medicine, not radiology: Manabe had, in fact, previously been president of the Japanese Society of Internal Medicine (*Nihon naika gakkai*). Radiology had to be a business of radiology specialists, Nakajima contested, but the council was divided on the issue.

The next day was the general assembly of the society, which gathered several hundreds of doctors. During the opening address by acting president Taiga Saito (an independent practitioner in Kyoto and former assistant professor at Kyoto University), doctors from the imperial universities of Kyushu and Osaka, along with their closest allies, heckled the speaker and left the room. They then organized a demonstration in front of the Faculty of Medicine of Kyoto University, where the general assembly was taking place. Their demand was clear: They wanted the society to be led by specialists.

These dissident doctors were large in number, totaling 462 in August 1933.[155] A meeting of the opposition took place at the Osaka University Hospital on June 25, 1933, with Nagahashi presiding. The attendees appointed a temporary 10-member committee and chose Koichi Fujinami as the president of the new society: the "Japanese Society of Medical Radiology" (*Nihon hoshasen igakkai*).[156] The statutes of the society were exactly the same as those of the Japanese Society of Radiology, and the new organization also launched the publication of its own journal (*Nihon hoshasen igaku gakkai zasshi*) in 1933 (Table 6).

Although the committee basically consisted of doctors from Kansai and Western Japan, the overarching conflict was not a regional one but rather a struggle over the status of specialists. Members of Kyoto University (in Western Japan) participated in meetings of the Japanese

Table 6 Temporary committee of the Japanese Society of Medical Radiology, 1933 (*Source* Goto, *Nihon hoshasen igaku shiko*, vol. 2, p. 220, *Dainihon hakashi roku*, Izumi, *Nihon kingendai igaku jinmei jiten*, and *Kaiin shimei roku*)

Name	Professional career
Koichi Fujinami, president	Professor of radiology at Keio University
Masamichi Nagahashi	Professor of radiology at Osaka University
Yoshisada Nakajima	Professor of radiology at Kyushu University
Kakuichi Ando	Professor at Okayama Medical College
Saiichi Koike	Head of the department of radiology of Kanazawa Prefectural Hospital
Toshimitsu Takeda	Assistant professor at Okayama Medical College
Tomio Nishioka	Army doctor
Itsuma Suetsugu	Assistant professor at Nagasaki Medical College
Yutaro Sakurai	Lecturer at the department of radiology of Keio University
Shimao Shimasaki	Head of the department of radiology of Gifu Prefectural Hospital

Society of Radiology (the original group), while some doctors from Keio University (in Tokyo) aligned with the offshoot Japanese Society of Medical Radiology. These two societies negotiated their participation in the meetings of the Japanese Medical Science Society (*Nihon igakkai*) and organized special sessions on radiology on these occasions. In this "cold-war" atmosphere, Japanese radiologists held two separate sessions at the April 1934 meeting: a morning session for the Japanese Society of Radiology (the JSR) and an afternoon session for the Japanese Society of Medical Radiology (the JSMR).[157]

The difference between these two societies was, in fact, a small divergence of opinion in the professional concerns and issues pertaining to the organization of the specialty. In 1935, the members of the JSMR discussed measures to take in order to promote the development of chairs at universities and independent departments at hospitals. From this perspective, the presence and domination of professors from other medical disciplines at Tokyo and Kyoto universities was incompatible with the autonomization process.

However, after few years of open conflict, the leaders of the Japanese Society of Radiology took a step toward conciliating the dissidents by appointing Nakaizumi—who had been promoted two years earlier to professor of radiology at the University of Tokyo—as president in 1936. He was sensible to professional concerns and able to restore dialogue between the radiologists and practitioners from other disciplines. During his inauguration speech at the general assembly on April 1, 1936, he stressed his views on the matter:

> The opposition between our societies is very regrettable. It is necessary to unite them again. I would like to discuss matters frankly and forget completely personal feelings. The year 1940 is upon us, and our country is preparing for the Olympics. We must come together from throughout Japan and organize an international conference of radiology in Japan. In working toward that goal, we reunify our societies of radiology.[158]

The following year, the JSR proposed to the JSMR the idea of holding a joint meeting at the annual meeting of the Japanese Medical Science Society.[159] The JSMR also agreed to hold its 1937 annual meeting at the Faculty of Medicine at the University of Tokyo.[160] This rapprochement was obviously made possible by the two societies' common view of specialty autonomization, which reflected a change of opinion within the JSR. In 1938, both societies set up a joint commission in charge of submitting a petition to the authorities on the independence of medical specialties.[161] The commission included Sukehiro Higuchi (Jikei University of Medicine, Tokyo), Koshiro Iwasaki (the Army), Masanori Nakaizumi (the University of Tokyo), and Chichio Tamiya (Chiba University). In March 1939, it addressed a petition to the ministries of Education and Health, as well as to the deans of the faculties of medicine at imperial universities, calling for the creation of chairs of radiology to train enough specialized radiologists for hospitals and health centers. One major issue was to ensure that X-ray equipment would not endanger the safety of nursing staff and patients; the Ministry of Interior's decree on rules to control medical X-ray equipment, issued on August 2, 1937, stipulated that the curriculum vitae of the head doctor—including information on his training—would need to be transmitted to the authorities.[162] If the state considered radiologists' training important to guaranteeing the security of staff and patients using X-ray devices, it was necessary to make sure that faculties of medicine provided proper education.[163]

The reception of this petition is unknown, but the number of chairs of radiology did not change after 1939. However, the Ministry of Education began to acknowledge radiology as a specific discipline. In 1940, after the societies merged, the scientific division of the department of special affairs of the Ministry of Education (*Monbusho senmongakumu-kyoku kagakuka*) became the official head office of the newly formed academic society, uniting the former rival associations.[164]

The two societies of radiology thus came together and give birth to the Japanese Society of Medical Radiology (*Nihon igaku hoshasen gak-kai*), whose first president was Professor Manabe.[165] A large society with a membership of 920 members in 1941,[166] the group did not include anything along the lines of collective goals in its statutes. After the first meeting of the council in July 1940, however, members decided to continue lobbying in favor of the development of independent chairs.[167] Soon thereafter, two representatives of the society delivered a new petition on the issue to the head of the department of special affairs of the Ministry of Education.[168] The new association continued to pursue these aims until 1942, when the war effort put a clamp on the activities of societies across the board. The key point here, though, is that professional concerns had found a spot on the agenda for the new society.

7   Conclusion

The autonomization of radiology as a medical discipline in Japan during the first part of the twentieth century saw the field become a specialization without official certification, whereas certification was a core component of the process in both Germany and the United States. The emergence of a medical specialty appears to be an issue specific to individual doctors. The state and society maintained a hands-off approach, even while some radiologists mobilized external actors—including manufacturers of X-ray equipment and X-ray technicians—to put their discipline in a better position to autonomize.

The birth of radiology as a specialty in Japan was thus a process that unfolded in two main phases. During the first period, which spanned from the 1890s to the 1920s, the central issue was to make medical doctors more aware of the possibilities of radiology as a supporting technology for medical activities, especially in diagnostic applications. Some professors at the University of Tokyo, notably Tashiro, played a key role through their influence on the Japanese medical world. X-ray technology also bestowed career-building opportunities on a group of young doctors, like Fujinami and Urano, who established themselves as the first specialists in the discipline. Chairs of radiology began to appear in this context, as well, thereby diffusing general knowledge to new generations of doctors and helping train the first wave of specialists. A society of radiology also formed in 1923, again with the objective of disseminating know-how. Radiology gradually became autonomous in medical science and practice.

The second period covered the 1930s and 1940s. Radiology shifted from progressive autonomization to real specialization and then into a foundational structure for professional claims. New generations of radiologists wanted to rescue their discipline from stagnating as a supporting tool for other specialized fields, such as surgery and orthopedics, and secure footing for their field as a recognized specialty. This mutation was the source of deep conflicts between doctors, a spate of strife that eventually calmed down with the opening of a chair of radiology at the University of Tokyo. The period of upheaval made radiology stronger, though, as the field emerged as an acknowledged specialty from then on. Radiologists also intensified their lobbying against the state at the end of the 1930s and during the war to protect their autonomy.

Looking beyond the issues of professionalization and specialization, this chapter also shed light on the emergence of a new social group that played a major role in the transformation of medicine into a profitable business: radiologists, who represented an omnipresent force in this process. At first, they constituted an important customer base for the manufacturers of X-ray devices and contributed to the diffusion of new medical technologies across the hospital system. Demand among radiologists consequently had a particular impact on the type of equipment that manufacturers, especially Tokyo Electric and Shimadzu, developed. Moreover, radiologists were important intermediaries between the medical world and Japanese society. In the hospital context, they embodied medical modernity and contributed to the expansion of X-ray use by patients. Finally, radiologists and their work had a profound effect on hospital management and competitiveness within the hospital system. The cost of X-ray equipment pushed hospitals along an endless pursuit of larger resources and gave way to escalating competition between hospitals (see Chapter 4).

NOTES

1. "Segi Yoshikazu", *Dainihon hakase roku*, vol. 4, p. 848.
2. Ikai, *Byoin no seiki*, pp. 97–126.
3. Reiser, "Technology, Specialization, and the Allied Health Professions" and Premuda, "La naissance des spécialités médicales".
4. Rosen, "Changing Attitudes of the Medical Profession to Specialization".
5. Weisz, *Divide and Conquer*.
6. Ibidem, pp. 192 and 229.
7. For the US, see Starr, *The Social Transformation of American Medicine*, pp. 220–225.
8. Stevens, *Medical Practice in Modern England*.
9. Ikai, *Byoin no seiki*, p. 284.
10. Yamazaki, *Igyo to horitsu*, pp. 26–47.
11. Kawakami, *Gendai nihon iryoshi*, p. 451.
12. Ikai, *Byoin no seiki*, p. 292.
13. Terasaki, "Senmon iseido no rekishi to genjo", p. 420 and Shimazaki, *Nihon no iryo*, p. 89.
14. Yoshida, "Ishi no kyaria keisei to ishibusoku".
15. Goto and Mori, *Nihon no oishasan kenkyu*, p. 35.
16. Matsu e.a., "Daigaku to kanren byoin", p. 504.
17. Goto and Mori, *Nihon no oishasan kenkyu*, p. 36.
18. Kawakami, *Gendai nihon iryoshi*, pp. 324–326.

19. Statutes of 23 March 1923, published by par Goto, *Nihon hoshasen igaku shiko*, vol. 1, pp. 220–221.
20. Dommann, *Dursicht, Einsicht, Vorsicht*.
21. According to the Virtual Museum of the Japan Medical Imaging and Radiological Systems Industries Association, http://www.jira-net.or.jp/vm/top-page.html (accessed 8 January 2015).
22. *Shimadzu seisakujo shi*, p. 353.
23. Dommann, *Dursicht, Einsicht, Vorsicht*.
24. Low, *Building a modern Japan*.
25. Kim, *Doctors of Empire*, Chapter 2.
26. Goto, *Nihon hoshasen igaku shiko*, vol. 1, p. 22.
27. Kataoka, *Rikugun guni chujo*.
28. Goto, *Nihon hoshasen igaku shiko*, vol. 1, p. 22.
29. Ibidem, p. 51.
30. Ibidem, pp. 40–41.
31. Izumi, *Nihon kingendai igaku jinmei jiten*, p. 386.
32. Goto, *Nihon hoshasen igaku shiko*, vol. 1, p. 53.
33. *Tokyo daigaku igakubu hyakunen shi*, p. 308.
34. Goto, *Nihon hoshasen igaku shiko*, vol. 1, p. 92.
35. *Chuo tetsudo byoin shi*, p. 308.
36. Naito, *Kyukyu shochi*.
37. Izumi, *Nihon kingendai igaku jinmei jiten*, p. 443.
38. Ibidem, p. 181.
39. Abe, "Osaka daigaku akaibuzu no soritsu to kokuritsu daigaku bunshokan", p. 4.
40. *Irigaku ryoho zasshi*, vols. 1–12, 1914–1921.
41. Segi and Hayashi, "Urano tamonji hakase no tsuioku to no shogai", p. 71 and Aoyanagi, *Iyo ekkusu sen sochi hattatsushi*, p. 36.
42. Otori, "Ko fujinami koichi", *Dainihon hakushi roku*, vol. 2, p. 222.
43. http://www.deutsche-biographie.de/sfz33622.html and University Library of Vienna, on-line biographical information, http://ub.meduni-wien.ac.at.
44. Tamaki, "Nihon saisho no hoshasen ika".
45. Goto, *Nihon hoshasen igaku shiko*, vol. 1.
46. National Diet Library, OPAC.
47. Toshiba Medical, *21 seiki he no kakehashi*, pp. 4–5.
48. Goto, *Nihon hoshasen igaku shiko*, vol. 1, p. 160.
49. Fujinami, "Waga kuni ni okeru rentogen gaku shinpo no jotai".
50. Ibidem, p. 16.
51. Ibidem.
52. Goto, *Nihon hoshasen igaku shiko*, vol. 1, p. 127.
53. Goto, *Nihon hoshasen igaku shiko*, vol. 2.
54. Furuya, *Rentogen ryoho shinron*.

55. Ibidem, p. 18.
56. Ibidem, p. 17.
57. Segi and Hayashi, "Urano tamonji hakase no tsuioku to no shogai", *Danihon kakushi roku*, vol. 3, p. 517.
58. *Kyoto daigaku hyakunenshi*, p. 855.
59. *Osaka kaisei byoin*, p. 148.
60. Goto, *Nihon hoshasen igaku shiko*, vol. 1, p. 148.
61. Ibidem, p. 169.
62. Urano, *Rentogen shashin zufu*.
63. Shimadzu seisakujo, *Eigyo hokokusho*, list of shareholders, 1929–1930.
64. Segi and Hayashi, "Urano tamonji hakase no tsuioku to no shogai", p. 71.
65. Kawakami, *Gendai nihon iryoshi*, p. 201.
66. *Nihon igakkai bunkakai shoshi*.
67. Goto, *Nihon hoshasen igaku shiko*, vol. 1, pp. 217–219.
68. *Nihon rentogen gakkai zasshi*, vol. 1, no. 1, 1923, p. 183.
69. *Shimadzu seisakujo-shi*, p. 37.
70. Goto, *Nihon hoshasen igaku shiko*, vol. 1, p. 220.
71. Ibidem, p. 220 and 1970, p. 212.
72. *Rentogen gaku zasshi*, vols. 1–3, 1928–1930.
73. Goto, *Nihon hoshasen igaku shiko*, vol. 2, p. 84.
74. *Ika kikai gaku zasshi*, vol. 1, no. 3, 1923.
75. Shinmura, *Nihon iryo shi*, pp. 234–237; Kawakami, *Gendai nihon iryoshi*, pp. 197–203 and 319–326.
76. Goto, *Nihon hoshasen igaku shiko*, vol. 1, p. 124.
77. Ibidem, p. 169.
78. Ibidem, p. 137.
79. Ibidem, p. 191.
80. Bartholomew, *The Formation of Science in Japan*, pp. 243–244, *Keio gijuku daigaku igakubu 60 nen-shi*.
81. Bartholomew, *The Acculturation of Science in Japan*.
82. *Keio gijuku daigaku igakubu 60 nen-shi*, pp. 22–29.
83. Izumi, *Nihon kingendai igaku jinmei jiten*, p. 530.
84. Goto, *Nihon hoshasen igaku shiko*, vol. 1, p. 226.
85. Own calculation based on Goto, *Nihon hoshasen igaku shiko*, vols. 1 and 2.
86. *Kyushu daigaku igakubu hoshasenkagaku kyoshitsu 50 nen-shi*, pp. 25–26.
87. Izumi, *Nihon kingendai igaku jinmei jiten*, p. 437.
88. *Osaka daigaku igaku denshu hyakunenshi*.
89. Burrows, *Pioneers and early years*, p. 183.
90. Nagahashi, *Rentogen shindan to chiryo*.
91. Izumi, *Nihon kingendai igaku jinmei jiten*, p. 358.
92. Ibidem, p. 432.
93. Nakaizumi, "Tokyo teikokudaigaku igakubu hoshasenka no setsubi".

94. *Tokyo daigaku igakubu hyakunen shi*, p. 439.
95. Ibidem, p. 440.
96. *Kyoto daigaku hyakunen-shi: bunkyoku-shi hen*, pp. 855–859.
97. *Kaiin shimei roku*, p. 209 and Goto, *Nihon hoshasen igaku shiko*, vol. 2, p. 173.
98. Izumi, *Nihon kingendai igaku jinmei jiten*, p. 79.
99. Ibidem, p. 327.
100. *Nihon daigaku igakubu 50 nen-shi*, p. 300.
101. *Tokyo jikeikai ika daigaku hyaku nen-shi*, pp. 788–789.
102. *Nihon ika daigaku no rekishi*, p. 217.
103. Cases quoted by Goto, *Nihon hoshasen igaku shiko*, vols. 1 and 2.
104. Ibidem.
105. Goto, *Nihon hoshasen igaku shiko*, vol. 1, p. 100.
106. Fujinami, "Waga kuni ni okeru rentogen gaku shinpo no jotai".
107. Goto, *Nihon hoshasen igaku shiko*, vol. 1, p. 75.
108. Kresta, "Bankin no rentogen hosenkai".
109. Goto, *Nihon hoshasen igaku shiko*, vol. 1, p. 123.
110. Fujii, "Rentogen kankyu no jumyo to hason no genin".
111. Goto, *Nihon hoshasen igaku shiko*, vol. 1, p. 220.
112. Fukuda, "Rentogen-sen ni tsuite".
113. Goto, *Nihon hoshasen igaku shiko*, vol. 1, p. 236.
114. Ibidem, pp. 159–160.
115. Goto, *Nihon hoshasen igaku shiko*, vol. 2, p. 146.
116. *Shimadzu seisakujo shi*, p. 49. The numbers are unknown for the following years. In 1923, a similar course for dentists was organized.
117. *Shimadzu seisakujo shi*, p. 49.
118. Ibidem, p. 50.
119. Goto, *Nihon hoshasen igaku shiko*, vol. 1, p. 168.
120. Larkin, "Medical Dominance and Control" and Larkin, "Health Workers", p. 538.
121. Shumsky, "The Municipal Clinic of San Francisco" and Bridgman Perkins, "Shaping Institution-Based Specialism".
122. Nixon, "Professionalism in Radiography", p. 31.
123. Howell, *Technology in the Hospital*.
124. Decker and Iphofen, "Developing the Profession of Radiography", p. 264.
125. Hoing, *A History of the ASXT, 1920 to 1950*.
126. Dommann, *Dursicht, Einsicht, Vorsicht*, pp. 139–192 and Droux, *L'attraction céleste*, Chapter 5.
127. Dommann, *Dursicht, Einsicht, Vorsicht*, p. 139.
128. Ibidem, pp. 139–192.
129. Thomas and Banerjee, *The History of Radiology*, p. 27.
130. Kitadono, "Rentogen sochi sosa gijutsu no ikusei".

131. *Isei hyakunen shi*, p. 433.
132. *50 nen no ayumi*, p. 20.
133. Momose, *Showa senzen no nihon*, pp. 343 and 368.
134. *Hokkaido ekkusu-sen gishi*, p. 23, "Kaneko Junji".
135. *Toseki, Shimadzu.*
136. *Toseki*, p. 8.
137. Ibidem, p. 13.
138. Ibidem, p. 198.
139. Ibidem, pp. 13–14.
140. Own calculation based on *Toseki*, p. 213.
141. Historical Statistics of Japan, http://www.stat.go.jp/english/data/chouki/, document no. 24–28. General hospitals do not include psychiatric hospitals.
142. *Isei hyakunen shi*, pp. 433–434.
143. *30 shunen kinen-shi*, p. 36.
144. "Segi Yoshikazu".
145. *30 nen-shi*, p. 29.
146. *Isei hyakunen shi*, p. 429.
147. *30 nen no ayumi*, p. 176.
148. *Nihon rentogen gijutsu-in gakkai zasshi*, vol. 1, no. 1, 1944, p. 2.
149. *Isei hyakunen shi*, p. 429.
150. Goto, *Nihon hoshasen igaku shiko*, vol. 2, p. 173.
151. Ibidem, p. 212.
152. Ibidem, p. 173.
153. Goto, *Nihon hoshasen igaku shiko*, vol. 2, pp. 212–214, *Nihon rentogen gakkai zasshi*, vol. 11, no. 7, 1934.
154. Goto, *Nihon hoshasen igaku shiko*, vol. 2, p. 212.
155. Ibidem, p. 220.
156. Ibidem.
157. Ibidem, p. 257.
158. Ibidem, p. 339.
159. Ibidem, p. 391.
160. Ibidem, p. 399.
161. Ibidem, p. 439.
162. *Jitsuyo iji hoki*, pp. 148–150.
163. Text quoted by Goto, *Nihon hoshasen igaku shiko*, vol. 2, pp. 484–485.
164. Statutes of the Japanese Society of Medical Radiology, art. 3, quoted by Goto, *Nihon hoshasen igaku shiko*, vol. 2, p. 537.
165. Ibidem, p. 528.
166. Ibidem, p. 573.
167. Ibidem, p. 540.
168. Ibidem.

CHAPTER 4

Cooperation Between Firms and Doctors

1 Introduction

Dr. Shichiro Hida appeared in the previous two chapters both as the inventor of an X-ray machine for Shimadzu and as a doctor involved in the promotion of radiology as a specialty. His position as an intermediary between the health equipment industry and medical doctors was strengthened by his action as an entrepreneur. In 1915, Hida and his brother Shigeru, the owner of a small trading firm, founded an X-ray manufacturing and marketing company that would continue operating into the 1950s.[1] The development of the X-ray device for Shimadzu during World War I (WWI) probably made Hida and his brother conscious of the potential that business could hold. Still, the brothers' enterprise was not at the frontier of innovation; it rather represented the adaptation of foreign technology to the Japanese market. Neither the Hida brothers nor their company Hida Electric Industry registered any patents from 1918 through 1945. However, Hida Shigeru did obtain certification for twelve utility models between 1925 and 1938, and his company Hida Electric Industry secured two more in 1942 and 1943. The property rights for the models came from the Japanese authorities for minor innovations, mostly improvements of existing products (see below).

This example raises interesting questions concerning innovation in the medical device industry during its formative years. What was the nature of cooperation between doctors and manufacturers in developing instruments and machines for medical practice? Did companies employ

© The Author(s) 2018
P.-Y. Donzé, *Making Medicine a Business*,
https://doi.org/10.1007/978-981-10-8159-0_4

practitioners to codevelop devices? Did doctors register patents for their innovations? If they did, what did they do with the patents—use them to help found a new company or sell them to manufacturers?

The answers to these questions are vital to understanding the dynamics of medicine and its transformation into a fast-growing business. Considering that medical doctors were far from passive consumers of new technology, the process of technological innovation in medicine during the first part of the twentieth century warrants close examination. Literature in the field of the history of medicine, influenced by the STS (science and technology studies) approach, has placed special emphasis on innovation by individual doctors and the importance of their insertion in social networks in establishing a visible position and broader market for their products among practitioners. In some particular cases, scholars have stressed also the proximity with mechanics and small companies in the instrument industry as crucial to the process of developing medical devices. Generally speaking, this approach focuses on individuals and neglects the action of large enterprises. Scholars tend to conceive innovation as a bottom-up process emerging from the medical doctor contingent.[2]

While this base of literature is naturally a foundation for further investigation, the perspective of business history that I use in this book requires a slightly different point of view. Chapter 1 explained that large enterprises, whether they be multinational (Siemens and General Electric) or domestic (Shimadzu), were major actors in the manufacture of X-ray devices. Consequently, it is essential to analyze their activity as well as their relations with medical doctors.

Works on national innovation systems (NIS) offer a useful tool for approaching innovation in the medical device industry in Japan during the first part of the twentieth century.[3] NIS-focused researchers have considered innovation as the product of activity by various organizations (universities, enterprises, army, and state-owned organizations) and individuals, ascribing a strong significance to the relations between them. In the case of Japan, Minoru Sawai showed that, in many industries, the state took the lead in orchestrating cooperation between academia, business, and the military during the interwar period[4]: In various cases, the government set up specific associations and research groups to promote joint research. Sawai did not focus specifically on medicine in his seminal work; he mentioned only the state's move to organize a research group on X-ray equipment in 1943, but the group consisted exclusively of private company representatives and did not include any members from universities, public bodies, or the army.[5] The general lack of joint research in the medical industry during World War II (WWII) did not mean that there was no cooperation between firms and doctors throughout the first part of the twentieth century. Sawai's general framework provides a useful resource for delineating the organization of research and product development in the X-ray equipment industry.

The Japanese medical instrument industry as a whole, including the X-ray equipment field, featured deep, widespread cooperation between craftsmen and doctors. Joint research groups existed as early as 1902, with various associations coordinating joint research projects until WWII.[6] In 1923, the idea of supporting the progress of medicine through the alliance of medical doctors, manufacturers, and traders led to the creation of the Japanese Society for Medical Instrumentation (*Nihon ika kikai gakkai*).[7] The first committee of the association included 9 individuals and 2 firms, one of which was Shimadzu.[8] As early as December 1923, meanwhile, members involved in X-ray device business created an autonomous section (*denki bukai*). During its first meetings, the section gathered representatives from manufacturers of equipment (Matsumoto Seisakujo, Okura Roentgen, and Tokyo Electric (TE)), trading companies (Matsumoto Kikaiten), and medical doctors (Koichi Fujinami, Tsugushige Kondo, and Sazo Ujihara). They soon organized meetings with the Japan Electric Association (*Denki kyokai*) and cooperated particularly with Siemens, TE, and Shimadzu. There were thus some collective discussions and joint activities for the co-development of X-ray equipment during the 1920s, as there were for other kinds of medical instruments. One major difference separated X-ray equipment from other medical instruments, however: although joint research continued and developed for medical instruments, research and development (R&D) for X-ray devices was almost exclusively the domain of large companies. Competition between multinational enterprises (MNEs) and a handful of domestic firms was the driving force behind innovation, leaving scant room for individuals and craftsmen.

This chapter analyzes the dynamics of relationships between radiology equipment manufacturers and medical doctors through a survey of intellectual property right registrations (patents and utility models) in Japan through 1945. Although patents do not represent the level of innovativeness of a nation or a company but rather the strategies that companies and individuals adopt regarding innovation, legal protection, and commercialization, economic and business historians often use patents to study—and sometimes measure—innovation.[9] In this chapter, I thus use patents from both a quantitative and a qualitative perspective to shed light on the various strategies of various actors in the X-ray equipment industry. The patent documents that I introduce, accessible online on the website of the Japanese Industrial Property Digital Library,[10] include a broad range of useful information, such as type of innovation (which part of the X-ray equipment the patent is for), name and location of the inventor, name and location of the patent's owner (if different from the inventor), and date and number of the patent. By identifying both the inventor and the owner of a patent or a utility model, the documents make it possible to investigate the relations between medical doctors (inventors) and manufacturers (owners).

The chapter comprises five sections. Section 1 introduces the Japanese patent system and its major characteristics. Section 2 provides a statistical overview of intellectual property rights for X-ray equipment registered in Japan through 1945, emphasizing the general evolution of this phenomenon. Sections 3 (foreign MNEs), 4 (Shimadzu), and 5 (other domestic actors) analyze the product development strategies of the most important actors.

2   The Japanese Patent System

The roots of intellectual property rights in Japan go back to the Edo period, when an early patent system took shape and formed a structure that shared many qualities with the systems in place in Europe at the time. The authorities implemented a monopoly system for the commercial exploitation of inventions that operated only at the provincial level and excluded foreigners.[11] However, the contemporary Japanese government shied away from technological innovation and even promulgated a law prohibiting innovation (*Shinki hatto*) in 1721.[12] In this context, the forcible opening of Japan in 1853 triggered a dramatic change and raised two questions: how to unify intellectual property at a national level and how to handle foreign access to the system.

Indeed, it soon became obvious that Japan's industrial development and the security of the country's independence would require the protection of inventions. Although a consensus on this point was quick to emerge, industrial circles swiftly expressed their opposition to reciprocal rights for foreigners. In the late 1860s, Japanese jurists began to disseminate information nationwide on Western systems for the protection of inventions and trademarks, leading to a public debate in 1870 on the need to adopt such systems. As there were no foreign multinationals in the country, the question of whether or not to guarantee patent protection for such firms did not arise.[13] Nevertheless, Japan went ahead to adopt—primarily at the state's urging—an active policy of technology transfer, mainly in the fields of arms, shipbuilding, textiles, and machines. During the 1860s and 1870s, the bulk of technology transferred to Japan was channeled through foreign engineers employed by various public or private firms.[14] As the costs of employing these engineers were extremely demanding, however, these firms lobbied the state to protect their new acquisitions, enabling them to retain the edge that the technologies gave them in the domestic market.[15] Their main contact in the administration was Eiichi Shibusawa, who was a key figure in the industrialization of Japan and eventually became known as the "father of Japanese capitalism."[16] Along with building a career in private industry, he did a short stint with the Ministry of Finance as the head of the Office of Reform (1869–1873). It was there that he promoted the idea of patent laws to protect the inventions acquired from foreigners.[17]

A centralized system for granting monopolies over inventions was enacted between 1871 and 1872 and later suspended in 1884. Meanwhile, the regional authorities (prefectures) resumed their practice of granting these monopolies, but only at the local level. As these procedures drew only limited interest in a country that was undergoing economic unification, the centralized system saw only 326 application submissions during that period.[18] However, such systems were not deemed useful until the early 1880s. It was trademarks—not inventions—that demanded prompt legislation in response to several disputes between Western exporters and Japanese merchants, who used copied trademarks without protection for consumer goods (beer, soap, and drugs) during the 1870s and 1880s.[19] These conflicts gave rise to an 1884 law governing the protection of trademarks and designs.

The question of national patent laws once again came to the fore after Japan entered a period of industrial growth and strengthened its business tides with Western companies. Even though there was no authorization for foreign direct investment (FDI) flows to Japan, the state sought to integrate the country into the international system in order to work together with foreign companies and benefit from new technologies.[20] Legislation on the patenting of inventions saw the light of day in 1885, with the adoption of the Patent Monopoly Act.[21] A first draft bill, submitted by the Ministry of Agriculture and Trade in 1883, was designed to secure Japan's integration into the international system. The authorities adopted a very open attitude toward multinationals but ran afoul of independent entrepreneurs seeking to protect their infant industry. Consequently, Parliament—where industrialists' interests were well represented—rejected the initiative; in the end, the 1885 law granted rights to Japanese nationals only.[22] Lawmakers did adopt certain limitations, however, including a ban on patenting medicine, a 15-year time limit on maximum protection, and the rendering of patents invalid in the event of military needs.[23] The government decreed a new law on the protection of intellectual property in 1888 in order to cover inventions, trademarks, and designs with a single legislative instrument.

Lawmakers amended this piece of legislation extensively in the late 1890s to enable FDIs in Japan.[24] The Japanese government also signed bilateral patent agreements with the United States and the United Kingdom (1897), allowing citizens from the two countries to register patents in Japan, and later signed the Paris Convention for the Protection of Industrial Property in 1899.[25] Furthermore, during the second part of the 1890s, Japan recovered its right to impose custom duties and adopted a protectionist policy whose main objective was to ensure that the internationalization of the patent protection system would spur not a huge influx of imports but rather investment and production in Japan.[26]

Besides, as a backward economy, Japan also allowed and encouraged copying to support its technological development. The government thus introduced a new law on the protection of utility models, using the German system as a foundation, in 1905.[27] Japan's definition of utility models enabled it to protect goods that were not "innovations" as such but featured a new form or structure.[28] The authorities sought to encourage the technological development of industry, even if the goods or procedures that it protected were not sufficiently novel to warrant patent registration. These utility models were primarily used for imitations of foreign products, making it possible to legalize technological hybridization or even imitation.[29] Whereas patents held influence over the capital goods industry, production processes, and high-tech goods, primarily, utility models mainly protected ordinary consumer goods, all of which were imitations of imported products.[30] Moreover, the rights were mainly held by Japanese nationals. The period from 1905 to 1930 saw the registration of 140,699 utility models, of which only 629 were filed by foreigners (0.5% of the total).[31] During the same period, the number of patents registrations came to 67,782, of which 46,766 were held by Japanese (68.9%). Thus, Japanese nationals registered three times as many utility models as they did patents.

Consequently, the patenting of medical instruments happened within a twofold system (patents and utility models) that began permitting submissions from foreigners in the late 1890s and made it possible to protect both new products and minor innovations (like imitations or adaptations of products for the Japanese market).[32] Companies and individuals worked to obtain intellectual property rights in the X-ray equipment field using all the available possibilities under this legal framework, which enabled the implementation of various strategies for acquiring knowledge, innovating, and turning profits.

3 PATENTING X-RAY DEVICES: A STATISTICAL OVERVIEW

The statistics on X-ray device patents and utility models registered in Japan through 1945 not only reflect the development of this industry but also underline the field's specificity within the medical instrument industry. X-ray devices indeed demonstrated a growing prevalence within the general field of medical instruments and equipment over the course of four phases, growing from no patents in 1885–1901 to 4.3% of all patents in 1902–1925, 14.6% in 1926–1937, and 20.8% in 1938–1945. The development of patenting in the X-ray machine industry had strong ties to the emergence of foreigners and companies within the patent system. Figure 1 gives an overview of this development, providing details to support discussion and illustrate the strategies of various actors (individuals, companies, Japanese, and foreigners). The findings reveal two major features: one pertaining to patents and one to utility models.

First, there was a total of 236 patents related to X-ray devices, most of which were registered in the mid-1920s and thereafter; only 18 were obtained before 1925 (7.6%). The most important actors were companies, which registered 72% of the total (170 patents). The X-ray device industry had been a high-tech sector since its creation, and R&D occurred mostly within firms—patenting activity was not the outcome of individual craftsmen and doctors. However, the intensity of the patenting activity in the area points to both varying innovation capabilities and different patent strategies, which form the basis for the discussion in

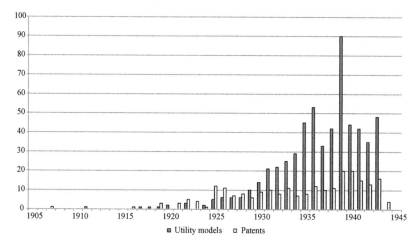

Fig. 1 Numbers of patents and utility models for X-ray devices, 1885–1945 (*Source* Industrial Property Digital Library, www.ipdl.inpit.go.jp (last accessed 27 May 2013))

the next section. Some companies registered large numbers of patents, such as the US firm GE and its subsidiaries (77 patents) or the Kyoto-based company Shimadzu (33). Other firms like Philips (10), Siemens (7), and Westinghouse (5) registered few patents despite their positions as global players in the field. There were also many Japanese companies that engaged in this area, but except for Shibuya Roentgen (11) and NEC (7), they lacked the organizational capabilities to be real innovators. Eleven small Japanese companies had only one or two patents.

The 46 individuals who registered patents were also relatively isolated, with only a few serial innovators among them. The individuals held an average of 1.4 patents, and only two of them had more than two patents. The largest owner was Kikuta Koizumi (8 patents), an artisan who founded Shibuya Roentgen in 1928.[33] The second individual with more than two patents was Masanori Nakaizumi (3 patents), a medical doctor and professor of radiology at the University of Tokyo.[34] He himself owned the property rights to his patents upon registration, which means that his patents were the results of his research at his own laboratory—not the product of any cooperation with a company. Moreover, the group of individual patent holders was almost exclusively Japanese: the number of foreigners with patents amounted to just six (four German, one American, and one Dutch), four of whom had obtained their patents before 1925—during the formative years of the industry, before it became a fast-growing business.

Finally, X-ray patent data make it possible to identify targets of innovation more precisely. As tubes were the most important part of the equipment, vital in ensuring the dosage and strength of the X-rays, they were a major source of patenting activity. The first patent registered in this field was the famous patent for the Coolidge tube, registered by GE in Japan in 1919 (no. 34'628). Tubes alone accounted for a total of 63 patent registrations (26.7%), mostly from companies (66%).

Second, utility models greatly outnumbered patents (with a total of 588 registrations), but their growth started later: there were only 12 utility model registrations before 1925 (2%) and 33 during the years from 1925 to 1929 (5.6%). Consequently, the increase in utility model registrations came in the wake of growth in patent volume. The development of the X-ray equipment business obviously encouraged many artisans, doctors, researchers, and companies to enter the field and attempt to improve the existing technology and equipment. This sparked rapid growth in utility model registrations during the 1930s. The profile of utility model registration holders is essentially the same as the breakdown of patent holders, however.

Companies represented a slightly lower share of all utility model registrations (378 utility models, 64.3%), but they were still dominant actors. Here, too, different capabilities and strategies were in play. GE's Japanese subsidiaries (Shibaura and TE, which merged in 1939 to form Toshiba) had a total of 100, while Siemens possessed only two, Philips one, and Westinghouse one. Several Japanese companies were active in submitting many utility models, although most of them held nearly no patents: Shimadzu had 101 utility models, Shibuya Roentgen 50, Goto Fuundo 33, Kawanishi Machine 19, Hitachi 11, and Dai-Nihon Roentgen 10. There were also 17 other companies with fewer than 10 utility models.

The 98 individual utility model owners held 2.1 utility models on average, a higher per-capita volume than individual patent holders had. However, the number of serial innovators was also low. The only people to own more than five models were Raizo Kubota (22 models), an artisan who founded his own company under the name Kubota Manufacturing, Musashi Sakata (7, unidentified), and Shigeru Hida (12), the owner of the Hida Trading company and brother of the famous radiologist Shichiro Hida, who was a University of Tokyo graduate and a doctor at the School of Medicine of the Army.

The most significant feature of utility model activity was the scarcity of foreigners, who accounted for only 16 registrations among both companies and individuals (2.8%). Interestingly, GE did not directly register any utility model in Japan; the company's Japanese subsidiaries took charge of those efforts, even for some innovations realized in the United States. Utility models were thus essentially a way for Japanese individuals and companies to enter the field of X-ray business—a high-tech industry dominated by a small number of MNEs—through imitations and adaptations of foreign products.

This basic statistical analysis emphasizes how companies were the dominant actors in filing patents and utility models for X-ray devices. However, that major force covered a wide range: a large variety of firms engaged in these filing activities. In addition, there was still room for individuals to participate in innovation and become actors in X-ray device business. The next section discusses the strategies that companies and individuals adopted in patenting in the X-ray machine industry, with a special emphasis on the role of medical doctors.

4   FOREIGN MULTINATIONALS

The two main foreign MNEs involved in the business of X-ray machines in Japan—as was the case elsewhere in the world—were the US company GE and the German firm Siemens. The analysis of the dynamics of this industry in Chapter 1 demonstrated that the two firms pursued completely different strategies as they expanded into the Japanese market, notably in relation to product development, which hurt Siemens' competitiveness and market share during the 1920s. By exploring the companies' patent strategies in Japan, this section lays out the very different perspectives that the companies took on cooperation with Japanese employees and helps explain why Siemens was unable to develop specific devices for the market in question.

First, GE established its presence in Japan through two joint ventures—TE (established in 1905) and Shibaura Works (1910)—and became a major player in the electrical appliance industry.[35] As Shigehiro Nishimura has shown, GE transferred patent management to its Japanese subsidiaries: TE and Shibaura could decide by themselves which US patents they wanted to protect in their country. Moreover, as technology and know-how gradually made their way to Japan via transfers, GE's subsidiaries engaged in R&D and applied for their own patents and utility models.[36] In the field of X-ray machines, they registered a total of 76 patents and 100 utility models in Japan.

Figure 2 shows the nationalities of inventors behind patents registered in Japan by TE and Shibaura. Most of these patents were for innovations carried out in the United States (71.1%). From 1928 onward, however, patents began naming Japanese inventors, a change that reflected the gradual acquisition of knowledge and implementation of R&D organizational structures at Japanese subsidiaries. In 1929, TE was the Japanese firm with the largest R&D center, employing a total of 45 researchers at that time and 216 by 1934.[37] Of course, these figures include all of the company's researchers, not just those engaged in R&D for medical instruments. In all, TE and Shibaura patents listed a total of nine Japanese inventors active in electro-medical machines; none of them were medical doctors—all were engineers. Shodo Tanaka and Hamaji Yoshida, graduates of the Faculty of Sciences of the University of Tokyo and the Faculty of Engineering of Kyoto University, respectively, appeared in five patents.[38] The proportion of Japanese inventors

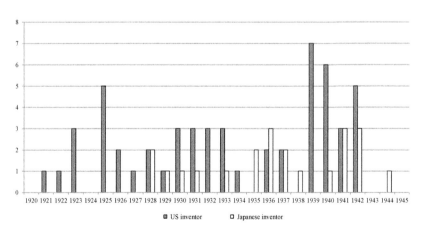

Fig. 2 Patents registered in Japan by Tokyo Electric and Shibaura in the field of X-ray equipment by nationality of inventor, 1920–1945 (*Source* Industrial Property Digital Library, www.ipdl.inpit.go.jp (last accessed 27 May 2013))

was even higher in the utility model field (83%). This legal instrument was obviously used for adapting devices and equipment to the Japanese market, but medical doctors are absent from the lists of inventors. Few of the utility models focused on high-tech parts such as tubes (15% of all utility models), cathodes (9%), or full equipment (2%). Rather, most of the minor innovations were for the electric system (29%) and the metal accessories supporting tubes (24%)—in other words, parts for making X-ray equipment smaller and lighter, while using Western high-technology.

This suggests that the learning process for developing X-ray machines at GE fell within the classical framework of international technology transfer at an MNE. This strategy helped TE become a major player in X-ray equipment in Japan during the 1930s.

One must wonder, however, what relationships TE and Shibaura had with medical doctors. Internalizing knowledge related to medical practice and the use of X-ray equipment in hospitals must have been a key to improving devices and answering doctors' needs. Although TE and Shibaura controlled their own patent strategies, they actually worked closely with radiologists and practitioners as advisors. For example, TE presented the first prototype for an X-ray tube in Japan in 1915 thanks to a cooperative connection with Koichi Fujinami, then the head of the department of radiology at Juntendo Hospital (see Chapter 2).[39]

Siemens, meanwhile, followed a completely different strategy. Through its subsidiary for electro-medical equipment Siemens-Reiniger-Werke (SRW), the German MNE controlled the Japanese X-ray equipment market at the beginning of the twentieth century and wanted to avoid transferring production and knowledge to Japan, registering only seven patents and two utility models—all developed in Germany—from 1900 to 1945. Even when it launched a joint venture with the Japanese medical instrument trader Goto Fuundo to found Goto Fuundo Manufacturing (GFM) in 1932 in hopes of regaining some of the market share it had lost during WWI and the 1920s, Siemens tried to transfer as few technologies as possible to Japan. Moreover, it wanted to control potential innovations realized within GFM as well as possible cooperation arrangements with other firms. The 1932 agreement on the establishment of the joint venture included a long article on innovation, which mentioned notably that "inventions and other propositions for improvements proceeding from the supervisors or employees shall be communicated by Factory to SRW immediately, at the latest by the time when the protection rights for such inventions or improvements are applied for in Japan. To utilize such inventions and improvements and to acquire protection rights outside of Japan, SRW is authorized exclusively."[40] It also stipulated that the "Factory shall not acquire the rights of other inventions and protection rights unless SRW explicitly agrees to each such case. In case SRW expresses its agreement, it will advise Factory as to the acquisition. Factory shall do its best to help SRW acquire these rights for utilization outside of Japan under at least the same advantageous conditions. It depends on the decision of SRW whether or not it accepts the conditions."[41]

Hence, GFM had few chances to develop and held only two patents through 1945. Its parent company, Goto Fuundo, had only two patents, of which at least one was for an invention made by Kosaku Kawamura, who became a member of the board after WWII and a president of the Osaka Medical Equipment Society in 1954.[42] However, this company did hold rights to a high number of utility models (33). No doctor, however, appears in their credits, and all of the inventors were Japanese. All the utility models were also obtained for low-tech parts of X-ray equipment, like metal supports for X-ray tubes, as was the case for GE's subsidiaries. For Siemens, this strategy embodied the technological competitiveness that it enjoyed in the field of X-ray machines and stemmed from a desire to dominate the market through the excellence of its products; as it transferred the assembly of consistently top-level X-ray machines to GFM, Siemens would thus prevent domestic manufacturers that did not have the necessary organizational capabilities to develop such equipment from copying them. Japanese partners limited their intervention to the development of minor parts of equipment. Consequently, Siemens did not see patenting as a necessary measure. However, Siemens' decision to focus solely on the high-end market stopped the company from being able to answer Japanese doctors' calls for cheaper and simpler equipment and precipitated a dramatic loss in market shares.

5   The Successful Co-development Strategy of Shimadzu

Japanese companies became important players in the development of X-ray machines in the mid-1920s, but only a very limited number of them had a real R&D strategy and registered more than a few patents.

The biggest patent holder was the Kyoto-based scientific instrument maker Shimadzu. Founded in 1875, this family business began to enjoy significant growth in the field of X-ray devices in the mid-1920s and largely dominated the corresponding market until the end of WWII, thus challenging the monopoly position Siemens had exerted until WWI. Shimadzu's success relied essentially on its ability to adapt Western technology to the Japanese environment and offer cheaper, smaller, and simpler equipment to Japanese doctors and hospitals. Working together with medical doctors was a key element of this strategy to codevelop new products suitable for the Japanese market. Shimadzu's property right holdings embody this cooperative approach.

The company registered a total of 33 patents and 101 utility models through 1945. However, the learning process at Shimadzu was very different from that at GE, as Shimadzu did not cooperate very much with foreign MNEs. None of the inventors mentioned were foreigners. Instead, Shimadzu relied on the internalization of domestic knowledge via the employment of university graduates and cooperation with private research institutes and medical doctors.

Collaboration with Dr. Shichiro Hida, one of the pioneers of radiology in Japan, made it possible for Shimadzu to obtain the first patent for an X-ray device in 1916 (no. 29'665). In the 1920s, Shimadzu beefed up its organizational R&D capability by hiring engineers in charge of developing new X-ray devices and established itself in 1924–1925 as the leading producer of X-ray equipment in Japan. The number of staff at its R&D center grew from 12 in 1929 to 125 in 1934. Although not all the employees focused on X-ray devices, this rapid development reflects the attention that management devoted to in-house research.[43] Moreover, Shimadzu outsourced some R&D activities to researchers from the Faculty of Engineering at Kyoto University. For example, joint research with Yoshio Onishi led to the registration of two patents in 1938 and 1939 (nos. 129'184 and 134'076).[44]

However, the most important feature of Shimadzu's research strategy was the collaboration with doctors. Although most of the inventors mentioned in the firm's patents and utility models were actually engineers and technicians, collaboration with medical practitioners from various backgrounds was also an important avenue of innovation. Joint research projects with Tamonji Urano—a promoter of radiology in Japan, the head of the X-ray division at Osaka Kaisei Hospital, a lecturer at Kyoto University, and a shareholder in Shimadzu (see Chapter 2)—led to the registration of a patent for an X-ray tube in 1933 (no. 101'414), thus reducing the dependence on TE for the supply of high-quality tubes.[45] Another important partner was Toshimitsu Takeda, assistant professor at Okayama Medical College. Takeda wrote research papers on the improvement of X-ray device security[46] and authored a bestseller on X-ray technology that came out in 1935 and went through 11 editions through 1951.[47] In 1938, Shimadzu registered both a patent (no. 125'679) and a utility model (no. 13-14038) for his innovations.

Shimadzu's cooperation with other doctors included works with Michimaro Takahashi, a medical doctor in the Navy (utility model no. 6-8819 in 1931), Tsuneo Hayano, the former head of the department of radiology of Kurashiki Chuo Hospital in Okayama Prefecture (utility model 11-8280 in 1936), Yoshihiko Koga, a radiologist at Tohoku University who developed equipment for the mass radiography of groups in the mid-1930s (utility model no. 15-15839 in 1937), and the dentist Hisashi Numata (patent no. 146'700 in 1941). Moreover, Shimadzu also cooperated with X-ray technicians like Osaka Kaisei Hospital's Masami Nomura, who worked intensively on the improvement of radiological equipment (utility model no. 11-2328 in 1936).[48] None of these practitioners had exclusive links to Shimadzu; some, in fact, applied for patents and utility models in their own names. For Shimadzu, this brand of collaboration was an important way of internalizing knowledge about X-ray devices and the needs of practitioners. The approach is undoubtedly one of the major reasons why Shimadzu was able to launch new kinds of equipment and compete effectively with Siemens and GE.

6   OTHER DOMESTIC ACTORS

Besides Shimadzu, there were also a handful of small- and medium-sized companies involved in the field of X-ray equipment. Most focused on assembly or the manufacture of specific parts such as X-ray tubes, which led them to register some patents. Kenji Ito is a case in point. Born in 1885, he took a job with Iwashiya Iwamoto, a major medical instrument trading and manufacturing company, in 1911 and later became the head of the X-ray machine department in 1915. The following year, he started his own company, Tokyo Medical Electric (*Tokyo igaku denki KK*, later renamed Ito Co.), where he developed some electro-medical devices, including X-ray devices, and secured a patent for new equipment in 1942 (no. 153'823). He became famous publishing books to support the use of household medico-electric appliances and promoted self-medication, notably through the publication of books.[49]

Other examples of these firms include Shibuya Roentgen (founded in 1928 and close to the Hitachi Group), Dai-Nihon Roentgen, Kawanishi Machine, Hitachi, and Morikawa. The first was a small assembly-maker founded in 1928 by Kikuta Koizumi and supported by Hitachi, which took it over in 1951.[50] Through 1945, it registered a total of 9 patents and 49 utility models. These figures clearly attest to the will to develop new equipment suitable for the Japanese market. The small company employed a graduate in physics from the University of Tokyo, Nobuo Mochita,[51] but there is no evidence that the firm cooperated with medical doctors. Dai-Nihon Roentgen was also very active in R&D, securing a total of 10 utility models and 1 patent for an innovation that the company codeveloped with Kazuma Tateishi (no. 109'635, registered in 1935), the founder of Omron Corporation. Finally, Kawanishi Machine (19 utility models), Hitachi (10), and Morikawa (7) held no patents and did not cooperate directly with medical doctors. These examples of Japanese companies engaged in the development and the improvement of X-ray devices show that the case of Shimadzu, which cooperated intensively with medical doctors, was an exception among domestic producers.

Although enterprises had far and away the largest share of patents and utility models, individuals also submitted many applications for intellectual property rights to X-ray equipment-related innovations. Most were unidentified or from the sector of general medical instruments and mechanics—in other words, small- and medium-sized companies. Some of them obviously developed and improved equipment to respond directly to the needs of medical doctors, as had been the case for individuals working on innovations in other instruments.[52] This was true of Raizo Kubota (2 patents and 22 utility models), for example, a mechanic who worked in a medical instrument workshop in Tokyo. Kubota would later found his own company, Kubota Manufacturing, in 1920 to develop X-ray equipment for a professor of Tokyo University.[53] Such cooperative relationships may have existed, but there is too little evidence to define the role of medical doctors in this mode of partnership.

Hence, my focus in the following discussion is on medical doctors who have been identified through the use of various directories.[54] My analysis aims at shedding light on the profile of the doctors who patented X-ray innovations, an objective that might uncover possible explanations of their individual patent strategies. In my view, these doctors employed two major approaches.

First, there were doctors with strong academic and professional goals. Radiology was an emerging and not yet fully acknowledged specialty in Japan during the interwar period. Several of the doctors who promoted radiology as a new medical field engaged in developing and improving equipment on their own. From this perspective, one could conceive of patenting as a way to strengthen the position of radiology as a specialty, with technology providing a justification for the specificity of the discipline. One could also conjecture that these doctors patented their inventions with the intentions of selling them to manufacturers afterward.

The best example is obviously Masanori Nagaizumi, who was the first professor appointed to the chair of radiology at the Faculty of Medicine of the University of Tokyo in 1934 (see Chapter 2). He registered three patents between 1936 and 1940 and collaborated with TE to develop and improve several devices.[55] Other doctors followed this model at a local level or for specific sub-specialties. Born in the Kobe region, Chichio Tamiya graduated from Tokyo University in 1920 and built his career in the department of internal medicine at his alma mater until moving to Niigata College of Medicine (1925), where he organized a department of medicine as an assistant professor. He then spent three years in Germany and Austria, where he specialized in radiology and applied for a patent from abroad (no. 72678 in 1927). After moving back to Japan in 1928, he became a proponent of the use of radiology in internal medicine and devoted himself to academia. Toshio Kurokawa was assistant professor in internal medicine at Tohoku University when he registered a utility model for the improvement of equipment for taking X-ray pictures (no. 11-472 in 1936). He may have also had ties to Shimadzu, as he used the Shimadzu patent officer to fill out the form for his utility model. Above all, though, he was a scholar: he published and coauthored a book about the radiography of the digestive system in 1936[56] and became one of the most prominent advocates of cancer research in Japan after WWII. Another doctor was Noburu Terauchi, a doctor who specialized in dentistry. He started his career in 1912 heading up radiography as an assistant professor at Tokyo Dental University.[57] He later registered a patent in 1926 (no. 68'694) and published several books on the use of radiology in dental medicine.[58] These activities helped establish Terauchi as a leading figure in the application of radiology in dental medicine.

The other approach to patenting focused on securing rights for business reasons, allowing doctors to make money selling their innovations to various partners. Tokio Nishioka, a doctor in the army who became professor at Osaka University after WWII, is a good example. In the early 1930s, he registered a utility model (no. 7-6102 in 1932) and a patent (no. 109'133 in 1935) that do not specify any company owner. However, he changed his strategy in the mid-1930s and started working for private companies, obviously aware of the financial benefits his innovations could generate. He developed five utility models for Osaka-based Dai-Nihon Roentgen between 1936 and 1938 and then three others for Shimadzu in 1940 and 1941. Hisashi Numata presents a similar case. A specialist in radiography for dental medicine, he applied for a total of five utility models from 1933 to 1936. Two were registered together with Kikuta Koizumi, the founder of Shibuya Roentgen, in Tokyo, and another one was sold to Shimadzu. As a researcher and an entrepreneur, Numata founded his own research institute, the Numata Medical Institute (*Numata igaku kenkyujo*), after WWII.[59]

Of course, the distinction between academic-oriented and business-oriented patent strategies is not absolute; I drew the division to stress the various objectives that medical doctors sought. Advancing the progress of science, driving the development of an industry, and making money were not contradictory aims—they all resulted from the entrepreneurial spirit in the broad sense. At any rate, the different career paths of these doctors fell in line with the two main goals I have emphasized here.

7   Conclusion

The patenting of X-ray devices in Japan during the first part of the twentieth century was mostly a corporate venture. X-ray equipment was part of a high-tech industry, and the knowledge required to develop and improve radiological equipment extended beyond the scope of medical science and practice. Electricity and vacuum tube technologies were key elements of innovation and competitiveness in the X-ray machine business, which is why large companies with R&D facilities dominated the industry. Despite their technological leverage, not all MNEs followed the same patent strategy. While GE protected its innovations and transferred patent management to Japan on a large scale, Siemens preferred to keep most of its inventions secret and patented its products only sparingly. Thus, patenting activity represented the strategy of a given company or individual, not necessarily the corresponding actor's level of innovativeness.

Whatever their patent strategies, neither GE nor Siemens collaborated intensively with Japanese medical doctors to develop and improve X-ray equipment. No doctors appear among the inventors listed on their patents and utility models, which basically consist of engineers from the respective companies either in their home countries (GE and Siemens) or in Japan (GE). Both companies surely worked closely with doctors in hopes of attracting buyers. For example, GE's subsidiary TE actively organized training courses for radiologists beginning in the late 1910s and sent representatives to the meetings of the Japanese Society of Radiology since its foundation in 1923.[60] Still, the practical substance of this relationship apparently extended no further than marketing activity. Foreign MNEs trusted their technological advantage to develop new equipment.

In this context, Shimadzu was able to achieve brilliant success precisely because it worked together with medical doctors to meet the needs of the medical community.[61] The company's capacity for inventing new devices and, in particular, adapting existing equipment to the specificity of Japanese medical market—via smaller, lighter, and cheaper products—rested on intensive cooperation with doctors. Shimadzu's patents and utility models mention doctors as inventors, even if they were not company employees. Many of them were working at universities, at hospitals, or as independent practitioners, fortifying the growth of a domestic company.

Shimadzu's product development strategy was, however, unique among domestic manufacturers. Other Japanese medical instrument companies do not appear to have worked so closely or intensely in collaborations with medical doctors. It is also important to stress that few doctors patented X-ray device-related innovations on an individual basis, but it is difficult to make a proper evaluation of how representative these doctors were and what they did with their intellectual property rights.

The above analysis of cooperation between X-ray equipment producers and medical doctors, based on a survey of patents and utility models, sheds light on the source of Shimadzu's competitive advantage in the domestic market. Working together with doctors made it possible to adapt global technology to their needs. This chapter also showed that the 1920s, especially the second part of the decade, was a turning point: the number of patent and utility model registrations for X-ray technology began to surge, and TE (GE's subsidiary) began securing patents for innovations by Japanese engineers instead of simply importing from the United States. At the same time, Shimadzu became the leading supplier of equipment on the Japanese market (Chapter 1), while radiologists engaged in a process of professionalization (Chapter 2). Operating in the context of these findings, the next two chapters tackle the impact of the relevant economic, social, and technological changes on the management of hospitals and the organization of the health system as a whole.

NOTES

1. Goto, *Nihon hoshasen igaku shiko*, vol. 1, p. 127 and *Nihon ika kikai mokuroku*, p. 336.
2. Stanton, *Innovations in Health and Medicine*; Schlich and Tröhler, *The Risks of Medical Innovation*; Timmermann and Anderson, *Devices and Designs*; and Anderson, Neary and Pickstone, *Surgeons, Manufacturers and Patients*.
3. Lundvall, *National Innovation System*and Nelson, *National Innovation Systems*.
4. Sawai, *Kindai nihon no kenkyu kaihatsu taisei*.
5. Ibidem, pp. 190–191.
6. Donzé, "The Beginnings of the Japanese Medical Instruments Industry".
7. *Ika kikai gaku zasshi*, vol. 1, no. 1, p. 1.
8. *Ika kikai gaku zasshi*, vol. 1, no. 2.
9. Cantwell, *Technological Innovation and Multinational Corporations* and Cantwell and Andersen, "A Statistical Analysis of Corporate Technological Leadership Historically".
10. http://www.ipdl.inpit.go.jp (last access 25 January 2015).
11. Tomita, *Shijo kyoso kara mita chiteki shoyuken*.
12. Kinoshita, "Edoki ni okeru gijutsu hattatsu".
13. Mason, *American Multinationals and Japan*.
14. Burks, *The Modernisers*.
15. Tamura and Suzuki, "Nihon tokkyo seido gaishi".
16. Jones, *Debating the Responsibility of Capitalism*.
17. *Kogyo shoyuken seido hyaku nen shi*, vol. 1, p. 17.
18. Ibidem, p. 20.
19. Ibidem, pp. 35–36.
20. Donzé, "The International Patent System and the Global Flow of Technologies".
21. *Nihon sangyo gijutsu shi jiten*, pp. 15–16 and *Tokkyo seido 70 nen shi*, p. 44.

22. *Nihon sangyo gijutsu shi jiten*, pp. 15–16.
23. *Tokkyo seido 70 nen shi*, p. 44.
24. *Kogyo shoyuken seido hyaku nen shi*, pp. 98–103.
25. *Tokkyo kara mita sangyo hatten shi*, p. 2.
26. *Tokkyo seido 70 nen shi*, pp. 31–32.
27. Richards, "Petty Patent Protection".
28. *Tokkyo seido 70 nen shi*, p. 72.
29. Models are sometimes confused with designs. A design is a new product, whereas a model is a new application of an existing product. *Tokkyo kara mita sangyo hatten shi*, p. 4.
30. Ibidem, p. 12.
31. *Historical statistics of Japan*, document no. 17–10.
32. Donzé, "Patents as a Source for the History of Medicine".
33. Koizumi, *Waga kuni ni okeru X-sen kan no ayumi*.
34. Izumi, *Nihon kingendai igaku jinmei jiten*, p. 432.
35. Janssen and Medford, *Envision*.
36. Nishimura, "The Adoption of American Patent Management in Japan".
37. Sawai, *Kindai nihon no kenkyu kaihatsu taisei*, p. 47.
38. *Kaiin shimeiroku*, 1943, p. 250.
39. *21 seiki he no kakehashi*, p. 5.
40. Siemens Medical Archives, Erlangen (Germany), unmarked folder, Agreement between Goto Fuundo and SRW, 30 June 1932–25 November 1933, art. 16.
41. Ibidem.
42. Goto Fuundo, *Eigyo hokokusho*, 1950.
43. Sawai, *Kindai nihon no kenkyu kaihatsu taisei*, p. 47.
44. Abe, Oka and Onishi, "Denri denatsu kei no tokusei nitsuite".
45. Segi and Hayashi, "Urano tamonji hakase no tsuioku to no shogai".
46. For example, Takeda, "Dai yon shu ekkusu sen sochi non denka boshiki".
47. Takeda, *Rentogen gijutsu*.
48. Nomura, "Metoro kankyu to H gata kankyu no hikaku".
49. Ito, *Ichi-en no isha: ichimei shindenshi seimei-ron*.
50. National Diet Library, Archives of the GHQ/SCAP, ESS(C)11060-11062, Shibuya Roentgen Seisaku Sho, April 1950, *Hitachi Seisakusho-shi*, pp. 358–359.
51. *Kaiin shimeiroku*, 1943, p. 432.
52. Donzé, "The Beginnings of the Japanese Medical Instruments Industry".
53. According to the website of the company, http://www.kubotacorp.co.jp (accessed 16 January 2015).
54. *Kaiin shimeiroku*, 1936 and 1943; *Dainihon hakushi roku*, 1921–1930; and Izumi, *Nihon kingendai igaku jinmei jiten*.
55. *21 seiki he no kakehashi*, p. 6.

56. Kurokawa and Yamakawa, *Shokakan no rentogen shindan.*
57. *Tokyo shika daigaku hyaku nenshi.*
58. Terauchi, *Shika butsuri kagaku*, Terauchi, *Rentogen shikagaku.*
59. Numata, "Mukashi no X-sen kai no shuhen."
60. *Nihon rentogen gakkai zasshi*, 1923–1940.
61. Donzé, "The Beginnings of the Japanese Medical Instruments Industry".

CHAPTER 5

The Diffusion of Radiology and Its Effects on Hospital Management

1 INTRODUCTION

In 1918, Koichiro Masago, surgeon at the Wakayama Red Cross Hospital, went to Tokyo and spent half a year studying radiology at Juntendo Hospital under Dr. Koichi Fujinami. He then continued his training, spending three months at an army hospital in Tokyo, the University of Kyoto, and Kaisei Hospital in Osaka. During this period of specialization, he used X-ray devices made by various manufacturers and eventually chose a piece of equipment developed by Shimadzu for the Wakayama Red Cross Hospital, to which he returned in 1919. After this first radiological equipment came another new acquisition in 1923. In 1935 and the years thereafter, the X-ray devices underwent regular upgrades to more modern versions.

For the Wakayama Red Cross Hospital, the introduction of an X-ray device occurred during a deep transformation. Founded in 1905 via a takeover by the Red Cross of Wakayama Prefecture Hospital, newly privatized, the institution experienced a period of rapid growth and reorganization during the interwar years. Administrators expanded the hospital buildings several times (in 1917, 1918, 1925, 1927, and 1939) and made improvements to the technical environment; the installation of sterilization equipment (1912), a new operating room (1923), and the aforementioned X-ray devices are three examples. This infrastructural development made it possible for the institution to accept more and more patients. The total number of days of care went from 21,978 for hospitalizations and 64,791 for outpatients in 1914 to 68,023 and 206,977, respectively, in 1938, the last year before the Army took over the hospital. Expenses, meanwhile, grew from an average of 116,816 yen in 1908–1922 to 404,886 yen in 1938. Contributions from patients were the main sources of expenditure funding, with hospitalization and care fees accounting for a considerable proportion of revenue (74.7% of all resources in 1908–1922 and 83.7% in 1938). The accounting details are unknown, but new technology obviously attracted wealthy people who were ready and willing to pay substantial amounts of money for access to it. In addition, the hospital administrators offered new, special services for wealthy patients. In 1936, the hospital had five classes of paying patients, of which the first three received individual rooms.[1]

This example shows that understanding the development of the medical-technology infrastructure—at the heart of which was radiology—hinges on its management and financial dimension. This mutation was the core issue shaping the growth of the hospital system during the first third of the twentieth century in not only Japan but also Western Europe and the United States. Several monographs from American and British hospitals demonstrated that the new technology that made their way to hospitals in and after the 1890s was part of the general development of hospitals and their mutation toward organizations with management structures invoking the model of the modern enterprise.[2] Various historians have thus referred explicitly to Alfred Chandler in their studies; Steve Sturdy, for example, claimed that "the most important changes in medical practice were to be found in the sphere of what might best be termed medical administration."[3]

The most important concerns of this transformation related to the development of new medical technology such as radiology, clinical laboratories, and operating rooms. On the one hand, these technologies were costly; their acquisition was thus an important financial investment that institutions needed to recoup through various fees. On the other hand, the technologies also represented an opportunity to expand financial revenues by attracting wealthy-class patients—a segment that had traditionally preferred home-based care—to hospitals. As American historian Paul Starr states, "growth in the volume of surgical work provided the basis for expansion and profit in hospital care."[4] In Switzerland, the fees for the use of X-ray devices represented about 10% of the overall revenues at hospitals during the 1920s and the 1930s.[5]

In Japan, only a scant few researchers have tackled the transformation of hospitals. Most of the works are descriptive and follow a factual narrative, but they do provide rich data that outlines the general trends of the development of the hospital system from the 1870s to today.[6] These works provide the primary basis for the next section of this chapter. The only available academic study of the dynamics of the Japanese hospital system is the book that Shuhei Ikai published in 2010.[7] Adopting a comparative approach covering British, US, and Japanese cases, Ikai demonstrated that the Japanese hospital system has featured a high density of small, private hospitals in urban areas. For doctors, it was thus easy to access the hospital infrastructure by opening their own small hospitals; in the United States and United Kingdom, meanwhile, doctors tried to access existing institutions such as large urban hospitals. Ikai offers a liberal and positive view of the Japanese hospital system, which he asserts made it possible to achieve a high level of technological development and access to healthcare.[8] However, the work hardly discusses the technological dimension or the negative effects of competition (surplus equipment and pressure on revenues, for instance). The impact of technological changes on hospital management at both the individual (single-hospital) and collective (hospital-system) levels remains unaddressed.

As some of the above works on Western cases have noted, however, the relation between technological environment and hospital management is crucial. This chapter focuses on two essential points. It first analyzes the way in which new medical technology diffused through the Japanese hospital system, using the example of X-ray devices, and discusses the influence of the system's structure on the diffusion patterns. Second, it discusses the impact of the new technology on the management of hospitals. The main sources for my examination are various censuses and official reports, especially those by the Ministry of Health, as well as historical monographs that hospitals published to commemorate anniversaries. The chapter includes three sections. Section 1 introduces the main characteristics of the Japanese hospital system from an international comparative perspective. Section 2 then discusses the diffusion of radiology throughout the Japanese system, and Section 3 focuses on the impact of the technology on the management of several hospitals.

2   THE JAPANESE HOSPITAL SYSTEM BETWEEN 1870 AND 1945

The hospital, as an organization that admits and cares for the sick, was a new institution in Meiji-period Japan.[9] The contact and exchanges with Dutch doctors during the Edo period influenced Japanese medical science, leading to the development of anatomy.[10] The impact of these connections on health institutions was relatively limited, however, with most Japanese receiving care at home. One should also note that hospitals in Western Europe were, until the last third of the nineteenth century, essentially charitable institutions—facilities organized and developed by philanthropists and churches in the spirit of Christian outreach.[11]

Consequently, the new "hospital" institution came to Japan in the 1860s and experienced rapid development during the following decade after the Meiji government moved to adopt German medicine. For the authorities, hospitals were training institutions—both for doctors and nurses—as well as a channel for acquiring new medical technology from abroad and diffusing it throughout the country. One of the first hospitals in Japan was a military hospital in Yokohama, which opened in 1868, moved to Tokyo shortly thereafter, and later became the hospital of the University of Tokyo after the school's foundation (1877).

The government, together with local authorities (cities and prefectures), played an important role in establishing the first network of hospitals in Japan. Between 1874 and 1883, the number of public hospitals went from 22 to a peak of 357.[12] Most of them were linked to medical schools and used for training purposes. Training policy, rather than the implementation of a network of healthcare centers, was the driving force behind hospital development. At the same time, the authorities opened specialized hospitals (for psychiatry, tuberculosis, sexual diseases, and epidemics, etc.), in line with sanitation policy. Private hospitals also emerged during this period, of course. These private institutions included a broad range of organizations, from the private clinics of the first graduates of the University of Tokyo to nonprofit institutions like Red Cross hospitals (of which there were nine in 1910).[13] In 1883, private hospitals amounted to 43.2% of the 632 hospitals in Japan. The hospital system was thus predominantly public.

However, this system underwent a major change in the middle of the 1880s: the tide shifted toward privatization as Minister of Finance Matsukata emphasized a policy of austerity. As was the case in other sectors, such as the sale of the Nagasaki shipyard to Mitsubishi (1887) and the silk mill Tomioka to Mitsui (1893), the government sold public enterprises to private companies. This phenomenon was also evident in the field of healthcare. In 1887, Matsukata decided not to give any subsidies to public schools of medicine under municipal or prefectural control from 1888 onward. Consequently, the corresponding schools were privatized or closed in the following years except for three institutions (in Aichi, Kyoto, and Osaka).[14] The resulting decline of public hospitals, whose number dropped to 214 in 1890 and 170 in 1900, led to a general decrease in the number of hospitals. The number stayed below the 1883 peak until 1898, when the count reached 678, but that increase was largely the product of the development of private hospitals (with private institutions representing 76.4% of the total in 1898).

The crisis of the Japanese hospital system during the years 1885–1895 was the result of a paradigm shift: hospitals changed from training organizations to healthcare organizations, and this coincided precisely with the appearance of new technology such as sterilization equipment, X-ray devices, and mobile operation tables. The new phase of development in the hospital system had roots in market mechanisms and free competition, no longer in state intervention. Healthcare, to the authorities, was essentially equivalent to an ordinary business.[15]

The structure and the organization of the hospital system obviously had a major impact on the way in which and the speed at which new technology like radiology spread. Here, I thus need to touch on the macroeconomic evolution of the Japanese hospital system between 1890 and 1940. The context had three major characteristics.

First, there was a generalized and constant growth in the number of hospitals, which multiplied by a factor of around six during across the five decades in question—rising from 577 in 1890 to 3226 in 1940 (see Fig. 1), with considerable growth coming after World War I (WWI). The overall expansion had two important features. First, it relied essentially on private hospitals; the private share of the hospital system as a whole was 62.9% in 1890 and then grew exponentially to cross the 80% threshold in 1903, 90% in 1912, and 95% in 1926. Next, the hospital system grew increasingly dense—its growth outstripped that of the population. The average number of people per hospital dropped from 69,154 in 1890 to 60,871 in 1910, 41,275 in 1920, and 22,298 in 1940. For hospitals, this change brought a marked decrease in numbers of potential customers and thereby stoked stronger competition with other establishments over patients.

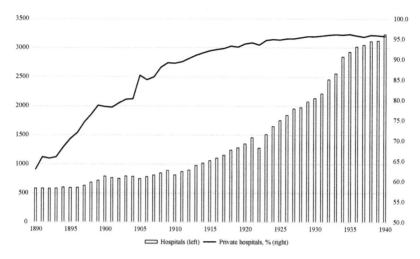

Fig. 1 The Japanese hospital system, number of hospitals and share of private hospitals, 1890–1940 (Source *Historical Statistics of Japan*, vol. 5, pp. 170–171)

Second, this densification of the hospital system came not only from the increasing number of hospitals but also from the growing number of beds (see Fig. 2). Statistics on the numbers of hospital beds for the years prior to 1913 (and 1910 for public hospitals) are unfortunately unknown, a lack that naturally limits the perspective of my analysis. As the strong densification of the hospital system occurred particularly during the interwar years, however, the figures are important. The total number of beds went from 36,856 in 1913 to 101,883 in 1940, following a path of stable growth. The sizable difference between public and private hospitals deserves closer inspection. The average number of beds at public institutions was 92.3 during the years 1913–1940, but private hospitals only had an average of 31.3 beds over the same period. Private institutions also saw a slight decrease in their bed counts after WWI (from 34 in 1920 to 29 in 1940). The limited numbers of beds at private hospitals point to increasing competition, meaning that small private institutions drove the growth of the hospital system. Shuhei Ikai explained that the opening of a small hospital was a way for Japanese doctors to access new hospital infrastructure, while their American and British colleagues used the services of large urban hospitals open to independent practitioners.[16]

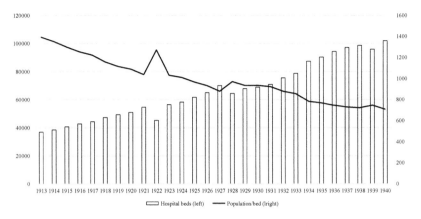

Fig. 2 The Japanese hospital system, number of beds, 1913–1940 (Source *Historical Statistics of Japan*, vol. 5, pp. 170–171. *Note* The decrease in 1922 is due to the Great Kanto Earthquake, which prevented comprehensive census taking. Data on Tokyo and Kanagawa are missing for this year)

Third, the spatial dispersion of hospitals was another important element. In 1883, there was strong opposition between urban areas, which had a high proportion of private hospitals, and the countryside, where public hospitals were sometimes the only medical institutions in existence.[17] Doctors who opened their own hospitals tended to establish themselves in cities, where the market was the largest—and thus the most competitive. The Japanese historiography has traditionally emphasized the high concentration of doctors and healthcare institutions in cities, to the detriment of small towns and villages, until World War II (WWII).[18] In 1935, Tokyo proper (which represented 9.2% of Japan's total population) had 316 hospitals, or 10.8% of the total. According to the data on the actual number of hospitals, then, there was not really a significant concentration of institutions in the national capital. However, Tokyo accounted for 15% of all hospital beds and 18.6% of all medical doctors.[19] The concentration of healthcare in Tokyo actually arose from the fact that hospitals in Tokyo were, on average, larger than those elsewhere in the country. The overwhelming presence of doctors in the city spawned numerous surgeries (medical offices) and small clinics (*shin-ryōjo*). In 1935, 15% of all Japanese clinics were in Tokyo.

This brief analysis of the evolution of the Japanese hospital system between 1890 and 1940 aimed to shed light on the importance of small private hospitals, which were concentrated in urban areas. The system also operated on the principles of market mechanisms and free competition between hospitals, which is why they were so numerous in cities—the wealthy demographics made cities attractive markets. This market-oriented character of the Japanese hospital system also led ruling classes and major entrepreneurs to organize various kinds of charitable institutions to compensate for the imperfections of the market and offer hospital care to the poor. One example was the Saiseikai Foundation, which was created by the emperor in 1911. In 1929, the organization possessed a total of 41 healthcare centers throughout the country.[20] Other institutions for the working classes were the hospitals founded during the interwar years by farmers' unions, cost-price health centers (*jippi shinryōjo*), and the philanthropic hospital of the Mitsui *zaibatsu*, which opened in 1904. However, these institutions were largely exceptions to the rule within a hospital system that fully embraced the laws of the free market.

Competition in the healthcare business intensified due to the presence of many clinics (*shinryōjo*) in addition to the existing hospitals (*byōin*). Clinics were actually "tiny hospitals"—an extension of private surgeries—and are not part of the statistical data above. The official distinction between the two kinds of institutions (clinics and hospitals) first took form in 1933, with the number of beds determining institutional status: Hospitals were establishments with at least ten beds, and clinics were those with fewer than ten. This definition was in force until 1948, when policymakers raised the cutoff raised to 20 beds.[21] In 1934, Japan had a total of 35,014 clinics, of which 98.9% were private. Their concentration in urban areas was important: 14.7% were based in Tokyo (which was home to 9% of the national population).[22]

To finish this overview, Table 1 provides an international comparison for the years 1927–1929. Statistics that make it possible to compare different hospital systems around the world prior to WWII are very rare. For the data in Table 1, I used values from directories on public health published by the League of Nations in 1930. The figures reveal two major findings. First, Japan had the third-largest number of hospitals, trailing the United States and Germany. However, this was essentially a function of having a large population; Japan did have a particularly high density of hospitals per inhabitant. In terms of hospital density, several small countries (Denmark, Finland, New Zealand, Norway, and Switzerland) had higher levels than Japan. Second, the statistics show that Japan had

Table 1 International comparison of hospital systems, 1927–1929 (*Source* League of Nations, *International Health Year-book 1930: Reports on the Public Health Progress of Thirty-Four Countries and colonies in 1929*, Geneva, 1932)

	General hospitals	Hospitals/ Million people	Beds	Beds/ Hospital	Beds/10,000 people	Year
Czechoslovakia	250	17.1	35,451	141.8	24.3	1929
Denmark	177	50.6	17,462	98.7	49.9	1928
Egypt	28	2.0	3848	137.4	2.7	1929
Finland	176	49.0	5606	31.9	15.6	1928
France	1301	31.6	151,514	116.5	36.7	1929
Greece	67	10.7	4948	73.9	7.9	1929
Hungary	176	20.5	15,324	87.1	17.9	1929
Germany	3842	60.6	374,260	97.4	59	1929
Japan	2059	32.9	62,451	30.3	10.0	1929
Latvia	65	33.0	4988	76.7	25.3	1929
Lithuania	41	17.8	1889	46.1	8.2	1929
Mexico	258	15.8	15,724	60.9	9.6	1927
Netherlands	230	29.6	34,902	151.7	44.8	1929
New Zealand	87	59.4	6661	76.6	45.5	1929
Norway	182	64.9	10,986	60.4	39.2	1928
Poland	707	24.3	61,028	86.3	21	1929
Switzerland	192	48.0	18,590	96.8	46.5	1928
Turkey	5	0.3	450	90.0	0.3	1929
United States	4925	40.4	361,079	73.3	29.7	1929

the lowest average number of beds per hospital. Besides emerging countries (Egypt, Greece, Lithuania, Mexico, and Turkey), Japan was the only nation with a bed density of lower than 10 beds per 10,000 people. Germany had a density of 59 beds per 10,000 people, and the United States had a density of 29.7. From an international perspective, therefore, the Japanese hospital system had a very high number of hospitals. With that background in mind, we can now discuss the interwar diffusion of medical technology through an investigation of X-ray equipment.

3   THE DIFFUSION OF X-RAY EQUIPMENT IN THE JAPANESE HOSPITAL SYSTEM

Considering the organization (competition) and the structure (numerous small hospitals) of the Japanese hospital system, one would expect a broad, quick diffusion of new technology, as such resources conferred a competitive advantage on the establishments that held them. However, there are nearly no quantitative sources on conditions prior to WWII that enable precise analyses of the diffusion of radiology throughout the country. Table 2 uses data from various sources, particularly articles by Koichi Fujinami, the main promoter of radiology in Japan.

Despite the minimal amount of data, this table makes it possible to deduce the general dynamics of the diffusion of X-ray equipment in Japan. First, the figures reflect the slow beginnings of the new technology's spread. The historiography usually focuses on the early introduction of the first radiological equipment at a few large hospitals in Japan; the hospitals of the universities of Tokyo and Kyoto, for example, acquired their devices in 1899 and 1900,[23] respectively. The army, meanwhile, ordered equipment from Siemens in 1898, while the navy decided five years later to equip its hospitals with the new technology.[24] A handful of prefectural hospitals, such as those in Fukuoka, Kumamoto, and Gifu, installed X-ray equipment at the turn of the century. Finally, independent doctors who purchased X-ray devices were extremely rare before WWI. The atypical case is that of Dr. Masakiyo Ogata, an Osaka-based obstetrician, who had X-ray equipment in 1903.[25] All these examples are exceptions, however. In 1912, there were less than a hundred pieces of radiological equipment in Japan, which had a total of 895 hospitals at the time.

The years 1912–1921 present the first phase of growth, with the number of equipment in service going from less than 100 to about 800. Technological innovation is a key factor in explaining this change:

Table 2 Number of X-ray equipment in Japan, 1912–1940 (Source *Ika kikai shinpō*, vol. 1, 1917, pp. 32–33 (1917); Koichi Fujinami, "Waga kuni ni okeru rentogen gaku shinpo no jōtai," *Ikai jiho*, vol. 1332, 1920, p. 16 (1912 and 1918); Koichi Fujinami, "Waga kuni ni okeru rentogen gaku oyo ni kansuru shokan," *Rentogen geppo*, vol. 1, 1921 (1921); Tatsuo Shiga, "Teito ni okeru shinryō ekkusu-sen sōchi no chōsa," *Nihon igaku hōshasen gakkai zasshi*, vol. 1, no. 2, 1940, p. 205 (1940))

Year	Japan	Tokyo
1912	<100	–
1917	500	–
1918	450	–
1921	800	–
1940	–	>1'300

General Electric (GE) launched the Coolidge tube, which underwent development during WWI and dramatically improved the quality of X-ray-driven diagnostics. Moreover, Shimadzu marketed its first devices during the 1910s. In an article penned in 1920, Fujinami, who was himself close to the manufacturers of the devices, claimed that the monthly volume of orders to manufacturers at the time had surpassed the yearly volume for the years before 1914.[26] In 1921, though, Fujinami put these statistics in clearer perspective. Although he estimated that the total number of equipment in Japan was about 800, he maintained that "half of them work, while the other half are merely decorative or used improperly."[27] Radiology as a medical specialty was in its early stages, and few doctors knew the correct usage methods for the technology—assets that they had acquired in order to strengthen the positions of their hospitals and clinics as high-standing healthcare institutions.

The last set of available data is limited to Tokyo city for the year 1940. The figures come from a survey by Dr. Tatsuo Shiga, an employee of the Division of Medicine of the Service of Hygiene of the municipality of Tokyo. He counted more than 1300 pieces of equipment of any kind (radioscopy, radiotherapy, devices for dentists, or portable devices, etc.).[28] It is difficult to compare this data with the other collections, which covered the entire country. However, considering that Tokyo was home to about 15% of the hospitals and clinics in Japan in 1940, it is obviously no exaggeration to estimate the total number of X-ray devices in the country in the thousands—perhaps close to 8000 (assuming that the Tokyo share was also 15%).

Consequently, the 1920s and the 1930s were two decades of dramatic growth in radiological equipment, whose market density increased by a factor of ten. New brands of healthcare institution—clinics specializing in radiology and collective medico-technical centers—also appeared during this period. The first type saw major development in urban areas through launches by promoters of radiology, like Atsushi Nagamachi (1923), Yoshikazu Segi (1925), Shuichi Sugishita (1925), and Takeo Inoue (1925) in Tokyo, as well as Sho Hoshiro in Fukuoka (1926).[29] Major examples of the second new type of institution include the Aichi Scientific Medical Treatment Center (*Aichi Rigaku Ryōhōjo*), a joint stock company founded in 1922 by a group of doctors in Nagoya,[30] and the Hygiene Center of Tokyo City (*Tokyo-shi Eisei Shikenjo*), an institution founded in 1900, which installed X-ray equipment open to the doctors of the city in 1923.[31]

The small set of data on this point highlights the dynamics of the diffusion of radiology throughout Japan but does not provide any information on the technology's geographical breakdown, particularly the possible concentration in urban areas. The annual reports of the Bureau of Hygiene since 1937 offer some details on the various departments of medical specialties in Japanese hospitals, classified according to the size of the conurbation: cities (*toshi*), towns (*machi*), and villages (*mura*). Of course, this census does not give any information on the X-ray equipment itself but rather simply points to the presence of radiology departments at hospitals—clinics are not included. Still, the document does provide a good overview of the geographical distribution of radiology as a specialty in 1937.[32] That year, there were 662 radiology departments in Japan, representing 21.7% of all hospitals. The divide between the numbers of departments at public (46) and private (616) hospitals corresponds to the relative shares of these institutions within the hospital system.

The dispersion of these departments by conurbation type reveals a strong concentration in cities. Cities held 65.1% of the total radiology departments, compared to just 27.2% in towns and 7.7% in villages. As for the size of hospitals, the information shows that the existence of a large hospital was not a necessary condition for the presence of a radiology department. Most departments were in hospitals of 30 beds or fewer (60.6%), while hospitals with more than 100 beds accounted for only 8.3% of the total number of radiology departments. Consequently, departments of radiology were most prominent at small, private hospitals in urban areas—the locations where the healthcare market was most competitive. The intense competition between hospitals was obviously a major driving force for the diffusion of X-ray equipment.

4   THE IMPACT OF THE NEW TECHNOLOGY ON HOSPITAL MANAGEMENT

The next point for discussion is how new technology such as radiology affected hospital management. The atomized structure and strong competitiveness of the Japanese hospital system favored a fast diffusion of X-ray equipment because it gave a competitive advantage to hospitals with the new resources. The equipment was an investment, however, which entailed amortization. According to the official price list published in 1934 by the Tokyo Medical Device Association, the diagnostic X-ray device model Heian (produced and sold by Shimadzu) cost 10,000 yen at the time.[33] In comparison with the average yearly income of a worker in the cotton industry (about 410 yen that year), X-ray expenses underscore the importance of the investment (about 25 times the yearly salary of a worker).[34] The acquisition of X-ray equipment was not impossible, of course, but it required a well-conceived financial plan. The question, then, is how hospital managers designed commercial strategies to ensure the technological development of their institutions. In Japan, hospital archives make it difficult to investigate this issue in depth; most hospitals do not have—or do not allow access to—accounting documents on the interwar period. Hospitals did not publish annual reports with full sets of financial data, unlike most Western hospitals, which began releasing such documents in the mid-nineteenth century to publicize their activities and attract new charitable support. Thus, there is no reliable way of making an exhaustive and detailed analysis of hospital management in Japan, particularly of the conditions at private hospitals. However, numerous public hospitals published books about their own histories as anniversary commemorations, and these volumes usually included statistical and factual data on the evolution of their respective institutions' finances. These books constitute the main sources for this section, which presents a representative sample of various kinds of public and nonprofit (charitable) private hospitals.

4.1   Osaka City Citizen Hospital[35]

Founded in 1925 in Abeno, a dense, southern suburb of the city, Osaka City Citizen Hospital (*Osaka Shiritsu Shimin Byōin*) was one of the largest healthcare centers in the Kansai area at the time. In 1944, the institution became the Osaka City School of Medicine Hospital. It was a modern hospital, boasting a capacity of 500 inpatients and 500 outpatients, and possessed the newest technology—including an X-ray room. A general public hospital created for the population of Osaka city, the institution strove to address social policy and promote access to modern healthcare among the working classes. Indeed, the hospital's statutes mentioned free hospitalization for people who received public assistance and members of families with annual financial resources of less than 800 yen.

However, this social objective was not incompatible with the business dimension. The hospital needed cash and organized itself to attract patients who could afford paying for hospitalization and medical treatments. When it opened, Osaka City Citizen Hospital thus adopted a three-class structure of paying patients that ranged between 1.5 and 3 yen per day (the daily salary of a worker in the textile industry was about 1.5 yen)[36] and various fees for medical examinations, operations, drugs, and materials.[37]

The revenues for 1930 encapsulate the importance of paying patients for the hospital.[38] Hospitalization fees amounted to 125,962 yen and represented 39.6% of all resources that year. Class-A patients, who paid 3 yen a day, provided 43,362 yen, or 34.4% of hospitalization fees and 13.6% of all revenues. Moreover, paying patients were important because they could afford the use of new medical equipment for which they incurred charges. The average fee for an operation was nearly 40 yen, and operations accounted for 9.2% of all resources. The fees for using infrastructure and materials represented nearly one-third of all income (32.7%). Wealthy patients were thus important because they received large amounts of care and thereby assisted in the amortization of the medical equipment.

The statistics on the number of days of treatment by patient type, as Table 3 shows, also reflect the importance of paying patients and capture the dynamics of the hospital's development. As the hospital opened in October 1925, the data for 1925 do not figure into the comparison. The valid figures for hospitalizations show a rather stable number of patients from 1926 to 1933, with an average of 90,700 total days per year. The absence of a general growth trend suggests that the hospital was operating at close to full capacity after opening. However, the values reveal a slight increase in the rate of paying patients from 1926 to 1927 (which averaged 50.4%) to a peak in 1929 (65.4%) and around 55% in 1931–1933. The enforcement of the Health Insurance Act in 1922 (see Chapter 5) had an obvious impact. However, even if insured patients represented a growing proportion of the paying patients, they were still a small minority—just 7.3% of paying patients in 1933 had insurance coverage, and the hospitalization fees from insured patients were only 4.2% of all revenues in 1930.

Outpatients also had a growing significance, as Table 3 suggests. The number of treatment days for this patient category experienced a general growth, rising from 109,247 days in 1926 to 147,414 days in 1933.

Table 3 Patients of Osaka City Citizen Hospital, number of days of care, 1925–1933 (Source *Kindai toshi no eisei kankyō* (*Osaka*), Tokyo: Kingendai, vol. 15, 2007, pp. 159–161)

	1925	1926	1927	1928	1929	1930	1931	1932	1933
Hospitalization, total	12,970	90,170	87,733	91,122	80,832	86,452	95,538	90,281	103,745
Paying patients, as a %	39.1	49.8	51.0	60.2	65.4	59.8	56.7	56.9	53.8
Insured patients, as a % of paying patients	–	–	1.5	5.5	5.7	6.1	Unknown	Unknown	7.3
Outpatients, total	20,421	109,427	101,241	133,327	133,470	149,549	149,090	123,380	147,414
Paying outpatients, as a %	24.2	50.8	58.4	67.9	76.1	74.4	66.9	80.5	70.0

Note In grey, the share of paying patients, as a %

Across this entire period, overall outpatient treatment was 44% longer than that of hospitalized patients. Moreover, they comprised a larger and growing proportion of paying patients, going from 50.8% in 1926 to 70% in 1933 at an average of 68.1%. These patients largely came to the hospital to use its updated medical technology. For example, in 1930, the department of radiology registered 4200 days for outpatients, of which only 768 were free of charge. These numbers indicate that 81.8% of the users paid for the technology.[39] Members of the middle and wealthy classes thus used the public hospital instead of independent doctors and small hospitals as a means of securing healthcare. There was, therefore, a direct competition with the private sector.

4.2   Two General Public Hospitals in the Countryside: Iwase General Hospital and Hikone City Hospital

The next section turns the focus to general public hospitals in the countryside, where the demand for private hospital care was lower than in metropolises like Tokyo and Osaka. The examples of two hospitals in the prefectures of Fukushima (north of Tokyo) and Shiga (between Kyoto and Nagoya) make it possible to highlight a relatively similar dynamic to the pattern that emerged in large cities.

First, Iwase General Hospital (Fukushima) is a good illustration of the relations between the development of hospitalization capacity, the modernization of equipment, and the increase of resources.[40] The institution, originally Fukushima Prefecture Hospital, was opened in 1872 and then sold to Iwase City in 1890. At the beginning of the twentieth century, the institution was a small hospital that focused especially on isolating contagious patients and providing a training center for the local nursing school, which opened in 1913. It was thus a tool of the local public health policy. Although the hospital expanded its buildings installed its first X-ray device in 1917, it remained relatively small: In 1924, there were 20,782 days of hospitalization and 51,699 days of outpatient care—numbers far lower than those at Osaka City Citizen Hospital for the same year.

However, Iwase General Hospital adopted a new growth strategy in the mid-1930s by expanding its capacity, opening a second ward building in 1934 (which probably included individual rooms for wealthy patients), and then installing new radiology equipment in 1936. This figure behind this policy was Dr. Chikara Nagai, a graduate of the Faculty of Medicine at the University of Tokyo, who became the director of the hospital in 1928 and stayed in charge until 1947. Nagai worked together with a team of 11 doctors, a pharmacist, and an X-ray technician. Due to the initiatives that took shape under Nagai, the number of hospitalization days and outpatient care days grew to 35,008 and to 117,642, respectively, in 1940.

The management of the hospital adopted a new financial policy, as well (see Fig. 3). The evolution of the institution's resources and profit rates underline two major points. First, resources began experiencing substantial growth in 1934 after having remained stagnant for a decade. Second, the growth of the profit rate—the balance of accounts as a percentage of resources—started to increase in the early 1930s and peaked at 30.2% in 1939. The specific details on the hospital's resources are unknown, but one could obviously argue that the hospitalization of new kinds of paying patients drove the growth of resources after the institution's transformation in the mid-1930s. The principle of the management was to turn enough profits to invest in the perpetual modernization of the infrastructure. Management enlarged the hospital's bed capacity again in 1940 and installed a new operating room in 1941.

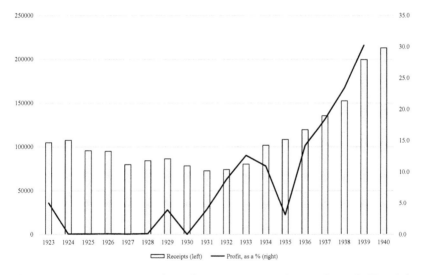

Fig. 3 Receipts in yen and profit rate as a %, Iwase General Hospital, 1923–1940 (Source *Kōritsu Iwase Byōin hyaku nen shi*, Fukushima: Iwase byoin, 1972, pp. 196–197)

Hikone Prefecture Hospital (Shiga) followed a very similar development trajectory.[41] The institution launched operations in 1891 and belonged to Shiga Prefecture until 1937, when Hikone City assumed administrative control. Until WWI, it was a small and basic hospital (36 beds in 1901) with departments of surgery, medicine, and, beginning in 1914, obstetrics.

The first inklings of transformation emerged in the aftermath of the war, with the installation of X-ray equipment (1919), the opening of an ENT department (1921), the creation of an ophthalmology department (1922), and a small extension that brought the capacity to 55 beds in 1923.[42] The number of patients grew slightly, rising from 6980 days of hospitalization and 34,918 days of outpatient care in 1923 to 7734 and 34,975, respectively, in 1926. Although the social origins of the patients are unclear, the resource structure (see Table 4) shows that, in 1919, the sales of drugs generated more money than operations did. The hospital was a traditional healthcare institution, not a medico-technological platform. The amount of revenues from hospitalizations, with an average daily cost of 2.2 yen in 1926, also prove that the middle classes used the hospital. The institution acquired a new Shimadzu X-ray device in 1928, as well.[43]

The real move toward a new phase of development, an effort that focused on resources from wealthy patients, came with the opening of a new 75-bed building in 1933. At the time, the hospital had a total of 40 beds in individual wards (for the first and second classes), while the remaining 35 beds were in three common wards.[44] Other facilities at the institution included a room for radiology and a laboratory. In 1938, the hospital purchased a new X-ray device from Shimadzu and decided to introduce a minimum fee of 4 yen for the use of the equipment.[45]

Table 4 Resources of Hikone Prefectural Hospital, 1919–1937 (Source *Hikone Shiritsu Byōin Hyakunen-shi*, Hikone: Hikone Shiritsu Byōin, 1991, pp. 84 and 133)

	1919	1926	1937
Revenues, total, in yen	39,596	62,928	94,445
Hospitalization, as a %	29.7	27.4	29.2
Drugs, as a %	31.4	30.5	23.5
Operations, as a %	29.1	34.8	39.4
Diagnostics, as a %	3.3	2.4	2.4
Others, as a %	6.6	4.8	5.5

Despite the new technological fixtures at the hospital, the share of revenues from the use of diagnostic technology stayed stable and low at around 2% of all resources. However, there was a major change in the resource structure between 1919 and 1937 as drug sales fell and operation fees—which had become the largest category during the early 1920s—rose. These trends point to the notion that the local population began using the hospital in new ways. The institution was no longer a general-purpose healthcare center but rather a medico-technological platform used for specific purposes. The number of patients grew quickly and reached 14,124 days of hospitalization and 54,869 days of outpatient care in 1937.

4.3 Charitable Hospitals

This final section focuses briefly on the case of charitable hospitals, which were private nonprofit organizations. Due to the lack of a Christian philanthropy tradition in Japan, this kind of hospital—widespread in Western Europe and the United States—was an extreme minority. However, Japan's industrialization and urbanization from the end of the nineteenth century onward impoverished the working classes and gave way to social action seeking the integration and control of poor people. Philanthropic paternalism thus emerged in Japan from the backdrop of maintaining social order and had an impact on the development of hospitals. Several institutions were created to offer healthcare to the working classes; one such organization was the Kaiseikai society, which originated in 1909 and strove to help poor people get access to healthcare centers before opening its own hospitals.[46] Cost-price health centers (*jippi shinryōjo*), which began appearing in 1911, were another example of social activism in the hospital field.[47] Also deserving mention are the various hospitals founded by industrial enterprises for their own employees, such as the hospitals organized by Kobe Railways (1915), Fujikoshi (1934), Hitachi (1938), and Toyota (1938). Although all of these institutions aimed to offer free or cheap healthcare to the working classes, some opened their doors to middle classes in hopes of increasing their resources and financing their technological development.

The Mitsui Philanthropic Hospital (Izumibashi Philanthropic Hospital from 1919 to 1943), founded by the Mitsui *zaibatsu* and opened in Tokyo in 1909, presents an excellent case for discussing the relation between charitable institutions and the healthcare market.[48]

Funded by its *zaibatsu*, captains of industry like Eiichi Shibusawa (the "father of Japanese capitalism"), and the imperial family, the hospital was designed for use by the poor, directed by famous professors from the prestigious Faculty of Medicine at the University of Tokyo, and equipped with the most modern technology—a department of radiology was opened in 1914. The general direction of the establishment was entrusted to Professor Yoshinori Tashiro, a proponent of radiology in Japan (see Chapter 2). For funding, the hospital relied almost exclusively on private donations and earnings from assets. In 1937, the institution's total expenses of 485,342 yen were covered by its own earnings (36.7%), a loan from the Mitsui holding company (*Mitsui Gōmei*, 25.8%), and the institution's own ample funding (37.3%). Direct financial resources from patients amounted to just 1030 yen—a mere 0.2% of the total expenses.[49] The model of management for the Mitsui Philanthropic Hospital was thus completely different from the structure that public general hospitals employed. Mitsui Philanthropic Hospital was the epitome of elites devoting attention to the poor.

The facility opened in 1909 with a capacity of 125 beds and initially offered free healthcare for up to 200 outpatients a day.[50] Outpatients actually represented the largest patient category receiving care at the establishment. While the number of hospitalization days went from 26,540 in 1910 to 34,013 in 1930, outpatient care days rose from 298,777 to 305,986 across the same time frame.[51] Outpatients outnumbered hospitalized patients by a factor of nearly ten, a proportion far larger than the same ratio at general hospitals. The hospital's department of radiology was also mostly for outpatient use and proved increasingly popular, serving 843 patients in 1915 and then 4780 in 1925 before peaking at 6583 in 1932.[52] As people from outside the poorer classes began taking advantage of this free service, however, the hospital decided in November 1933 to introduce fees for the use of X-ray devices. The impact of the new fees on the establishment's resources was insignificant (200 yen of the total revenue in 1937, or 0.04% of the overall budget), but the pricing plan enabled the hospital to keep its focus on caring for the poor. The introduction of the fee led to a rapid decrease in the number of outpatients in radiology (4748 in 1934 and 3869 in 1938), with the middle classes turning instead toward general hospitals.

The social policy and massive assets of Mitsui Philanthropic Hospital explain its decision not to extend care to the middle classes or pursue external funding. This was, however, an exceptional choice, one that owed a great deal to the particular nature of the institution and was definitely not representative of charitable hospitals on the whole. Some other charitable institutions without the financial resources of Mitsui Philanthropic Hospital had to open their establishments to the middle classes. One example was Nissay Hospital in Osaka, one of the oldest and largest charitable hospitals in the city.[53] A private association founded in 1924 by the insurance company Nippon Life opened a small healthcare center the following year, which was later transformed into a general hospital in 1931. Nissay Hospital offered free care to poor patients but was also accessible to the middle classes for certain fees.[54] It experienced considerable growth during the second part of the 1930s, with the number of hospitalization days increasing from 6768 in 1936 to 50,059 in 1940 and outpatient care days going from 19,093 to 82,801 during the same period.[55] Based on the historical documents detailing the hospital's resources since 1939, management relied essentially on contributions by patients and fees for the use of X-ray devices, which amounted to 10.6% of all revenues in 1939.[56] Nissay Hospital is thus a case of a charitable institution whose management style was similar to the approach of public general hospitals. The development of the institution's medico-technological infrastructure and its care for the poor depended on payments from members of the middle classes.

5   Conclusion

The end of the nineteenth century saw the beginnings of new developments in medical technology, which included X-ray equipment—the focus of this chapter—as well as laboratories and operating rooms. These advances were powerful catalysts of change in the nature of hospitals, which truly became medico-technological platforms and work tools for doctors. Thus, hospitals established themselves at the heart of the health system and entered a phase of high growth during the interwar years.

This transformation was not only a technological and professional metamorphosis but also a managerial and financial one. The acquisition and the renewal of technical equipment like X-ray devices, in addition to the new construction and successive extension of hospital buildings, made it necessary for institutions to secure larger amounts of financial resources. As was the case in Western Europe and the United States during the same period, financial contributions from patients became the main resources of hospitals in Japan. Even public hospitals, such as the cases in this chapter, received either no or very few direct subsidies from the state. Alongside hospitalization fees, hospitals also charged for the use of medico-technological equipment. The continuous modernization of medical devices attracted new categories of patients to public general hospitals, where financial contributions were always crucial. Financial resources came from wealthy people, of course, for whom hospitals organized new services like individual wards. There were also outpatients, who often used diagnostic equipment (X-ray devices and laboratories) and became more and more numerous over time.

This chapter used several case studies to look at the transformation of hospital management and organization through a microeconomic lens. Despite the sample lacks of private hospitals, for which it has been unfortunately impossible to find accounting archives for the interwar years, the examples in this chapter all exhibited a similar phenomenon and a common objective in hospital management: the quest for profitable patients. This strategy led to stronger competitiveness within the hospital system, especially as Japanese hospitals were numerous, small, and concentrated in urban areas. Consequently, two additional key issues emerge: how this competitiveness influenced the evolution of the hospital system as a whole, first of all, and how institutions worked to solve the negative effects of the competitiveness (which tended to diminish prices and thus undercut hospital revenues). These questions form the focus of the next chapter.

Notes

1. *Wakayama sekijuji byoin*, pp. 45, 71–73, 88–89, 102, 106–108, 872–875 and 886–887.
2. Rosner, *A Once Charitable Enterprise* and Howell, *Technology in the Hospital.*
3. Sturdy, "The Political Economy of Scientific Medicine", p. 128.
4. Starr, *The Social Transformation of American Medicine*, p. 157.
5. Pierre-Yves Donzé, "De la charité à l'entreprise".
6. Fukunaga, *Nihon byouin shi*, Sugaya, *Nihon no byoin.*
7. Shuhei, *Byoin no seiki no riron.*
8. Ibidem, pp. 209 and 256–259.
9. Sugaya, *Nihon no byoin.*
10. Macé, *Médecins et médecine dans l'histoire du Japon.*
11. Bremner, *Giving.*
12. *Historical statistics of Japan*, vol. 5, p. 170.

13. Sugaya, *Nihon no byoin*, p. 71.
14. Ibidem, p. 60.
15. Kamikawa, *Gendai nihon iryoshi*.
16. Shuhei, *Byoin no seiki no riron*.
17. Ibidem, p. 66.
18. Ibidem and Kamikawa, *Gendai nihon iryoshi*.
19. *Historical Statistics of Japan*, vol. 5.
20. Sugaya, *Nihon no byoin*, p. 93.
21. Ibidem, pp. 9–10.
22. *Eiseikyoku nenpo*, 1934, pp. 204–205.
23. Goto, *Nihon hoshasen igaku shiko*, vol. 1, p. 26.
24. Ibidem, pp. 22 and 26.
25. Ibidem, p. 42.
26. Fujinami, "Waga kuni ni okeru rentogen gaku shinpo no jotai", p. 16.
27. Fujinami, "Waga kuni ni okeru rentogen gaku oyo ni kansuru shokan".
28. Shiga, "Teito ni okeru shinryo".
29. *Dainihon hakushi roku*, vols. 2–4 and Goto, *Nihon hoshasen igaku shiko*, vol. 1, p. 272.
30. Goto, *Nihon hoshasen igaku shiko*, vol. 1, p. 205.
31. Ibidem, p. 225.
32. *Eiseikyoku nenpo*, 1937, pp. 220–229.
33. *Tokyo ika kikai kumiai mokuroku*, p. 414.
34. Wada and Hara, *Kingendai nihon keizaishi yoran*, p. 99.
35. *Kindai toshi no eisei kankyo (Osaka)*.
36. Wada and Hara, *Kingendai nihon keizaishi yoran*, p. 99.
37. *Kindai toshi no eisei kankyo (Osaka)*, pp. 149–150.
38. Ibidem, pp. 152–158.
39. Ibidem, pp. 162–163.
40. *Koritsu iwase byoin*.
41. *Hikone shiritsu byoin*.
42. Ibidem, p. 74.
43. Ibidem, p. 93.
44. Ibidem, p. 110.
45. Ibidem, p. 115.
46. Aoyanagi, *Shinryo hoshu*, pp. 342–343.
47. Ibidem, p. 353.
48. *Mitsui kinen byoin hyakunen no ayumi*.
49. Mitsui Archives, A027-1-2, Annual report of Izumibashi Philanthropic Hospital, 1937.
50. *Mitsui kinen byoin hyakunen no ayumi*, p. 22.
51. Mitsui Archives, A027-10, *Zaidanhojin Izumibashi jizen byoin 30 nen-ryakushi*, 1939, pp. 23–25.

52. Ibidem, pp. 40–41.
53. *Nihon seimei saiseikai*, pp. 40 and 53–55.
54. Ibidem, p. 32.
55. Ibidem, pp. 68 and 91.
56. Ibidem, p. 91.

CHAPTER 6

Regulating the Healthcare System

1   Introduction

In 1879, following demands from a group of private doctors, Tokyo authorities decided to limit the treatment of nonpoor outpatients in municipal hospitals. To doctors, the low-cost care available at these institutions represented unfair competition.[1] Relations between private doctors and public hospitals continued to be difficult during the two last decades of the nineteenth century until the 1906 adoption of the Medical Practitioners Act (*ishi-hō*), which consecrated private doctors as the foundation of the health system and brought Japan into what Takeshi Kawakami called the "golden age of private medicine."[2] When new medical technology such as X-ray devices, laboratories, and sterilized operation rooms became equipment necessary for medical practice, private doctors thus accessed the infrastructure by opening clinics and small private hospitals.[3]

As Chapter 4 discussed, this new technology had a deep influence on hospital management. Moreover, the impact extended beyond hospitals as single organizations. Indeed, the competition that existed between the various healthcare organizations in a single space—usually a city or a district—made it necessary to acquire the latest medical technology in order to remain competitive and attract patients. This was a major engine of technological development and innovation in the Japanese medical market. However, competition also made it necessary to lower or at least limit the increase of hospital and medical prices in order to

© The Author(s) 2018   153
P.-Y. Donzé, *Making Medicine a Business*,
https://doi.org/10.1007/978-981-10-8159-0_6

continue attracting patients. Consequently, the endless modernization of medico-technical equipment, given the competition surrounding the healthcare system, led to a contradiction proper to the system itself—a situation that Karl Marx called the tendency of the rate of profit to fall. In this context, how was it possible to ensure the maintenance of the health system and its ability to continue growing?

This question is not exclusive to Japan; the patterns are evident elsewhere in industrialized countries during the same period and in a very similar form, although the conditions in Japan were particularly intense due to the atomized structure of the hospital system. In Western Europe and the United States, the regulatory intervention of the state, most common during the interwar years, transcended this contradiction proper to free market-based hospital medicine. The intervention took various forms, ranging from the nationalization of hospitals and the planning of national needs to systems based on the introduction of minimum prices (hospitalization, use of medico-technical equipment, and fees for doctors, for example) that ensured institutional functionality. In the case of France, for example, Jean-Paul Domin demonstrated that competitiveness on the healthcare market led medical doctors to organize within a national association (1884) that pressured the authorities into declaring that care for the poor would not be free of charge any longer but rather under local government control (1898). After 1918, the hospital system experienced significant growth thanks to health insurance, which made it possible for a large proportion of the population to access hospital care and afford the costs. It was only under the Vichy regime (1940–1944), however, that the state became an authoritarian regulator of the entire hospital system, a policy that the government pursued after 1945 through the institution of social security and the adoption of fixed prices negotiated with doctors and hospitals.[4] Discussing the case of France, scholar Olivier Faure also showed the existence of a very important private sector for hospitals. It experienced fast growth starting in the 1930s, essentially based on the hospitalization of middle-class members of a mutual insurance company that had contracts with private clinics and doctors.[5] Until World War II (WWII), the French hospital market thus featured regulation without strong state intervention. The situation was similar to the cases in most Western countries, like Germany or Switzerland.[6] In the United States, however, there was a growing opposition between public and charitable hospitals serving poor people on the one hand and for-profit hospitals for wealthy people on the other.

There was state regulation, but it was under a two-system framework.[7] It was quite similar in the United Kingdom, where the philanthropy crisis delayed the modernization of the hospital infrastructure during the 1920s and 1930s and gave way to the nationalization of the health system in 1948.[8]

As for Japan, a mid-1960s study by Marxist historian Takeshi Kawakami highlighted how medicine had shifted from a purely capitalist system during the years 1870–1914 to a gradual "socialization of healthcare" (*iryō no shakaika*) during the interwar years.[9] While the Japanese hospital system was based on the development of small private institutions belonging to and under the management of doctors, Kawakami emphasized that the introduction of health centers with cost prices (*jippi shinryōjo*) for the middle class (first opened in Tokyo in 1911; a total of 153 centers were opened throughout the country by 1929),[10] the adoption of the Health Insurance Act (*kenkō hoken hō*), and the introduction of the National Health Insurance Act (*kokumin kenkō hoken-hō*) enabled working classes to benefit from new medical technology while private doctors focused on wealthy and profitable patients. Consequently, Kawakami exposed a dual system quite close to the conditions in the United States during the same period. However, his examination does not detail the process of regulation enough to clarify the situation of medical doctors and private hospitals.

This chapter focuses on the regulation of hospitals and medical care in Japan until WWII, aiming to answer the following questions: How were hospital managers and private doctors able to organize the hospital market in order to sustain continuous development? What was the role of the state in this process? The chapter comprises three sections. The first tackles the introduction of official prices for medical treatment; the second analyzes the role and impact of health insurance; and the third discusses the regulatory intervention of the state.

2 The Organization of the Supply of Healthcare

Although private institutions—especially small hospitals and independent doctors—accounted for an overwhelming share of the healthcare system, that does not mean that the system was based on purely free-market mechanisms. As the association of private doctors in Tokyo employed interventionist measures against the municipal authorities, an approach that I mentioned at the beginning of the chapter, the organization of the supply of healthcare resulted from relations and negotiations between various interest groups. This section analyzes the historical development of the regulation of medical and hospital prices up until WWII.

To begin, a short statistical overview of the medical profession between 1900 and 1940 would be beneficial. Official censuses carried out by the Bureau of Hygiene (Ministry of Health since 1938) provide helpful data. In Japan, doctors represented the main lobbying organization that succeeded in discussing the regulation of the healthcare market with sanitary authorities. Unlike Western Europe and the United States, Japanese hospitals did not have an organized association, and the political weight of health insurance was weak. During the four first decades of the twentieth century, however, the medical profession in Japan underwent a deep transformation.

First, Fig. 1 shows the total number of medical practitioners in Japan over time, as well as the average number of people per doctor, which helps illustrate changes in competitiveness in the healthcare market. The figures reveal four distinct phases. First, the years 1901–1918 were a period of constant increase in the number of practitioners, which went from 32,977 to a peak of 46,109; the market thus saw strong densification (1349 people per doctor in 1901 and 1186 in 1918). The hospital

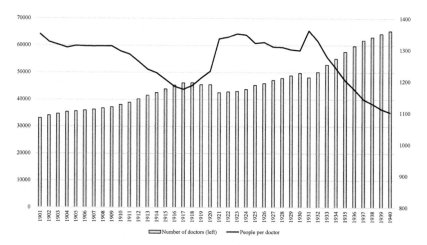

Fig. 1 Number of medical doctors and density of the medical market, 1901–1940 (Source *Eiseikyoku nenpō*, Tokyo: Eiseikyoku, 1901–1936 and *Eisei nenpō*, Tokyo: Koseisho, 1937–1940)

field also saw growth in the number of small private hospitals over the same period (see Chapter 4). Second, the post-World War I (WWI) era (1918–1921) corresponds to a short phase of decline in the number of doctors (42,464 in 1921) and a strong decrease in the average size of the market (1334 people per doctor). This lull in the competition was brief, however: The two subsequent decades witnessed a growing number of doctors in two different phases. In the third period, from 1921 to 1930, the number of doctors increased (49,680 practitioners in 1930), but the density stagnated (1323 people per doctor on average). Still, as Shuhei Ikai noted, this growth did not occur in a uniform fashion across Japan—new doctors tended to concentrate in cities and find employment in hospitals. On the one hand, the number of towns and villages without doctors grew from 1960 in 1923 to 3231 in 1930. On the other hand, while the number of independent doctors remained stable between 1913 and 1927 (at around 32,000), the number of doctors with hospital appointments doubled during the same period (from 5295 in 1913 to 10,656 in 1927).[11] The healthcare market in cities became highly competitive and concentrated more and more around hospitals. Fourth and finally, the years 1931–1940 represented a phase of significant growth in both the number of doctors (65,332 in 1940) and market density (1101 people per doctor in 1940). The trends observable in the previous period grew stronger, with towns and villages without doctors growing even more numerous (3655 in 1939), independent doctor numbers increasing (34,806 in 1936), and more doctors flocking to hospitals(19,191 in 1936).[12] Two other key points to note are that medical specialties like radiology emerged in this context and that X-ray equipment entered a high-diffusion phase.

A brief discussion of the evolution of medical-doctor training, which had a strong influence on the nature of competitiveness of the healthcare market, is also necessary. Figure 2 shows numbers of doctors by their "pathways" of training in Japan up to WWII.[13] The first pathway corresponds to doctors who were in practice before the implementation of the law on medicine in 1875. These doctors held neither modern certifications nor diplomas but still retained the authorization to continue practicing. Although this pathway represented the largest group of doctors through 1907, it later experienced a steep drop from 63% of all practitioners in 1900 to 29.8% in 1910, 12.1% in 1920 and then less than 5% after 1927. Second, there were doctors who lacked any specific academic training but passed a state examination that originated in 1875.

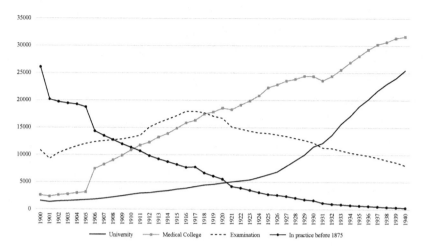

Fig. 2 Medical doctors in Japan by training, 1900–1940 (Source *Eiseikyoku nenpō*, Tokyo: Eiseikyoku, 1900–1936 and *Eisei nenpō*, Tokyo: Koseisho, 1937–1940)

The doctors who followed this pathway generally had basic practical training or academic backgrounds in various medical schools, albeit not always at state-recognized institutions. This category of doctors experienced significant growth until WWI and was the largest group between 1909 and 1917. The suppression of this certification system in 1916 led to the gradual decline of the second pathway; in 1940, it represented only 12.2% of all medical doctors. Third, the graduates of state-recognized medical colleges, either private or public, formed a growing category after the adoption of the Medical Practitioners Act (1906), which extended the number of state-recognized institutions.[14] This third pathway exhibited steady growth in real numbers and a very strong increase in relative numbers through 1925 (accounting for 28.6% of practitioners in 1910 and 49.4% in 1925). Until the mid-1920s, they were the primary drivers of Japan's increasing medical density. During the second part of the 1920s, however, they entered a phase of stagnation in relative numbers (49.1% of practitioners on average from 1925 to 1940) as the fourth doctor pathway emerged. The new group comprised graduates of the faculties of medicine at imperial universities (mostly Tokyo, but also Kyoto, Tohoku, Kyushu, Hokkaido, Osaka, and Nagoya) and the elite of the Japanese medical world. The size of the fourth pathway stayed small until the early 1920s, with doctors in the segment finding most of their positions at large, public institutions such as hospitals, universities, the military, and the central administration. They did not compete directly against other practitioners. However, the situation changed during the 1920s as the "medical elite" portion of the medical population began to grow from just 10.5% of practitioners in 1920 to 23.1% in 1930 and 39% in 1940. They also regularly ventured out on their own as independent doctors and owners of small hospitals, contributing to the escalating competitiveness of the healthcare market.[15]

Consequently, this quantitative overview of the evolution of the medical profession in Japan corroborates the notion that the healthcare market became increasingly competitive during the interwar years. In addition, the hospital system underwent major densification the 1920s and 1930s—a development that resulted in intensifying competition between independent doctors and hospitals that offered outpatient care at the time.[16] The presence of strong competition in a free-market context would normally have led to pressure on medical prices and, by extension, doctor earnings. Efforts to organize the doctor community, which began at the end of the nineteenth century, aimed specifically at preventing that logical outcome from happening.

Although the 1875 law on medicine forbade the sale of drugs by medical doctors, the practice was still widespread at the beginning of the twentieth century. It went back to the Edo period (1603–1868), during which all the services offered by doctors were included in a broad designation called the "cost of drugs" (*kusuri-dai*).[17] The new law introduced a separation between the cost of drugs and price of consultation. Medicine thus became a real service—a form of intellectual work—that warranted remuneration as such.[18] The progressive professional autonomization of pharmacists, which the developing drug industry buoyed, gave way to an important and long-lasting conflict with doctors. The discord was so strong that, in 1925, the state adopted a new law on pharmacists (*yakuzaishi-hō*) and stopped accepting the sales of drugs by doctors, which the government had tolerated up to that point due to a lack of pharmacists.[19] In terms of the organization of the healthcare market, the policy forced doctors to redefine the nature of their fees more precisely and relinquish the idea of *kusuri-dai*.

However, the 1875 law did not abandon doctors to purely free-market competition. The principle of official prices for medical treatments was one part of the legislation; each prefecture had official price lists, which doctors and local authorities agreed upon.[20] Four years later, the Bureau of Hygiene of the Home Ministry presented lists from Prussia to serve as examples.[21] Thereafter, prefectural authorities published lists of minimum and maximum prices for medical treatments. The local associations of doctors, which took shape between 1875 and 1882, were very active in this process, publishing their own lists and negotiating the specifics with authorities. Medical prices were thus under regulatory control at the end of the nineteenth century, and the fierce competition of the medical market had no negative impact on revenues.

Hospitals, meanwhile, collected hospitalization fees from the outset, with prices generally varying according to several classes of patients. These fees covered hospital costs but did not include drugs or doctor fees. For example, the rules of Osaka Prefecture Hospital in 1878 mentioned the possibility of offering Western meals to patients in the first and second classes with an additional daily fee of 1.5 yen, or more than twice the basic fee for the first class (0.6 yen). The following year, the same hospital specified that first- and second-class patients were to have individual rooms, while third-class patients were to stay in group rooms.[22] In Tokyo, private hospitals had begun implementing a broad variety of fees in the mid-1880s as the market segmented early and institutions set out on their quests for wealthy patients.[23] Since the implementation of a hospital system in Japan, then, these institutions competed over affluent patients. Moreover, there was no unified system of hospital fees—and the lack of any hospital association until WWII made its introduction unlikely.

The regulation of the healthcare market continued at the beginning of the twentieth century, with the control over fees growing more rigid and prefectures unifying their respective structures. On the basis of the 1906 law on medical practice, the Home Ministry adopted regulations governing the associations of doctors (*ishikai kisoku*), which established associations in each city and prefecture. These bodies set fees, minimum and sometimes fixed, for various medical treatments in agreement with local authorities.[24] Between 1907 and 1917, regional associations of doctors proliferated: New groups formed in Kyoto (1907), Shizuoka (1908), Nagano (1908), Kumamoto (1908), Aichi (1909), Yamaguchi (1909), Hiroshima (1911), Hokkaido (1914), and Tokyo (1917).[25] In 1919, the government required medical doctors to belong to regional associations.[26] Ikai argued that the graduates of imperial universities, particularly the University of Tokyo, exerted more and more control over these associations in the early 1920s. Their massive engagement in private medicine made it necessary for them to control the financial aspects of their business. Therefore, these associations unified fees within prefectures and later adapted the prices in accordance with price evolution. The competition between doctors was not over prices; doctors could not reduce fees.

However, during the interwar years, liberal medicine was blamed by a large number of politicians, bureaucrats, and intellectuals hoping to give the entire population access to the benefits of advances in medical science—especially new technologies like radiology. The "socialization of medicine" (*iryō no shakaika*), as many called it, progressed in the context of a recurring economic crisis during which attempts to reduce medical treatment fees were common.[27]

The opening of cost-price health centers (*jippi shinryōjo*), beginning in 1911, was a catalyst of intense debates over the cost of medicine. The fees at these cost-price centers amounted to just one-third of the prices recommended by the Japan Medical Association (*ishikai*).[28] Doctors tried to prevent the development of these facilities through a ban on the opening of healthcare institutions by nondoctors—a lobbying effort that ended successfully but still too late. Although the state decided in 1933 to subject the opening of hospitals and clinics by nondoctors to an official licensing procedure,[29] the number of cost-price health centers in Japan had already increased to 153 in 1929.

Despite the difficulties of the interwar years, the healthcare-market regulations that went into practice in the early 1920s created ideal conditions for doctors. The doctor population benefited from a system that guaranteed minimum fees for their work. The situation was quite different for hospitals, however, which were in a context of tight competition and relied mostly on patient contributions for their funding (see Chapter 4). Due to pressure from local associations of doctors, some hospitals joined doctor associations and gained the ability to fix hospitalization fees through negotiations with their respective associations and local authorities. This was the case for Hikone Hospital, which made itself an association member in 1920[30]; however, becoming an association member was neither compulsory nor a generalized process. Fixed fees were negotiated with health insurance associations since the introduction of the 1922 Health Insurance Act, and the growing population of healthcare policyholders enabled hospitals to apply fixed fees to a larger number of patients. Yet, it was only in 1943—amid the wartime mobilization effort—that the Ministry of Health introduced fixed hospital fees for all patients. After the war, one of the first actions of the Japan Hospital Association (founded in 1951) was to demand that the Ministry implement an official and unified increase of hospital fees.[31]

3   The Role of Health Insurance

In most Western countries, health insurance systems—whether private or public—have played a major role in the regulation of the healthcare market. Insurance providers have negotiated fixed fees for their patients with doctor and hospital associations, helping stabilize the pressure on prices and putting an end to price-based competition. That stabilization process relied centrally on premium payments from policyholders. In some cases, national governments have even subsidized insurance providers to reduce premium costs and thus facilitate the extension of policy coverage across wider segments of the population. In Japan, the Health Insurance Act (1922) and National Health Insurance Act (1938) constituted the basis of the system until WWII.[32]

3.1   The Health Insurance Act (1922)

The Health Insurance Act (*kenkō hoken hō*, 1922) was inspired by the German example and aligned with a social policy designed to maintain order in society.[33] The objective, in the context of the social and trade-union movements that characterized the post-WWI environment, was to guarantee access to healthcare for the poorest workers. The Act specifically applied to employees who worked for manufacturing and mining enterprises with more than ten workers and earned less than 1200 yen per year.[34] The salary provision, imported from the German model, was essential: The purport of the law was thus to support working classes, not the entire population. If one considers that the limit of 1200 yen represented more than twice the annual income of a male worker in the cotton industry at the time (estimated at 450–500 yen), however, the scope of the legislation was rather broad.[35]   Policymakers then extended the provision to employees in enterprises of more than five employees in 1934 and revised the Act in 1939 to include members of workers' families. The law led to a dual-institutional system. Enterprises employing more than 300 workers could open their own health insurance associations (*kenkō hoken kumiai*), while the government created public insurance for others. These various organizations negotiated contracts with doctors and hospitals; workers had no say in the agreements. Finally, in 1926, the state decided to subsidize these insurance programs.[36]

From the perspective of healthcare-market regulation, the law had two major effects. First, health insurance providers signed contracts with doctor and hospital associations—and thus defined fixed fees for various medical treatments. The Home Ministry published several editions of lists that prefectures had negotiated with medical and hospital associations.[37] Second, the financial contributions that insurance providers made toward healthcare costs (for hospitalization, drugs, operations, and the use of technological equipment, for example) had an upper limit until 1942. Providers did not reimburse all medical services, only covering a portion of the full range. This measure limited the possibility of the healthcare infrastructure developing endlessly on the backs of health insurance providers alone.

Consequently, the health insurance of industrial enterprises helped the healthcare market, albeit to a limited degree. The sector represented direct opposition to doctor associations that demanded higher fees for their services and tried to control fees among those who accepted contracts with insurance providers. These contracts were an opportunity for doctors to introduce the concept of "points" for each type of medical treatment and the idea of basing payments on point counts, which the prefectures defined with the regional associations of doctors. In 1943, when the state intervened authoritatively in health affairs, the Ministry of Health started to determine point values after first consulting doctors who had signed contracts with insurance providers, prefectural authorities, and regional medical associations.[38] This system of point-based fees enabled better control and the standardization of prices.

The 1933 official census by the Home Ministry provides some details about the state of health insurance associations belonging to private enterprises (*kumiai*).[39] There were 340 associations, mostly in the textile (132), machine (61), mining (48), and chemical (34) industries—the largest sectors of the manufacturing industry at the time. The geographical breakdown shows that the associations existed primarily in industrial cities: The prefectures of Osaka (52), Tokyo (50), and Aichi (34, where Nagoya is located) accounted for more than one-third of the sum. In total, these associations insured 569,856 workers, only slightly more than 10% of the entire workforce in the manufacturing and mining industries.[40] Consequently, many enterprises used the public insurance system to cover their employees. One must also note that most of these associations were small; on average, they had only 1676 members, and half (170) had less than 1000 members. Only six had more than 10,000 members: Tokyo City Electric Department (12,970), textile companies Toyo Spinning (34,637), Kanebo (31,731), Dai-Nihon Spinning (21,753) and Gunze (17,705), as well as the Mitsui Miike Mine (10,116). Thus, only a minority share of workers received coverage through insurance belonging to and under the direct control of their employers. Health insurance was not a tool for enterprises to implement a paternalistic strategy, unlike the cases of many companies in Western countries.[41]

3.2   The National Health Insurance Act (1938)

Social protection was bolstered in 1938 with the adoption of the National Health Insurance Act (*kokumin kenkō hoken-hō*), whose objective was to enlarge the share of the population benefiting from a policy through the integration of workers from agriculture and fish farming—two sectors that lay outside the scope of the 1922 law. As the country continued to militarize, a central aim of this new law was to improve health conditions across the entire population, particularly in the countryside. The foundation of a healthcare system based on free-market principles and the private action of independent doctors had led to a concentration of hospitals and doctors in cities. The idea of giving the rural population financial support for paying medical fees served to facilitate the business of doctors in the countryside.

This insurance structure operated on a decentralized system, with the creation of mutual insurance associations in villages and towns, or organized by professional unions. The associations had considerable autonomy regarding management (premiums, contracts with doctors and hospitals, and so forth).[42] In 1942 and 1943, about 95% of municipalities throughout Japan had such an association.[43] Membership was voluntary, however.

Lastly, following the creation of a Ministry of Health in 1938, health insurance coverage expanded to integrate workers from professions that had not yet been a part of the framework. In 1939, new laws gave birth to mutual insurance for the employees of maritime transportation (*sen'in hoken-hō*) and services (*shokuin kenkō hoken-hō*).

Figure 3 shows the number of people covered by the 1922 Health Insurance Act and the corresponding share of the total population. The figures, from Statistics Bureau data, do not include people covered by the new insurance systems created in 1938 and 1939. The graph clearly reveals the impact of the 1934 amendment to the law, which expanded coverage from industrial companies with at least ten workers to those with at least five workers. While the number of insured people averaged 1.8 million people from 1926 to 1933, it then entered a phase of growth, reaching 3.8 million in 1937 and 5.7 million in 1940. In 1944, some 10 million people were insured.[44]

The state played an important, but not essential, role in this development. First, a majority of insured people were members of public mutual insurance; their proportion fluctuated between 58 and 68% during the years 1926–1940, averaging 63.3%. Next, the state gave subsidies to all forms of insurance in a total sum that went from 3.2 million yen in 1930 to 6.1 million in 1940. These subsidies, however, represented a relatively small amount in comparison to the total premiums paid by the insured (33.2 million yen in 1930 and 121.3 million in 1940) and a constantly decreasing share thereof (from 9.6 to 5%).[45] The insured population

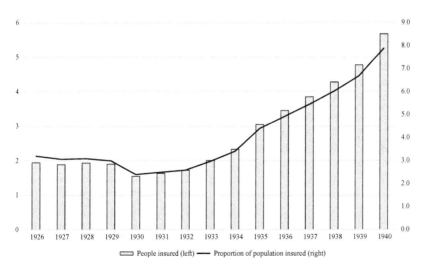

Fig. 3 Population covered by the 1922 Health Insurance Act, millions of people and share of total population (%), 1926–1940 (Source *Nihon chōki tōkei sōran*, Tokyo: Nihon Tōkei Kyōkai, 1987, tables 20-12-a/b)

formed the main basis for the financial growth of health insurance providers.

Despite this development, though, the proportion of the total population receiving coverage under the 1922 insurance system was low. The percentage was just 2.9%, on average, from 1926 to 1934 and reached only 7.9% in 1940. The health insurance system thus targeted specific categories (workers and employees) that lacked the financial means for accessing the healthcare infrastructure. Even if one were to add in the people covered by the 1938 and 1939 insurance provisions, the overall proportion remained relatively stagnant until 1940. That year, the total number of those covered by any kind of health insurance amounted to 9.8 million people—a mere 13.6% of the total population.[46]

These percentages are far lower than the corresponding figures in Western Europe during the interwar years. In France, for example, 20 million people—46% of the national population—had public or private health insurance in 1934.[47] Switzerland had a similar rate: In 1940, 48.8% of the population had health insurance coverage.[48] As for Germany, the estimated coverage rate in 1930 was 50%.[49] Even the United States, which tended to be "backward" on the issue in comparison with Western Europe, had a rate slightly larger than Japan: In 1945, the mutual and private associations Blue Cross and Blue Shield, which represented of the leading source of health insurance during the interwar years, had a total of 21 million members, or about 15% of the whole population.[50] In Japan, therefore, the health insurance system did not aim to give the middle class access to hospital treatment and then support the growth of the hospital and healthcare systems. Rather, it was basically a measure of social policy whose objective was to maintain social order. The chief aim was to create a safety net for the poorest workers.

The perspective of healthcare-market regulation brings a slightly different dimension into the topic, as insurance providers played an important role in introducing the idea of fixed fees for medical treatments and contributing to the unification of prices despite the opposition of independent doctors. In 1943, following the adoption of the National Medical Care Act (*kokumin iryō-hō*) within the context of a nationalist, militarist policy, the Ministry of Health's system of fixed fees took effect in the health system after doctors and hospitals had offered their input.[51] The proportion of the population with health insurance coverage, meanwhile, dramatically increased to 76% in 1943.[52]

4 THE REGULATORY INTERVENTION OF THE STATE

The associations of doctors and, to a lesser extent, health insurance providers had a major regulatory function in the healthcare market through the adoption of fixed fees. However, that action was possible only through state interventionism. The Japanese authorities adopted a legal order that enabled the institutionalization of the market, though the direct intervention of the state was extremely limited in the field of healthcare and medicine until WWII. Health policy had two main objectives: training doctors and fighting epidemics. Still, the organization of the healthcare market was not considered a major state responsibility, as the process rested on market principles.

Public health was one of the numerous fields of society and economy that underwent intense modernization under the new authorities after the Meiji Restoration (1868). Prussia served as a model for the effort. In 1870, the Japanese government asked Prussia to send two doctors to Tokyo to teach their skills in the state-owned medical school, which became the Faculty of Medicine at the University of Tokyo in 1877.[53] Doctor training was part of the public health policy itself, however. Training initiatives were originally the jurisdiction of the Ministry of Education. The Bureau of Medical Affairs (*imu-kyoku*), which opened in 1872 within the Ministry of Education, became part of the Home Ministry in 1875 and assumed a new name: the Bureau of Hygiene (*eisei-kyoku*).[54] In 1938, the organization became the Ministry of Health, which had a military objective to strengthen the nation.

The state's intervention in the health sector aimed first at improving the sanitary conditions of the country and protecting the weakest against illness and accidents. An objective of social policy thus led the state to take measures that had an impact on the organization of the healthcare market. One of the first actions in the field centered on factory work. The demanding working conditions and bad hygiene at textile factories at the end of the nineteenth century spurred a tuberculosis crisis, especially among young girls, who constituted cheap labor in the industry.[55] During the 1890s and 1900s, doctors raised the issue, leading to one of the first state interventions with an impact on health insurance. The Factory Act (*kōjō-hō*), adopted in 1916, introduced the provision stipulating that employers were to be responsible for work-related injuries and illnesses and, consequently, the corresponding healthcare costs.[56]

However, policymakers did not organize any specific accident insurance program after the passage of the law.

At the same time, the struggle against tuberculosis had essentially relied until then on the action of individuals and private associations. The largest was the Japanese Society for the Prevention of Tuberculosis (*nihon kekkaku yobō kyōkai*), founded in 1913.[57] In that context, the state enacted a law to prevent the spread of the epidemic (*kekkaku yobō-hō*, 1919). National lawmakers decided both to finance the construction and setup of sanatoria and to assume liability for the care of poor tuberculosis patients.[58] Sick individuals thus received state support outside the medical market. This was an exception, however, and their number was very limited; state intervention resulted principally from social and sanitary concerns. In 1930, there were 54 sanatoria for tuberculosis, a mere 1.5% of all healthcare institutions in Japan that year.[59] The interwar years saw increases working classes secure easier access to hospitalization and modern medical technology, although that development arose mostly from private action instead of state interventionism.

The first public intervention that affected the regulation of the healthcare market with any real heft came in 1933. The action resulted not so much from the Bureau of Hygiene bureaucracy's intentions to organize the market but rather from lobbying by independent doctors who wanted to limit competition. The new rules on health centers that the Home Ministry adopted that year introduced a legal distinction between a "hospital" (*byōin*, or a healthcare institution with ten beds or more) and a "clinic" or "healthcare center" (*shinryōjo*, an institution with fewer than ten beds) and gave the state control over the opening of institutions by nondoctors. Finally, the government adopted various measures aiming to guarantee the quality of healthcare and improve sanitary conditions (limiting the number of sick patients per room and isolating contagious individuals, for example), but these stipulations had no effect on the organization of the market.[60] This first state intervention was, on the whole, limited and indirect. The objective was to support the activities of doctors and improve the functioning of a market mechanism-oriented system.

Therefore, the state implemented an interventionist policy aiming at regulating the healthcare market after the creation of the Ministry of Health in 1938. This intervention occurred within the context of the militarization of Japanese society and economy, with the state aiming to control public health in order to strengthen the nation—and to ensure strong, healthy soldiers.[61] The National Medical Care Act (*kokumin iryō-hō*), which took effect in 1942, was the major avenue for advancing this new policy.[62] From the perspective of the regulation of the healthcare market, the government's initiative had two main consequences. First, it laid the groundwork for a nationwide network of public, government-financed hospitals, relying on two 500-bed central hospitals in Tokyo and Osaka, a 250-bed hospital in each prefecture, and 588 small (50-bed) hospitals throughout the country. The project saw only partial implementation, however, due to the war and the fervent opposition from independent doctors. The new authorities ended up halting the effort in 1947.[63] Second, the state introduced a generalized system of fixed fees for all medical treatments, including hospitalization. Each treatment was evaluated and given a number of points; the monetary value of each point was determined by the Ministry of Health, which adapted the value to price fluctuation. This system remained in force until 1948.[64] The idea to regulate the healthcare market through a system of treatment-specific credits formed the basis of today's healthcare system in Japan.

5   Conclusions

Although the healthcare market in Japan relied largely on private organizations until WWII, it did not function only according to the laws of the free market—it also operated under regulations resulting from the state's legal intervention. The approach to regulation had two objectives: to guarantee minimum prices for medical treatments for doctors and to provide the poorest workers with access to healthcare.

At first, from the end of the nineteenth century to WWI, prefectures had standardized fees for medical treatments. The key issue for doctors was to stand firm against the pressure to cut prices, and associations of doctors engaged actively in this process. Next, during the interwar years, health insurance took on a greater influence. As the emergence of new technology like X-ray equipment not only transformed medicine and hospitals but also spurred rising healthcare costs, the working classes had virtually no access to this advancing infrastructure. The state thus adopted a new legal framework to facilitate care for a broader range of people. Health insurance, despite covering only about 10% of population in 1940, had a regulatory impact on the healthcare market by negotiating fixed fees with doctors and some public hospitals.

The healthcare market was still largely based on competition, however, except for the domain of medical treatments prices. Few hospitals benefited from fixed hospitalization fees—a major source of revenue. In 1934, there were only 52 public hospitals that had contracts with health insurance providers guaranteeing fixed fees for insured patients.[65] While that number represented nearly half of all public hospitals (46.2%), it only amounted to a tiny share of all hospitals (1.8%).

Finally, my discussion emphasized the fact that the state played only a modest role in the regulation of the healthcare market until WWII. The government put its stock in the principle of a private market. The state's intervention was little more than a reaction against lobbying by the associations of doctors and a product of the need to take at least some measures for the working classes. There was no momentum behind the idea of organizing the entire healthcare market until the end of the 1930s. The creation of the Ministry of Health in 1938 thus represents a major turning point, one that coincides with the shift to a total-war economy.[66] The National Medical Care Act (1942) gave sweeping organizational powers to the government, which attempted a regulatory intervention in the health system—notably through the definition of fixed fees for all treatments. During the 1950s, the health system experienced a phase of reconstruction and reorganization, characterized by the government's focus on the growth of large public hospitals and the adoption of universal health insurance (1961) in light of the wartime experience and the British example. The continuity with the 1938 regime rested on the adoption of fixed fees for medical treatments and hospitalization, with the state and the various actors in the health system negotiating the values. This guaranteed the financial stability of the healthcare system and enabled the pursuit of its development. Until the late 1930s, the lack of rigid regulation made hospital revenues unstable due to the highly competitive nature of the market. This explains why hospitals felt it so necessary to acquire the most current medical technology in hopes of attracting patients—and why manufacturers of medical devices had to deliver equipment that fell within the limited budgets of small hospitals.

NOTES

1. *Isei hyakunen shi*, pp. 103–104.
2. Kawakami, *Gendai nihon iryoshi*, pp. 231–238.
3. Ikai, *Byoin no seiki no riron*.

4. Domin, *Une histoire économique de l'hôpital*.
5. Faure, *Les cliniques privées*.
6. Labisch and Spree, *Krankenhaus-Report 19. Jahrhundert* and Donzé, *L'ombre de César*.
7. Stevens, *In Sickness and in Wealth*.
8. Mohan, *Planning, Markets and Hospitals*.
9. Kawakami, *Gendai nihon iryoshi*.
10. Ibidem, p. 341.
11. Ikai, *Byoin no seiki no riron*, pp. 142 and 146.
12. Ibidem.
13. Sakai, *Rekishi de miru nihon no ishi no tsukurikata*.
14. Momose, *Showa senzenki no nihon*, p. 218.
15. *Byoin no seiki no riron*, Chapter 2.
16. Kawakami, *Gendai nihon iryoshi*, p. 11.
17. *Isei hyakunen shi*, Aoyagi, *Shinryo hoshu no rekishi*.
18. Kawakami, *Gendai nihon iryoshi*, p. 31.
19. Ibidem, pp. 211–213.
20. Aoyagi, *Shinryo hoshu no rekishi*, pp. 202–203.
21. *Naimu-sho Eiseikyoku zasshi*, vol. 13, 1878.
22. Aoyagi, *Shinryo hoshu no rekishi*, pp. 232–233.
23. Fukunaga, *Nihon byouin shi*, pp. 168–169.
24. Aoyagi, *Shinryo hoshu no rekishi*, p. 286.
25. Ibidem, p. 292.
26. Ibidem, p. 414.
27. Kawakami, *Gendai nihon iryoshi*, pp. 327–335.
28. Ibidem, p. 338.
29. Ibidem, pp. 341–342.
30. *Hikone shiritsu byoin hyakunenshi*, p. 74.
31. *Nihon byoin kai 30 nen shi*, p. 1.
32. Shimazaki, *Nihon iryo*, p. 114 and Sumiko, Hasegawa, Carrin and Kawabata, "Scaling Up Community Health Insurance".
33. Yoshihara and Wada, *Nihon iryo hoken seidoshi*, pp. 29–63.
34. Ibidem, p. 44.
35. Wada and Hara, *Kingendai nihon keizaishi yoran*, p. 99.
36. Yoshihara and Wada, *Nihon iryo hoken seidoshi*, p. 51.
37. For example, *Rodosha saigai fujo sekinin hoken jigyo nenpo*.
38. Yoshihara and Wada, *Nihon iryo hoken seidoshi*, p. 55.
39. *Kenko hoken kumiai yoran*, 1933.
40. In 1930, the workforce of these two sectors amounted at 5.0 million people. Historical Statistics of Japan, file 19-9-a, http://www.stat.go.jp/english/data/chouki/19.htm (accessed 5 December 2016).
41. Tone, *The Business of Benevolence*.

42. Shimazaki, *Nihon iryo*, pp. 65–80.
43. Ibidem, p. 44.
44. *Historical Statistics of Japan*, tables 20-12-a/b.
45. Ibidem.
46. Takaki, "Kokumin kenko hoken to chiiki fukushi", p. 252.
47. Domin, *Une histoire économique de l'hôpital*, vol. 1, p. 189.
48. *Statistisches Jahrbuch der Schweiz*, p. 257.
49. Carrin and Chris, "Social Health Insurance", p. 50.
50. Starr, *The Social Transformation of American Medicine*, p. 308.
51. Kawakami, *Gendai nihon iryoshi*, p. 57.
52. Takaki, "Kokumin kenko hoken to chiiki fukushi".
53. Kawakami, *Gendai nihon iryoshi*, pp. 91–96.
54. Ibidem, p. 114.
55. Aoki, *Kekkaku no shakaishi*, pp. 75–77.
56. Yoshihara and Wada, *Nihon iryo hoken seidoshi*, p. 12.
57. *Isei hyakunen shi*, p. 233.
58. Yoshihara and Wada, *Nihon iryo hoken seidoshi*, p. 21.
59. *Historical Statistics of Japan*, table 24-28, Hospitals by kind, 1910–2004.
60. Sugaya, *Nihon no byoin*, pp. 112–116.
61. Kasza, "War and Welfare Policy in Japan".
62. *Isei hyakunen shi*, pp. 293–295.
63. Sugaya, *Nihon no byoin*, 127–131 and   Sugiyama, *Senryoki no iryo kaikaku*, 191–192.
64. Kawakami, *Gendai nihon iryoshi*, p. 57 and 456.
65. *Rodosha saigai fujo sekinin hoken jigyo nenpo*.
66. Hara, "Wartime Controls".

CHAPTER 7

Conclusion

The objective of this book was to discuss why, when, and how medicine and healthcare became a business, drawing on the example of Japan during the first part of the twentieth century. In Japan, as was the case in Western countries, medicine and healthcare as market-based activities (paying/receiving payments to receive/provide care) were limited to niches until the mid-nineteenth century. Most doctors belonged to wealthy families that did not need to work to make a living, while the population used self-medication or traditional healers to recover from sicknesses.

Hence, the shift of medicine and healthcare toward the "business" sphere has roots in their commodification and the emergence and growth of a market-based healthcare system. Individuals (medical doctors) and organizations (hospitals, clinics, and surgeries, for example) were the forces in the market. They had to adopt strategies to ensure profitability and maintain competitiveness. The nature of the market (state-regulated, self-regulated, or free competition-based) has a deep influence on the strategical choices of the actors therein, as I discuss further below. In many cases, however, medical organizations had to face the issue of technological innovation. The new medical equipment developed at the end of the nineteenth century, including sterilization instruments, operating rooms, and X-ray devices, had a twofold impact. First, they contributed toward concentrating medical activities in hospitals and clinics; second, they came with costs that parties of some kind or another (patients, insurance providers, or the state) needed to cover. The transformation of medicine and

© The Author(s) 2018   173
P.-Y. Donzé, *Making Medicine a Business*,
https://doi.org/10.1007/978-981-10-8159-0_7

healthcare into a business—as a process of commodification—was thus tied to technological change. However, the relationships among technology, rising costs, business opportunities, and commodification are complex. This book explored the web of connections via a multifocal analysis. My case study demonstrated that, in Japan, the construction of a market-based healthcare system occurred during the 1920s and developed over the following decade. It was the outcome of the simultaneous—and dialectical—action of several individuals, groups, and organizations.

First, the manufacturers of medical equipment, particularly X-ray devices, were a major actor driving the change. X-ray devices were the first technology with an impact on the organization of the healthcare system. The nature and cost of X-ray equipment made it difficult for doctors to use the devices on house calls; instead, the devices needed to be installed in locations where doctors and patients would meet to use them: hospitals and clinics. Moreover, their high costs made them important investments that owners had to amortize by attracting more—or wealthier—patients. Similar to what happened in Western countries, manufacturers of medical equipment in Japan launched new types of X-ray devices during and after World War I (WWI). These new initiatives resulted from General Electric's development of the Coolidge tube in 1913, an innovation that enabled rays with high enough levels of precision for medical practice. The technological factor was not the only contributor, though. One must also acknowledge the major role of the domestic company Shimadzu (followed by Tokyo Electric in the early 1930s) in adapting X-ray technology to the conditions of the local market. These companies developed simpler, lighter, and cheaper equipment that was suitable for the Japanese healthcare market, where a large number of small private hospitals held the dominant position. The opportunities for equipment sales were abundant, but the technology needed to align with the needs and means of local hospitals. Siemens lost the Japanese X-ray device market, despite its dominant presence up until 1914, precisely because it did not adapt its equipment to local market conditions.

Second, the direct customers of this new technology—medical doctors who used X-ray devices—gradually organized to take control of the technology. During the 1920s and early 1930s, a new generation of practitioners, led by doctors Fujinami and Urano, established themselves as specialists in the use of radiological equipment. They had emancipated from surgeons, who had controlled the use of X-rays since the late 1890s, and forged a niche as radiologists, which represented a new kind of specialist. One of the results of this autonomization was the professionalization of the use of X-ray devices, notably through the training of technicians as assistants, with the cooperation of manufacturers like Shimadzu. The autonomization process also led to the diffusion of the technology throughout the country. The main objective of the professionalization of radiologists was not necessarily to pursue larger profits through the use of high-tech equipment, nor was it rooted in entrepreneurship: In fact, very few radiologists launched their own specialized clinics. The most important goal for this new generation of doctors was to secure employment in an increasingly competitive job market. Using a new technology as a specialty in itself was a way to create a new segment in the healthcare market. Moreover, doctors—radiologists, in particular—carried out joint research and development (R&D) with the manufacturers of medical devices, particularly Shimadzu, to codevelop and adapt medical technology for their own use. They needed cheaper and lighter equipment than what they could obtain from foreign multinational enterprises due to the sizes of their hospitals, which tended to be smaller than those in Western countries were.

Third, hospitals adapted their organizations and management practices to acquire new medical equipment like X-ray devices. The technology was an important investment, in a highly competitive environment, that hospitals needed to amortize. Attracting paying patients—mostly wealthy people, as health insurance was underdeveloped until World War II (WWII)—became a major issue for hospitals. They built private wards with high-grade services and opened outpatient services to offer X-ray diagnostics to a broader scope of customers. The technological and managerial transformation of hospitals during the interwar years made them major institutions, bastions at the core of the healthcare market. Of course, not all hospitals followed the same strategy. Some sought profits others focused on providing care to the people as charitable organizations, and most of the private hospitals in large cities were microfamily businesses. As Ikai demonstrated, self-employment was the most prevalent mode for Japanese doctors to access hospital infrastructure.[1] Whatever the nature of the hospital, however, financial stability was necessary; new technology, particularly X-ray devices, was thus a challenge from that perspective.

Fourth, the government stayed away from the healthcare market until WWII. Since the implementation of the modern state following the Meiji

Restoration (1868), the general consensus was that medicine and health-care were basically a private business save for controlling and fighting against epidemics like tuberculosis and training doctors. The state was not completely absent from the healthcare market. It financed some faculties of medicine (primarily at the Universities of Tokyo, Kyoto, and Kyushu) and owned several military hospitals. However, despite training doctors and controlling the access to the medical profession, it essentially let doctors organize themselves; the professionalization of specialists was a private matter, for the most part. Thus, the state hardly intervened to regulate the healthcare market. The first law on health insurance, which took effect in 1922, had a very limited scope. The most important measure, which first went into force during the 1900s, was the control of medical fees—a result of pressure from associations of doctors looking to benefit from minimal prices. Most of the healthcare market was unregulated prior to the late 1930s.

Consequently, the transformation of medicine into a business and its commodification resulted from the action of the medical device industry, doctors, and hospitals in a competitive and atomized healthcare market. Market mechanisms were the driving forces behind the diffusion of new medical technology that changed the very nature of hospitals in Japan during the first decades of the twentieth century.

Both the organization and the structure of the market impacted this change and supported the rise of the business-oriented model. The organization of the market can differ between full regulation by the state (control of the number of hospitals and distribution of medical equipment, fixed prices and fees, and no hospital and doctor choice for patients) and the laissez-faire approach. The structure of the market, meanwhile, can vary between a high concentration of hospitals and the presence of numerous small hospitals. These two features of healthcare markets can lead to various ideal-types, as Fig. 1 illustrates. The conditions in Japan during the first part of the twentieth century embody the most competitive form, with a high dispersion of hospitals in a minimally regulated environment. This explains the fast diffusion of technology (as a competitive advantage for hospitals that held it), the growing number of specialists and hospitals, the need to adapt foreign medical devices, and joint research between doctors and manufacturers. However, during and after WWII, the Japanese authorities adopted a more interventionist health policy that produced a growing proportion of health insurance coverage among the population

Organization

		Laissez-faire	Regulation
Structure	Dispersion	High competition	Competition
	Concentration	Competition	No competition

Fig. 1 Organization and structure of healthcare markets (*Source* Created by the author)

and involved the gradual control of prices and fees. The state regulation did not target hospital planning, however. Urbanization and population growth made it necessary to increase the hospital supply, and the government trusted market mechanisms for that. The number of hospitals in Japan (not including mental hospitals or sanatoriums for tuberculosis) went from 2939 in 1950 to a peak of 9006 in 1990, with the total number then gradually declining to 8493 in 2014.[2] Still today, Japan has one of the highest hospital-to-population ratios in the world. According to the Organization for Economic Cooperation and Development (OECD), Japan had 67.1 hospitals per million population in 2013, only trailing South Korea slightly (68.7). France was number three at 48.6 hospitals per million population, with Germany at 39.5, and the United States and the Netherlands at just 17.9 and 16.1, respectively.[3] This high hospital density led to regulated competition based not on prices, a state-controlled variable, but rather on the attraction of patients. The acquisition of new medical technology thus remains a major issue for hospital managers in striving to maintain competitiveness. Consequently, Japan has by far the world's largest density of medical equipment. In 2014, there were 107.1 CT scanners per million population in Japan. In comparison, the totals came out to 40.9 in the United States, 37.1 in South Korea, 35.3 in Germany, 15.3 in France, and 13.3 in the Netherlands.[4]

The Japanese path of development, which formed the focus of the analysis in this book, is not universal, however. Each national healthcare market has its own characteristics regarding organization and structure, which grow out of the historical evolution of hospital construction and development on the one hand and health policies on the other. In Western Europe and the United States, where hospitals were first founded as charitable institutions by philanthropists and local communities, healthcare markets are traditionally marked by a lower dispersion of hospitals—which are also larger on average than those in Japan—and consequently a lower degree of competition. These different conditions explain the lower density of medical equipment in the West. While the effects of new medical technology emerging into the healthcare system were similar throughout the world, prompting the commodification of medicine and healthcare, one must contextualize the patterns of this mutation and understand the courses of development in light of the local conditions in each country.

This book proposed an approach of business history to analyze the evolution of medicine during the first part of the twentieth century. It has implications for further research in neighboring fields. For historians of medicine, it offers an invitation to consider the business-related and economic dimensions of the transformation of medicine since the late nineteenth century. Even for those examining the social, cultural, and global issues dominating the discourse in the history of medicine today, the construction and development of healthcare as a market are valuable themes for consideration. The systemic and multifocal approach in this book can shed new light on other mutations of medicine and health, particularly the global diffusion and local adaptation of medical practice and technology. For business historians, on the other hand, the work shows how our field can contribute to a better understanding of the dynamics of sectors that have largely flown under the radar in the field of business history. The process of commodification of all aspects of social life, such as healthcare and medicine, is a major twentieth-century trend that has attracted more and more public attention for a decade. The new history of capitalism, born in departments of history, offers a perspective centered on the cultural and social dimensions of this "great transformation."[5] Business historians can contribute through analyses that demonstrate the mechanisms behind this major change and the key role that organizations have played.

NOTES

1. Ikai, *Byoin no seiki no riron.*
2. Historical Statistics of Japan, http://www.stat.go.jp/english/data/chouki/, document 24-28 (consulted 15 June 2017) and *The Statistical Handbook of Japan 2016*, p. 169.
3. http://stats.oecd.org (accessed 19 June 2017).
4. http://stats.oecd.org (accessed 19 June 2017).
5. Polanyi, *The Great Transformation*; Hilt, "Economic History, Historical Analysis, and the New History of Capitalism"; and Galambos, "Is This a Decisive Moment for the History of Business, Economic History, and the History of Capitalism?".

Bibliography

Primary Sources

Mitsui Archives, Tokyo
Mitsui Charitable Hospital (Izumibashi Charitable Hospital).
National Diet Library, Tokyo (NDL)
Archives of the GHQ/SCAP.
Siemens Corporate Archives, Berlin (SCA)
Documents about Japanese subsidiaries.
Siemens Medical Archives, Erlangen (MAE)
Correspondence with Goto Fuundo.

Published Sources

21 seiki he no kakehashi: okyakusama totomoni ayunda Toshiba iyo kikai kaihatsu no rekishi, Tokyo: Toshiba Medical, 1998.
30 nen no ayumi, Mito: Ibaraki-ken hoshasen gishi-kai, 1981.
30 nen-shi, Tokyo: Nihon hoshasen gishi kai, 1984.
30 shunen kinen-shi, s.l.: Iwate-ken hoshasen gishikai, 1978.
50 nen no ayumi, Tokyo: Nihon hoshasen gishi-kai, 1997.
130 nen no ayumi: 1872–2002, Osaka: Shiraimatsu, 2002.
Abe, Kiyoshi, Tsugio Oka, and Yoshio Onishi, "Denri denatsu kei no tokusei nitsuite", *Denki gakkai zasshi*, vol. 56, no. 574, 1936, pp. 552–553.
Chuo tetsudo byoin shi, Tokyo: Chuo Tetsudo Byoin, 1980.
Dainihon hakushi roku, Tokyo: Hattensha, vols. 1–5, 1921–1930.

Eiseikyoku nenpo, Tokyo: Ministry of Interior, Bureau of Hygiene, 1881–1938.

Fuji denki shashi, Tokyo: Fuji denki, 1957.

Fujinami, Koichi, "Waga kuni ni okeru rentogen gaku shinpo no jotai", *Ikai jiho*, vol. 1332, 1920, pp. 16–18.

Fujinami, Koichi, "Waga kuni ni okeru rentogen gaku oyo ni kansuru shokan", *Rentogen geppo*, vol. 1, 1921.

Fukuda, Shunichi, "Rentogen-sen ni tsuite", *Ika kikai gaku zasshi*, vol. 1, no. 2, 1923, pp. 67–75, no. 3, pp. 175–182 and no. 4, pp. 235–249.

Furuya, Shigeo, *Rentogen ryoho shinron*, Tokyo: Kokuseido shoten, 1925.

Goto, Fuundo, *Eigyo hokokusho*, 1950.

Goto, Goro, *Nihon hoshasen igaku shiko*, 2 volumes, Tokyo: Daijunikai kokusai hoshasen igaku kaigi, 1969–1970.

Hikone shiritsu byoin hyakunenshi, Hikone: Hikone byoin, 1991.

Historical Statistics of Japan, 5 volumes, Tokyo: Statistics Bureau, 1988.

Hitachi Seisakusho-shi, Hitachi, 1960.

Hoing, M., *A History of the ASXT, 1920 to 1950*, Saint Paul: The Bruce Publishing Co., 1952.

Hokkaido ekkusu-sen gishi: 50 nen no ayumi, Sapporo: Hokkaido ekkusu-sen gishi-kai, 1969.

Ika kikai gaku zasshi, 1923–1975.

Ika kikai shinpo, 1917–1919.

Irigaku ryoho zasshi, 1914–1921.

Iryo denki jippo, 1931–1940.

Isei hyakunen shi, Tokyo: Koseisho, 1976.

Ito, Kenji, *Ichi-en no isha: ichimei shindenshi seimei-ron*, Tokyo: Yukosha, 1938.

Izumi, Takateru, *Nihon kingendai igaku jinmei jiten, 1868–2011*, Tokyo: Igakushoin, 2012.

Janssen, Leon, and Gene Medford, *Envision: A History of the GE Healthcare Business*, Waukesha: Meadow Brook Farm, 2009.

Jitsuyo iji hoki: sanko horei mokuji oyobi bibo rantsuki, Tokyo: Kokuseido, 1939.

Kaiin shimei roku, Tokyo: Gakushikai, 1930–1945.

"Kaneko Junji", *Nihon hoshasen gijutsu gakkai zasshi*, vol. 29, no. 1, 1973, p. 1.

Keio gijuku daigaku igakubu 60 nen-shi, Tokyo: Keio University, 1983.

Kenko hoken kumiai yoran, Tokyo: Naimusho shakaikyoku hokenbu, 1933.

Kindai toshi no eisei kankyo (Osaka), Tokyo: Kingendai, vol. 15, 2007.

Kitadono Inji, "Rentogen sochi sosa gijutsu no ikusei", *Ika kikai shinpo*, vol. 1, 1917, pp. 32–33.

Kobe kogyo sha shi, Kobe: Kobe Kogyo, 1976.

Kogyo shoyuken seido hyaku nen shi, 2 volumes, Tokyo: Hatsumei kyokai, 1984–1985.

Koizumi Kikuta, *Waga kuni ni okeru X-sen kan no ayumi*, Tokyo: Softex, 1976.

Kojo tsuran, Tokyo: Shokosho, 1922, 1929 and 1935.

Koritsu iwase byoin hyaku nen shi, Fukushima: Iwase byoin, 1972.

Kresta, Otto, "Bankin no rentogen hosenkai", *Ika kikai gaku zasshi*, vol. 2, no. 9, 1925, pp. 482–489.

Kurokawa, Toshio, and S. Yamakawa, *Shokakan no rentogen shindan*, Tokyo: Kokuseido, 1936.

Kyoto daigaku hyakunenshi: bukyoku shihen, Kyoto: Kyoto University, vol. 1, 1997.

Kyushu daigaku igakubu hoshasenkagaku kyoshitsu 50 nen-shi, Fukuoka: Kyushu University, 1979.

Matsuda irigaku jippo, 1926–1930.

Matsushita, Denkichi (ed.), *Kindai nihon keizaijin taikei*, Tokyo, 1940.

Mitsui kinen byoin hyakunen no ayumi, Tokyo: Mitsui kinen byoin, 2009.

Momotani, Rokurouta, *Nihon ni okeru shimensu no jigyo to sono keiken reki*, Tokyo, 1955.

Nagahashi, Masamichi, *Rentogen shindan to chiryo*, Osaka: Nihon seimei saiseikai, 1927.

Naito, Raku, *Kyukyu shochi*, Tokyo: Tetsudo kyokokai, 1914.

Nakaizumi, Masanori, "Tokyo teikokudaigaku igakubu hoshasenka no setsubi", *Nihon rentogen gakkai zasshi*, vol. 10, no. 5–6, 1933, pp. 421–429.

Nihon byoin kai 30 nen shi, Tokyo: Nihon byoin kai, 1980.

Nihon daigaku igakubu 50 nen-shi, Tokyo: Nihon University, 1977.

Nihon hoshasen gijutsushi, Tokyo: Nihon hoshasen gijutsu gakkai, 2 volumes, 1989 and 2002.

Nihon igakkai bunkakai shoshi, Tokyo: Nihon igakkai, 1964.

Nihon ika daigaku no rekishi, Tokyo: Nippon Medical School, 2001.

Nihon ika kikai mokuroku, Nihon ika kikai mokuroku henshusho, 1952.

Nihon jinmei daijiten, Tokyo: Kodansha, 2009.

Nihon kanzei – zeikanshi shiryo, Tokyo: Ministry of Finances, 1960.

Nihon kogyo yokan, Tokyo: Kogyo no nihonsha, 1907–1941.

Nihon rentogen gakkai zasshi, 1923–1940.

Nihon rentogen gijutsu-in gakkai zasshi, 1944–1946.

Nihon seimei saiseikai 50 nen shi, Osaka: Nihon seimei saiseikai, 1979.

Nikkan kogyo shimbun, since 1922.

Nomura, Masami, "Metoro kankyu to H gata kankyu no hikaku", *Ika kikai gaku zasshi*, vol. 12, no. 9, 1934, pp. 443–446.

Numata, Hisashi, "Mukashi no X-sen kai no shuhen", *Nihon shika ishi gakkai kaishi*, vol. 8, no. 2, 1981, pp. 51–53.

Osaka daigaku igaku denshu hyakunenshi, Osaka: Osaka daigaku, 1978.

Osaka kaisei byoin: soritsu 100 shunen kinenshi, Osaka: Osaka Kaisei Hospital, 2000.

Otori, Ransaburo, "Ko fujinami koichi: sensei ryakureki oyobi byoreki", *Nihon ishigaku zasshi*, vol. 1315, 1943, pp. 217–219.

Rentogen gaku zasshi, vols. 1–3, 1928–1930.

Rentogen geppo, vols. 1–6, 1922–1923.

Rodosha saigai fujo sekinin hoken jigyo nenpo, Tokyo: Shakaikyoku, 1934.

Segi, Yoshikazu, *Nihon hoshasen gijutsu gakkai zasshi*, vol. 30, no. 3, 1975, pp. 248–249.

Segi, Yoshikazu, and Nobukatsu Hayashi, "Urano tamonji hakase no tsuioku to no shogai: Kyodai chuo rentogen shitsu soshi toji no koto", *Rinsho hoshasen no shoshi joho*, vol. 12, no. 1, 1967, pp. 71–74.

Seki, Seiichiro, "Rentogen sochi no kikaku tosei ni kanshite", *Ika kikain gaku zasshi*, vol. 17, no. 8, pp. 271–274.

Shiga, Tatsuo, "Teito ni okeru shinryo ekkusu-sen sochi no chosa", *Nihon igaku hoshasen gakkai zasshi*, vol. 1, no. 2, 1940, p. 205.

Shimadzu Seisakujo, *Eigyo hokokusho*, 1918–1945.

Shimadzu seisakujo shi, Kyoto: Shimadzu, 1967.

Siemens, Georg, *History of the House of Siemens*, 2 volumes, Freiburg/Munich: Karl Alber, 1957.

Siemens K.K., *100 Jahre Siemens in Japan*, Tokyo: Siemens, 1987.

Statistisches Jahrbuch der Schweiz, Berne: Eidgenossischen Statistischen Amt, 1941.

Takeda, Toshimitsu, *Rentogen gijutsu*, Tokyo: Hoshodo, 1935.

Takeda, Toshimitsu, "Dai yon shu ekkusu sen sochi non denka boshiki", *Ika kikai gaku zasshi*, vol. 16, no. 7, 1939, pp. 247–250.

Tamaki, Masao, "Nihon saisho no hoshasen ika: fujinami koichi", *Kenko bunka*, vol. 5, 1993, pp. 1–3.

Terauchi, Noburu, *Shika butsuri kagaku*, Tokyo: Shikagaku hosha, 1916.

Terauchi, Noburu, *Rentogen shikagaku*, second edition, Tokyo: Kawai shoten, 1941.

The Statistical Handbook of Japan 2016, Tokyo: Statistics Bureau, 2016.

Tokkyo bunrui betsu somokuroku, Tokyo: Tokkyocho, 1958.

Tokkyo kara mita sangyo hatten shi ni kan suru chosa kenkyu hokokusho, Tokyo: Tokkyocho, 2000.

Tokkyo seido 70 nen shi, Tokyo: Tokkyocho, 1955.

Tokyo daigaku igakubu hyakunen shi, Tokyo: Tokyo University Press, 1967.

Tokyo ika kikai dogyo kumiai mokuroku, Tokyo: Tokyo ika kikai dogyo kumiai, 1934.

Tokyo jikeikai ika daigaku hyaku nen-shi, Tokyo: Jikei University School of Medicine, 1980.

Tokyo shibaura denki kabushiki kaisha 85 nenshi, Tokyo: Toshiba, 1963.

Tokyo shika daigaku hyaku nenshi, Tokyo: Tokyo shika daigaku, 1991.

Toseki: soritsu 50 shunen kinenshi, Kyoto hoshasen gijutsu senmon gakkoga-kuyukai, 1977.

Toshiba Medical, *21 seiki he no kakehashi: okyakusama totomoni ayunda Toshiba iyo kikai kaihatsu no rekishi*, Tokyo: Toshiba Medical, 1998.

Urano, Tamonji, *Rentogen shashin zufu: naizo kensa ho*, Kyoto: Shimadzu, 1919.

Wakayama sekijuji byoin 80 nen shi, Wakayama: Wakayama sekijuji byoin, 1986.

Watanuki, Eisuke, "Ika denkiki ni kansuru chosa", *Denki shikenjo chosa hokoku*, vol. 95, 1939.

Yamada, Katsuhiko, "Nakabori Kouji meiyo komon no goseikyo wo shinonde", *Japanese Journal of Radiological Technology*, vol. 61, no. 9, 2005, p. 2.

Yamazaki, Tasuku, *Igyo to horitsu*, second edition, Tokyo: Kokuseido, 1917.

Academic Books and Articles

Abe, Takeshi, "Osaka daigaku akaibuzu no soritsu to kokuritsu daigaku bunsho-kan", *Osaka daigaku akaibuzu nyuzuleta*, no. 2, 2013, p. 4.

Aldous, Christopher, and Akihito Suzuki, *Reforming Public Health in Occupied Japan, 1945–1952: Alien Prescriptions?* London and New York: Routledge, 2012.

Anderson, Julie, Francis Neary, and John V. Pickstone, *Surgeons, Manufacturers and Patients: A Transatlantic History of Total Hip Replacement*, Basingstoke: Palgrave Macmillan, 2007.

Aoki, Junichi, *Kekkaku no shakaishi: kokuminbyo taisaku no soshikika to kekkaku kanja no jisso wo otte*, Tokyo: Ochanomizu shobo, 2004.

Aoyanagi, Seiichi, *Shinryo hoshu no rekishi*, Kyoto: Shibunkaku, 1996.

Aoyanagi, Taiji, *Iryo ekkusu sen sochi hattatsushi*, Tokyo: Koseisha, 2001.

Aoki, Junichi, *Kekkaku no shakaishi: kokuminbyo taisaku no soshikika to kekkaku kanja no jizzon wo otte*, Tokyo: Ochanomizu shobo, 2004.

Arns, Robert G., "The High-Vacuum X-Ray Tube: Technological Change in Social Context", *Technology and Culture*, vol. 38, no. 4, 1997, pp. 852–890.

Bartholomew, James R., *The Acculturation of Science in Japan: Kitasato Shibasaburo and the Japanese Bacteriological Community, 1885–1920*, Stanford: Stanford University Press, 1971.

Bartholomew, James R., *The Formation of Science in Japan: Building a Research Tradition*, New Haven and London: Yale University Press, 1989.

Blume, Stuart S., *Insight and Industry: On the Dynamics of Technological Change in Medicine*, London and Cambridge: MIT Press, 1992.

Boch, Rudolf (ed.), *Patentschutz und Innovation in Geschichte und Gegenwart*, Frankfurt am Main, etc.: Peter Lang, 1999.

Boersma, F. Kees, "Structural Ways to Embed a Research Laboratory into the Company: A Comparison between Philips and General Electric 1900–1940", *History and Technology*, vol. 19, no. 2, 2003a, pp. 109–126.

Boersma, Kees, "Tensions within an Industrial Research Laboratory: The Philips Laboratory's X-Ray Department between the Wars", *Enterprise & Society*, vol. 4, 2003b, pp. 65–98.

Bremner, Robert H., *Giving: Charity and Philanthropy in History*, Piscataway: Transaction Publishers, 1996.

Brown, Nik, and Andrew Webster, *New Medical Technologies and Society*, Cambridge: Polity, 2004.

Burks, Ardath W. (ed.), *The Modernisers: Overseas Students, Foreign Employees and Meiji Japan*, Boulder: Westview Press, 1985.

Burrows, Edmund H., *Pioneers and Early Years: A History of British Radiology*, St. Anne: Colophon, 1986.

Cantwell, John, *Technological Innovation and Multinational Corporations*, Oxford: Blackwell, 1989.

Cantwell, John, and Brigitte Andersen, "A Statistical Analysis of Corporate Technological Leadership Historically", *Economics of Innovation and New Technology*, vol. 4, 1996, pp. 211–234.

Carrin, Guy, and Chris James, "Social Health Insurance: Key Factors Affecting the Transition Towards Universal Coverage", *International Social Security Review*, vol. 58, no. 1, 2005, pp. 45–64.

Chandler, Alfred D., Jr., *Scale and Scope: The Dynamics of Industrial Capitalism*, Cambridge: Belknap Press, 1990.

Cherry, Steven, "Beyond National Health Insurance: The Voluntary Hospitals and Hospitals Contributory Schemes: A Regional Study", *Social History of Medicine*, vol. 5, no. 3, 1992, pp. 455–482.

Cherry, Steven, "Accountability, Entitlement, and Control Issues and Voluntary Hospital Funding c1860–1939", *Social History of Medicine*, vol. 9, no. 2, 1996, pp. 215–233.

Cherry, Steven, "Before the National Health Service: Financing the Voluntary Hospitals, 1900–1939", *Economic History Review*, 1997, pp. 305–326.

Cooter, Roger, and John Pickstone (eds.), *Companion to Medicine in the Twentieth Century*, London and New York: Routledge, 2003.

Craig, Barbara L., "The Role of Records and of Record-Keeping in the Development of the Modern Hospital in London, England, and Ontario, Canada, c. 1890–c. 1940", *Bulletin of the History of Medicine*, 1991, vol. 65, pp. 376–397.

Decker, Sola, and Ron Iphofen, "Developing the Profession of Radiography: Making Use of Oral History", *Radiography*, vol. 11, 2005, pp. 262–271

Deloitte, *2017 Global Health Care Outlook*, Deloitte Touche Tohmatsu Limited, 2017.

Domin, Jean-Paul, *Une histoire économique de l'hôpital (XIXe-XXe siècles): Une analyse rétrospective du développement hospitalier*, 2 volumes, Paris: Comité d'histoire de la sécurité sociale, 2008 and 2013.

Dommann, Monika, *Dursicht, Einsicht, Vorsicht: Eine Geschichte der Röntgenstrahlen, 1896–1963*, Zurich: Chronos, 2003.

Donzé, Pierre-Yves, *Bâtir, gérer, soigner: histoire des établissements hospitaliers de Suisse romande*, Geneva: Georg, 2003.

Donzé, Pierre-Yves, «De la charité à l'entreprise: les services de soins hospitaliers en Suisse romande (1880–1945)», in Hans-Jörg Gilomen, Margrit Müller, Laurent Tissot (eds.), *Les services - essor et transformation du «secteur tertiaire» (15è - 20è siècles)*, Zurich: Chronos, 2007a, pp. 287–301.

Donzé, Pierre-Yves, *L'ombre de César: les chirurgiens et la construction du système hospitalier vaudois (1840–1960)*, Lausanne: BHMS, 2007b.

Donzé, Pierre-Yves, "Studies Abroad by Japanese Doctors: A Prosopographic Analysis of the Nameless Practitioners, 1862–1912", *Social History of Medicine*, vol. 23, no. 2, 2010, pp. 244–260.

Donzé, Pierre-Yves, "The International Patent System and the Global Flow of Technologies: The Case of Japan, 1880–1930", in Christof Dejung and Niels Peterson (eds.), *The Foundations of Worldwide Economic Integration: Powers, Institutions, and Global Markets, 1850–1930*, Cambridge: Cambridge University Press, 2013a, pp. 179–201.

Donzé, Pierre-Yves, "Patents as a Source for the History of Medicine: The Example of the Japanese Medical Instrument Industry, 1885–1937", *Journal of the Japanese Society for the History of Medicine*, vol. 59, no. 4, 2013b, pp. 503–516.

Donzé, Pierre-Yves, "Multinational Enterprises and the Globalization of Medicine: Siemens and the Business of X-ray Equipment in Non-Western Markets, 1900–1939", *Enterprise & Society*, vol. 15, no. 4, 2014, pp. 820–848.

Donzé, Pierre-Yves, "The Beginnings of the Japanese Medical Instruments Industry and the Adaptation of Western Medicine to Japan (1880–1937)", *Australian Economic History Review*, vol. 56, no. 3, 2016, pp. 272–291.

Donzé, Pierre-Yves, and Ben Wubs, "Global Competition and Cooperation in the Electronics Industry: The Case of X-Ray Equipment, 1900–1970", forthcoming.

Donzé, Pierre-Yves, and Shigehiro Nishimura, *Organizing Global Technology Flows: Institutions, Actors, and Processes*, New York: Routledge, 2014.

Droux, Joëlle, *L'attraction céleste. La construction de la profession d'infirmière en Suisse Romande (19ᵉ-20ᵉsiècles)*, University of Geneva, unpublished PhD thesis, 2000.

Faure, Olivier, *Les cliniques privées: deux siècles de succès*, Rennes: Presses universitaires de Rennes, 2012.

Feldenkirchen, Wilfried, *Siemens, 1918–1945*, Columbus: Ohio State University Press, 1995.

Folland, Sherman, Allen C. Goodman, and Miron Stano, *The Economics of Health and Health Care*, seventh edition, Upper Saddle River: Pearson, 2013.

Foucault, Michel, *Naissance de la Clinique*, Paris: PUF, 1963.

Foucault, Michel, *Surveiller et punir*, Paris: Gallimard, 1975.

Frühstück, Sabine, *Colonizing Sex: Sexology and Social Control in Modern Japan*, Berkeley: University of California Press, 2003.

Fuchs, Victor R., "The Supply of Surgeons and the Demand for Operations", *Journal of Human resources*, vol. 13, 1978, pp. 35–56.

Fukunaga, Hajime, *Nihon byouin shi*, Tokyo: Pilar Press, 2014.

Fye, Bruce W., *Caring for the Heart: Mayo Clinic and the Rise of Specialization*, Oxford: Oxford University Press, 2015.

Galambos, Lou, "Is This a Decisive Moment for the History of Business, Economic History, and the History of Capitalism?", *Essays in Economic & Business History*, vol. 32, 2014, pp. 1–18.

Galambos, Louis, and Jane Eliot Sewell, *Networks of Innovation: Vaccine Development at Merck, Sharp & Dohme, and Mulford, 1895–1995*, Cambridge: Cambridge University Press, 1995.

Gelijns, Annetine, and Nathan Rosenberg, "The Dynamics of Technological Change in Medicine", *Health Affairs*, vol. 13, no. 3, 1994, pp. 28–46.

Getzen, Thomas E., "Population Aging and the Growth of Health Expenditures", *Journal of Gerontology*, vol. 47, no. 3, 1992, pp. 98–194.

Geue, Claudia, et al. "Population Ageing and Healthcare Expenditure Projections: New Evidence from a Time to Death Approach", *The European Journal of Health Economics*, vol. 15, no. 8, 2014, pp. 885–896.

Goebel, Thomas, "American Medicine and the 'Organizational Synthesis': Chicago Physicians and the Business of Medicine, 1900–1920", *Bulletin of the History of Medicine*, vol. 68, no. 4, 1994, pp. 639–663.

Gorsky, Martin, and Sally Sheard (eds.), *Financing Medicine. The British Experience since 1750*, London and New York: Routledge, 2006.

Goto, Rei, and Takeshi Mori, *Nihon no oishasan kenkyu*, Tokyo: Toyokeizai, 2012.

Grandshaw, Lindsay, "'Fame and Fortune by Means of Bricks and Mortar': The Medical Profession and Specialist Hospitals in Britain, 1800–1948", in Lindsay Granshaw and Roy Porter (eds.), *Hospitals in History*, London and New York: Routledge, 1989.

Hara, Akira, "Wartime Controls", in Takafusa Nakamura and Konosuke Odaka (eds.), *Economic History of Japan 1914–1945*, Oxford: Oxford University Press, 1999, pp. 247–286.

Hilt, Eric, "Economic History, Historical Analysis, and the 'New History of Capitalism'", *The Journal of Economic History*, vol. 77, no. 2, 2017, pp. 1–26.

Howell, Joel D., *Technology in the Hospital: Transforming Patient Care in the Early Twentieth Century*, Baltimore and London: The Johns Hopkins University Press, 1995.

Huisman, Frank, and John Harkley Warner (eds.), *Locating Medical History: The Stories and Their Meanings*, Baltimore and London: The Johns Hopkins Press, 2004.

Ikai, Shuhei, "Nihon ni okeru ishi no kyaria: i-kyoku seido ni okeru nihon no ishi sotsugo kyoiku no kozo bunseki", *Kikan shakai hosho kenkyu*, vol. 36, no. 2, 2000, pp. 169–178.

Ikai, Shuhei, *Byoin no seiki no riron*, Tokyo: Yuhikaku, 2010.

Jeremy, David (ed.), *International Technology Transfer: Europe, Japan and the USA, 1700–1914*, Aldershot: Edward Elgar, 1991.

Jeremy, David (ed.), *The Transfer of International Technology: Europe, Japan and the USA in the Twentieth Century*, Aldershot: Edward Elgar, 1992.

Jones, Edgar, *The Business of Medicine: The Extraordinary History of Glaxo, a Baby Food Producer, Which Became One of the World's Most Successful Pharmaceutical Companies*, New Delhi: Leads Press, 2004.

Jones, Geoffrey, *Debating the Responsibility of Capitalism in Historical and Global Perspective*, Harvard Business School Working Paper, 14-004, July 2013.

Kasza, Gregory J., "War and Welfare Policy in Japan", *Journal of Asian Studies*, vol. 61, no. 2, 2002, pp. 417–435.

Kataoka, Yoshio, *Rikugun guni chujo: haga eijiro hakase ni kansuru kenkyu*, Tokushima: Kataoka Yoshio, 1988.

Kawakami, Takeshi, *Gendai nihon iryoshi*, Tokyo: Keisoshobo, 1964.

Keating, Peter, and Alberto Cambrosio, *Biomedical Platforms: Realigning the Normal and the Pathological in the Late Twentieth-Century Medicine*, Cambridge and London: MIT Press, 2003.

Kevles, Bettyann Holtzmann, *Naked to the Bone: Medical Imaging in the Twentieth Century*, New York: Basic Books, 1997.

Kim, Hoi-Eun, *Doctors of Empire: Medical and Cultural Encounters between Imperial Germany and Meiji Japan*, Toronto: University of Toronto Press, 2014.

Kinoshita, Yasuhiro, "Edoki ni okeru gijutsu hattatsu", *Nihon kikai gakkai ron-bunshu*, vol. 80, no. 810, 2014, pp. 1–10.

Kira, Shiro, *Meijiki ni okeru doitsu igaku no juyo to fukyu: tokyo daigaku igakubu gaishi*, Tokyo: Tsukiji shokan, 2010.

Kudo, Akira, *Japanese–German Business Relations: Co-operation and Rivalry in the Interwar Period*, London and New York: Routledge, 1998.

Kudo, Akira, Nobuo Tajima, and Erich Pauer (eds.), *Japan and Germany: Two Latecomers to the World Stage, 1890–1945*, 3 volumes, 2009.

Labisch, Alfons, and Reinhard Spree (eds.), *«Einem jeden Kranken in einem Hospitale sein eigenes Bett». Zur Sozialgeschichte des Allgemeinen Krankenhauses in Deutschland im 19. Jahrhundert*, Frankfurt, Campus Verlag, 1996.

Labisch, Alfons, and Reinhardt Spree (eds.), *Krankenhaus-Report 19. Jahrhundert. Krankenhausträger, Krankenhausfinanzierung, Krankenhauspatienten*, Frankfurt: Campus Verlag, 2001.

Lane, Joane, *A Social History of Medicine: Health, Healing and Disease in England, 1750–1950*, London and New York: Routledge, 2001.

Larkin, Gerry V., "Medical Dominance and Control: Radiographers in the Division of Labour", *The Sociological Review*, vol. 26, 1978, pp. 843–858.

Larkin, Gerry "Health Workers", in Roger Cooter and John Pickstone (ed.), *Companion to Medicine in the Twentieth Century*, London: Routledge, 2003, pp. 531–542

Low, Morris (ed.), *Building a Modern Japan: Science, Technology, and Medicine in the Meiji era and Beyond*, Basingstoke: Palgrave Macmillan, 2005.

Lundvall, Bengt-Åke, *National Innovation System: Towards a Theory of Innovation and Interactive Learning*, London: Pinter, 1992.

Lynaugh, Joan, *The Community Hospitals of Kansas City, Missouri, 1870–1915*, New York and London: Garland, 1989.

Macé, Mieko, *Médecins et médecine dans l'histoire du Japon*, Paris: Les Belles-Lettres, 2013.

Mason, Mark, *American Multinationals and Japan: The Political Economy of Japanese Capital Control, 1899–1980*, Cambridge: Harvard University Press, 1992.

Matsu, Masataka e.a., "Daigaku to kanren byoin", *Keio igaku*, vol. 39, no. 6, 1962, pp. 503–511.

Michel, Sandrine, and Vallade Delphine, «Une Analyse de long terme des dépenses sociales», *Revue de la régulation* [online], June 2007, accessed 13 February 2017.

Miyamoto, Matao, and Makoto Kasuya, "Soron" in Matao Miyamoto and Makoto Kasuya (eds.), *Koza nihon keieishi I: Keieishi edo no keiken, 1600–1882*, Kyoto: Minerva, 2009, pp. 1–48.

Mohan, John, *Planning, Markets and Hospitals*, London and New York: Routledge, 2002.

Momose, Takashi, *Showa senzen no nihon: seido to jittai*, Tokyo: Yoshikawa, 1990.

Nakaoka, Tetsuro, *Nihon kindai gijutsu no keisei: dento to kindai no dainamik-usu*, Tokyo: Asahi Shimbun, 2006.

Nelson, Richard R. (ed.), *National Innovation Systems: A Comparative Analysis*, Oxford: Oxford University Press, 1993.

Newhouse, Joseph, "Medical Care Costs: How Much Welfare Loss?", *Journal of Economic Perspectives*, vol. 6, no. 3, 1992, pp. 3–21.

Nihon ishigaku zasshi, Journal of the Japanese Society of Medical History, since 1941.

Nihon sangyo gijutsu shi jiten, Tokyo: Shibunkaku, 2007.

Nishimura, Shigehiro, "The Adoption of American Patent Management in Japan: The Case of General Electric", in Pierre-Yves Donzé and Shigehiro Nishimura (eds.), *Organizing Global Technology Flows: Institutions, Actors and Processes*, New York: Routledge, 2014, pp. 60–79.

Nixon, S., "Professionalism in Radiography", *Radiography*, vol. 7, 2001, pp. 31–35.

Odagiri, Hiroyuki, and Akira Goto, *Technology and Industrial Development in Japan: Building Capabilities by Learning, Innovation, and Public Policy*, Oxford: Clarendon Press, 1996.

Ogawa, Sumiko, Toshihiko Hasegawa, Guy Carrin, and Kei Kawabata, "Scaling Up Community Health Insurance: Japan's Experience with the 19th Century Jyorei Scheme", *Health Policy and Planning*, vol. 18, no. 3, 2003, pp. 270–278.

Perkins, Barbara Bridgman, "Shaping Institution-Based Specialism: Early Twentieth-Century Economic Organization of Medicine", *Social History of Medicine*, vol. 10, no. 3, 1997, pp. 419–435.

Pickstone, John V., *Ways of Knowing: A New History of Science, Technology and Medicine*, Chicago: The University of Chicago Press, 2000.

Polanyi, Karl, *The Great Transformation*, New York: Farrar & Rinehart, 1944.

Porter, Michael E., and Elizabeth Olmsted Teisberg, *Redefining Health Care: Creating Value-Based Competition on Results*, Cambridge: Harvard Business School, 2006.

Premuda, Loris, "La naissance des spécialités médicales", in Mirko D. Grmek, e.a. (eds.), *Histoire de la pensée médicale en Occident*, vol. 3, 1999, pp. 253–269.

Reiser, Stanley J., "Technology, Specialization, and the Allied Health Professions", *Journal of Allied Health*, vol. 12, no. 3, 1983, pp. 177–182.

Reverby, Susan, "Stealing the Golden Eggs: Ernest Amory Codman and the Science and Management of Medicine", *Bulletin of the History of Medicine*, vol. 55, 1981, pp. 156–171.

Richards, John, "Petty Patent Protection", *Proceedings of Fordham University International Intellectual Property Law & Policy*, vol. 2, ch. 47, 1998.

Rosen, George, "Disease and Social Criticism: A Contribution to a Theory of Medical History", *Bulletin of the History of Medicine*, vol. 10, 1941, pp. 5–15.

Rosen, George, "Changing Attitudes of the Medical Profession to Specialization", *Bulletin of the History of Medicine*, vol. 12, 1942, pp. 343–353.

Rosenberg, Charles, "Inward Vision and Outward Glance: The Shaping of the American Hospital, 1880–1914", *Bulletin of the History of Medicine*, vol. 53, 1979, pp. 346–391.

Rosenberg, Nathan, "Economic Development and the Transfer of Technology: Some Historical Perspective", *Technology and Culture*, vol. 11, 1970, pp. 550–575.

Rosner, David, *A Once Charitable Enterprise. Hospitals and Health Care in Brooklyn and New York, 1885–1915*, Cambridge: Cambridge University Press, 1982.

Rossiter, Louis F., and Gail R. Wilensky, "Identification of Physician-Induced Demand", *Journal of Human Resources*, 1984, pp. 231–244.

Sakai, Shizu (ed.), *Rekishi de miru nihon no ishi no tsukurikata*, Tokyo: Nihon ishi gakkai, 2011.

Sawai, Minoru, *Kindai nihon no kenkyu kaihatsu taisei*, Nagoya: Nagoya University Press, 2012.

Schafer, James A., *The Business of Private Medical Practice: Doctors, Specialization, and Urban Change in Philadelphia, 1900–1940*, New Brunswick, NJ and London: Rutgers University Press, 2014.

Schlich, Thomas, *Surgery, Science and Industry: A Revolution in Fracture Care, 1950s–1990s*, Basingstoke: Palgrave Macmillan, 2002.

Schlich, Thomas, *The Origins of Organ Transplantation: Surgery and Laboratory Science, 1880–1930*, Rochester: University of Rochester Press, 2010.

Schlich, Thomas, and Ulrich Tröhler (eds.), *The Risks of Medical Innovation: Risk Perception and Assessment in Historical Context*, Oxon and New York: Routledge, 2006.

Shimazaki, Kenji, *Nihon no iryo: seido to seisaku*, Tokyo: Tokyo University Press, 2011.

Shinmura, Taku, *Nihon iryo shi*, Tokyo: Yoshikawa, 2006.

Shumsky, Neil Larry, "The Municipal Clinic of San Francisco: A Study in Medical Structure", *Bulletin of the History of Medicine*, no. 52, 1978, pp. 542–559.

Slade, Eric P., and Gerard F. Anderson, "The Relationship between Per Capita Income and Diffusion of Medical Technologies", *Health Policy*, vol. 58, no. 1, 2001, pp. 1–14.

Stanton, Jennifer, "Making Sense of Technologies in Medicine", *Social History of Medicine*, 1999, pp. 437–448.

Stanton, Jennifer (ed.), *Innovations in Health and Medicine: Diffusion and Resistance in the Twentieth Century*, London: Routledge, 2002.

Starr, Paul, *The Social Transformation of American Medicine: The Rise of a Sovereign Profession and the Making of a Vast Industry*, New York: Basic Book, 1982.

Stevens, Rosemary, "Sweet Charity; State Aid to Hospitals in Pennsylvania, 1870–1910", *Bulletin of the History of Medicine*, vol. 58, 1984, pp. 287–314 and 474–495.

Stevens, Rosemary, *In Sickness and in Wealth: American Hospitals in the Twentieth Century*, Baltimore and London: Johns Hopkins University Press, 1999.

Stevens, Rosemary, *Medical Practice in Modern England: The Impact of Specialization and State Medicine*, first edition: 1966, New Brunswick: Transaction Publishers, 2003.

Sturdy, Steve, "The Political Economy of Scientific Medicine: Science, Education and the Transformation of Medical Practice in Sheffield, 1890–1922", *Medical History*, vol. 36, 1992, pp. 125–159.

Sugaya, Akira, *Nihon no byoin*, Tokyo: Chuo Shinsho, 1981.

Sugiyama, Akiko, *Senryoki no iryo kaikaku*, Tokyo: Keisoshobo, 1995.

Takaki, Yasuo, "Kokumin kenko hoken to chiiki fukushi", *Kikan shakai hosho kenkyu*, vol. 30, no. 3, 1994, pp. 249–260.

Takenaka, Toru, "Business Activities of Siemens in Japan: A Case Study of German–Japanese Economic Relationships before the First World War", in Kudo Akira, Tajima Nobuom, and Erich Pauer (eds.), *Japan and Germany: Two Latecomers to the World Stage, 1890–1945*, vol. 1, Kent, 2009, pp. 114–149.

Takeuchi, Ryosuke, "Sengo takokuseki seiyaku kigyo no zainichi keiei: shakaiteki nettowaku tno renkei ni chumoku shite", *Keieishigaku*, vol. 47, no. 3, 2012, pp. 32–57.

Tamura, Tomio, and Nobuo Suzuki, "Nihon tokkyo seido gaishi", *Tokkyo kenkyu*, vols. 23–24, 1997, pp. 49–50.

Terasaki, Funio, "Senmon iseido no rekishi to genjo: senmon i no arikata", *Kyofu idai shi*, vol. 120, no. 6, 2011, pp. 419–428.

Thomas, Adrian M.K., and Arpan K. Banerjee, *The History of Radiology*, Oxford: Oxford University Press, 2013.

Thomasson, Melissa, "Economic History and the Healthcare Industry", in Robert Whaples and Randall E. Parker (eds.), *Routledge Handbook of Modern Economic History*, London and New York: Routledge, 2013, pp. 177–188.

Timmermann, Carsten, and Julie Anderson (eds.), *Devices and Designs: Medical Technologies in Historical Perspective*, Basingstoke: Palgrave Macmillan, 2006.

Tomita, Tetsuo, *Shijo kyoso kara mita chiteki shoyuken*, Tokyo: Dayamondo, 1993.

Tone, Andrea, *The Business of Benevolence: Industrial Paternalism in Progressive America*, Ithaca: Cornell University Press, 1997.

Tsukisawa, Miyoko, "Meiji shotō nihon ni okeru iryō gijutsu no inyu juyō katei: geka kigu ikuraseuru to jōshaku denkiki wo chūshin ni", *Nihon ishi gaku zasshi*, vol. 55, 2009, pp. 317–328.

Ueyama, Takahiro, "Capital, Profession and Medical Technology: The Electrotherapeutic Institutes and the Royal College of Physicians, 1888–1922", *Medical History*, vol. 41, 1997, pp. 150–181.

Umemura, Maki, *The Japanese Pharmaceutical Industry: Its Evolution and Current Challenges*, Oxon and New York: Routledge, 2011.

Wada, Ryoichi, and Akira Hara, *Kingendai nihon keizaishi yoran*, Tokyo: Tokyo University Press, 2007.

Webster, Andrew, *Health, Technology and Society: A Sociological Critique*, Basingstoke: Palgrave Macmillan, 2007.

Weisz, George, *Divide and Conquer: A Comparative History of Medical Specialization*, Oxford: Oxford University Press, 2006.

Wishart, James M., "Class Difference and the Reformation of Ontario Public Hospitals, 1900–1935: 'Make Every Effort to Satisfy the Tastes of the Well-to-Do'", *Labour/Le Travail*, vol. 48, 2001, pp. 27–61.

Wittwer, David G., and Philip C. Brown (eds.), *Science, Technology, and Medicine in the Modern Japanese Empire*, London and New York: Routledge, 2016.

Yamagishi, Takakazu, *War and Health Insurance Policy in Japan and the United States: World War II to Postwar Reconstruction*, Baltimore: The Johns Hopkins University Press, 2011.

Yamashita, Mai, *Iyaku wo kindaika shita kenkyu to senryaku*, Tokyo: Fuyoshobo, 2010.

Yongue, Julia, "Origins of Innovation in the Japanese Pharmaceutical Industry: The Case of Yamanouchi Pharmaceutical Company (1923–1976)", *Japanese Research in Business History*, vol. 22, 2005, pp. 109–135.

Yoshida, Atsushi, "Ishi no kyaria keisei to ishibusoku", *Nihon rodo kenkyu zasshi*, vol. 594, 2010, pp. 28–41.

Yoshihara, Kenji, and Masaru Wada, *Nihon iryo hoken seidoshi*, Tokyo: Toyokeizai, 2008.

Zweifel, Peter, Stefan Felder, and Markus Meiers, "Ageing of Population and Health Care Expenditure: A Red Herring?", *Health Economics*, vol. 8, no. 6, 1999, pp. 485–496.

Websites

Historical Statistics of Japan, http://www.stat.go.jp/english/data/chouki/.

Industrial Property Digital Library, www.ipdl.inpit.go.jp/homepg.ipdl.

Organization for Economic Cooperation and Development (OECD), http://stats.oecd.org/.

University Library of Vienna, on-line biographical information, http://ub.meduniwien.ac.at.

Virtual Museum of the Japan Medical Imaging and Radiological Systems Industries Association, http://www.jira-net.or.jp/vm/top-page.html.

http://www.deutsche-biographie.de/sfz33622.html.

World Health Organization (WHO), http://apps.who.int/nha/database/ViewData/Indicators/en.

INDEX

© The Editor(s) (if applicable) and The Author(s) 2018   195
P.-Y. Donzé, *Making Medicine a Business*,
https://doi.org/10.1007/978-981-10-8159-0

Printed by Printforce, the Netherlands